THE VOICE OF THIS STONE

THE VOICE OF THIS STONE

Learning from Volcanic Disasters Around the World

KEVIN SCOTT

Carpe Diem Books®
Portland, Oregon

Dedicated in memorium to
Richard J. "Dick" Janda (1938-1992)
Dwight R. "Rocky" Crandell (1923-2009)

First edition published 2019

ISBN: 978-1-7326775-1-7

Editor: Tricia Brown
Designer: Kelley R. Dodd, KRD Design & Illustration
Production Manager: Richard L. Owsiany, RLO Media Productions
Prepress: William Campbell, Mars Premedia
Publisher: Ross Eberman

Carpe Diem Books®

"Seize the Day—
Make the most of opportunities
with books!"

Carpe Diem Books
8136 NW Skyline Boulevard
Portland, OR 97229
www.carpediembooks.com
www.volcanicdisasters.com
503.936.6727
dick@carpediembooks.com
Printed in China

Cover photo: Mount St. Helens is reflected in Spirit Lake, May 19, 1982. (USGS photo by Lyn Topinka, Cascades Volcano Observatory)

Contents

Acknowledgments

I honor the United States Geological Survey for making many of these case histories possible. Its original mandated job of preparing a geological map of the nation has proved so successful that other agencies seek to become part of what has become the world's finest national science agency. To facilitate this, our mission statement is no longer "A Geological Map of the Nation," but "Science for a Changing World." What politician, looking for excuse to cut the budget, could argue with that?

Writing in the first person is a strategy that risk managers strongly recommend. They also find that personal experiences or stories can focus attention on the important points a scientist wants to make to emergency managers, to would-be developers in lahar pathways, and politicians who enact growth management boundaries. Hence, I have sought to keep your attention with stories of bears, war dogs, wolves, near-kidnappings, and helicopter mishaps. These, unfortunately, cannot be included in our scientific papers which, necessarily, are dry and tedious.

Above all, I want to honor the wonderful people I have met in the volcano hazard business. Here are a few of those who have helped me in preparing these essays of disasters, from reviewing chapters, to inviting me along on their field investigations, to simply inspiring me from a distance: Peter Baxter, Lucia Capra, Tom Casadevall, John Costa, Carolyn Driedger, Dan Dzurisin, Juan Manuel Espíndola, John Ewert, Cynthia Gardner, Julia Griswold, Chris Harpel, Rick Hoblitt, Richard Iverson, Jack Lockwood, José Luis Macías, Jon Major, Chris Newhall, John Pallister, Tom Pierson, Pat Pringle, Jon Riedel, Damiano Sarocchi, Ricardo Saucedo, Willie Scott, Claus Siebe, Kurt Spicer, John Scurlock, Roberto Sulpizio, David Tucker, James Vallance, Barry Voight, and Richard Waitt.

And a special thanks to my wonderful publishing team at Carpe Diem Books: Tricia Brown, Amazing Editor Extraordinaire; Kelley R. Dodd, KRD Design and Illustration; Richard L. Owsiany, RLO Media Productions; and William Campbell, Mars Premedia. I must also thank Darryl Lloyd, author of *Ever Wild: A Lifetime on Mount Adams*, for introducing me to Ross Eberman and Carpe Diem Books.

Nevado del Huila is the highest active stratovolcano in Colombia, but due to ever-present clouds at its peak, the actual height is unknown. (USGS)

Introduction

Descendants, Descendants . . .

In 1632, following a major eruption of Mount Vesuvius, the Spanish Viceroy erected stone billboards at the base of the volcano. "Descendants, descendants," they proclaimed, "listen to the voice of this stone." Their urgent advice: *When the ground shakes, do not delay, leave your possessions, evacuate now.* The Viceroy's motive was to save lives, as is mine in writing this book. I know that heeding it could save hundreds, probably thousands, or perhaps even tens of thousands in this century alone. This collection of volcano-disaster case histories is based on my many decades of research and experiences around the Pacific Rim of Fire (as well as Italy's Vesuvius and Campi Flegrei), where volcanos mark the boundary of heavy oceanic crust sliding beneath light continental crust, the dreaded subduction.

Our primordial fascination with volcanoes reflects the spectacular ways they behave and take large numbers of lives. Knowing about small details in volcano eruptions and collapses can be critical, as can the actions of those with the assigned or implicit duty to provide warnings and oversee evacuations.

In defining volcanic risk, the keystone is knowing how a volcano has behaved throughout its history. We do that with field geology, reading the layers and deposits of past eruptions and collapses. We know this history, at various levels of accuracy, for only about 10 percent of the world's roughly 1,500 active volcanoes. For that 10 percent, can we generalize on ways to warn those living on or near them and thus save lives and property? Strangely and curiously, no.

Volcanoes have very different personalities, even those that are adjacent like Mount St. Helens and Mount Rainier in the Cascade Range. And each has its own story to tell. We ignore those stories, both oral and written, at our peril. Examples?

- A day before incandescent clouds killed the people of Pompeii in 79 CE, a horseman rode completely around the Bay of Naples to get help from Pliny, the Roman navy commander.

- Barely five centuries ago, a large volcanic debris flow, or lahar, ran from Mount Rainier through what is now Tacoma and into Puget Sound. A Native American legend strangely coincides with some unusual features of that event.
- Andean villagers responded to possible devastation by evacuating to high ground, although the lahar they feared did not descend their valley, but the next valley beyond.
- A peculiar 2,500-year-old layer of gravel downstream from Mount St. Helens reveals that a prehistoric breakout of Spirit Lake, dammed by a debris avalanche, created a huge lahar. In turn, that lahar reveals that the 1980 blockage of Spirit Lake by a debris avalanche could fail and also form another huge lahar. To prevent this, President Ronald Reagan ordered the Corps of Engineers to accelerate lowering Spirit Lake's level using twenty-four-hour pumps, and then to stabilize it with a 2.6-km (1.6-mi) bedrock drainage tunnel.[1] Should the blockage fail, the resulting "flood" would have been more than three times what modelers were predicting.
- A strategy I propose in this book could have saved many of more than 20,000 people killed by lahars in Colombia in 1985, according to the U.S. Geological Survey (USGS) expert who interviewed survivors.

§

My lot has been fifty years as a geologist, not unusual but perhaps remarkable in that I was a career field geologist. This means I avoided the administrative positions—the "opportunities" that come the way of a bureaucrat. I admit to being a bureaucrat for most of my career, but with the finest national science organization in the world, the U.S. Geological Survey (USGS). That was preceded by brief but very fortunate employment by the oil company that made the first strikes in Alaska, and I was tempted to take their offer to finance my doctoral degree. After I retired from the USGS, I concluded my salaried employment as a senior international professor with the Chinese Academy of Sciences from 2009 to 2011.

What is special about field geology? It's hard work, for one thing. It can be dangerous. Close colleagues have died in plane crashes, river-running, and road accidents. Terrain can be challenging, from walking on tussock grass (like bowling balls) to slide-and-die ice slopes and those paved with ice-slick mountain heather. The most aggravating is terrain with horizontally growing alders—your boots rarely touch the ground. And then there are animals such as large bears and wolves. Please excuse my fascination with them, but they are a key part of what keeps this work stimulating.

I was educated at probably the peak of geological training for field work. The University of California, Los Angeles (UCLA), had a famous field-oriented curriculum. The mandatory summer-field course, mapping a 2-mi-wide strip across a Nevada mountain range, was torture. I survived with one of four A grades among fifty-two students, and that achievement—the answer to a single question in an interview with an oil company chief geologist—landed me my first professional job. Wisconsin, where I went for a Ph.D., had the quintessentially attractive graduate program, steeped in tradition and bonhomie.

By the time Mount St. Helens erupted in 1980, I had already traversed a series of project chiefships involving a dam failure, designing flood- and sediment-control reservoirs both large and small, Arctic stream behavior on the North Slope, and salmon-affecting bank erosion on the Kenai Peninsula. It was tutelage in the transport of sediment and doing a good job on time for another agency. That agency had contracted with the USGS to pay half the cost, focusing on the public interest. The public's interests—there's the rub—you had better do a good job because you will be judged by two agencies. With St. Helens, it came together—saving lives, exotic travel, friendships with foreign colleagues, and compassion for people living in dangerous places. And all in the context of decoding the fascinating history of the earth's surface.

The public interest is at the very heart of *The Voice of This Stone*, which takes a look at volcanoes around the Pacific Rim and compares them to the iconic Vesuvius and Campi Flegrei. Each chapter is a separate case history, either of a disaster or of a volcano with the potential for one. With one exception, I have been on the ground with my fellow men and women of the field-geologist tribe as a responding scientist. The Epilogue includes a list of critical details that will save lives in the future and the case histories from which they come. With each case study, we can decipher their history, in ways both simple and sophisticated, to prepare for the future.

NOTE:

1. Distances are given in both metric and English units in the introduction and first chapter; subsequently, distances are given mainly in units used in the papers cited.

Chapter 1

Alarms and False Alarms

Most of us are curious about our planet's past and its landscapes, and especially about the past cataclysms as evidenced in road cuts, stream valleys, and mountain ranges. For the risks of lahars and debris avalanches at some volcanoes, we may want to promote a version of the Japanese *tendenko*: When a tsunami threatens, save yourself first and without delay. In 2011, the Prime Minister of Japan had briefly considered evacuating 50 million people, destroying the country's economy, with the possible fallout related to reactor meltdowns (and potential loss of water in spent-fuel storage ponds) caused by tsunamis. The cause, which is entirely relevant for volcanic risks, is that engineers ignored geological history to build the reactors at criminally low elevations.

And there is the problem of false alarms—the bane of emergency managers. An eruption impends and warning is made, but nothing happens. There are several ways things go wrong. Worst case, a warning is either not made, or it is made too late to prevent death and destruction with evacuations. This can lead to guilt so profound that Japanese tradition advises ritual suicide, *hara-kiri*. Or, a warning is made but becomes a false alarm. Volcanic activity typically waxes and wanes, suggesting that an eruption impends, but then nothing happens. Simply calling for an evacuation can result in panic and loss of life, as wonderfully portrayed in the evacuation panic in the film *Dante's Peak*. After the movie's release, staffers at CVO (Cascades Volcano Observatory in Vancouver, Washington) decided how to grade the film (we gave it a B-) for the press that was ringing our phones. Among other things, the fictional evacuation chaos seemed realistic. The film is the most accurate of the volcano genre, thanks to retired USGS scientists as consultants.

Another variation in the history of false-alarm problems is an accurate evacuation warning that saves people from an initial eruption, but then that warning is lifted, probably with pressure from evacuees to return home. They do return home, and 2,000 are incinerated the next day in the true climactic eruption.

Barry Voight, distinguished emeritus professor of geology at Pennsylvania State, summarizes the "false-alarm problem" with the question, "What do you cry when there *may* be a wolf?" Ideally, you warn, but try to explain your lack of certainty. But people demand certainty, and the press can crucify bearers of uncertainty. You can try to discuss some past case histories as examples. In the best case, however, the false-alarm problem can be mitigated if you have prepared for a hazard over the long term. That is the first central theme here—forecasting the future from what has happened and then tuning warning and evacuation plans accordingly. Again, each volcano has its own story to tell and thus, so to speak, its own mitigation plans to recommend. Field geology is simply reading the story.

Long-term planning should "fit" the volcano. Hazard types vary in their impact, and volcanoes have personalities that make certain hazards more likely. For example, the huge prehistoric lahars that transformed from landslides at Mount Rainier have the size to fit the category of high-consequence, low-probability events. They would disable an economy of regional scale, *as would the evacuations to avoid their consequences*. Their probability, about every 500 to 1,000 years in later post-glacial[1] time, is near the frequency that some hydrologists and engineers will use in their planning, for example, of nuclear reactors. They are not in the "Black Swan" class,[2] meaning they were totally unexpected. Because evacuation is so difficult, or because there may be little or no volcanic activity as a warning, the USGS installed the world's first sophisticated *event-warning* system at Rainier. That is the detection of the actual hazard (it is happening now!).

This system is more important than ever because numbers of people at risk are expanding (despite land-use restrictions), so risk is continually increasing. Plus, the massive volcano's hot acid-water plumbing system is slowly weakening the edifice.

At some volcanoes, we may overly fixate on the question, "Will there be precursory activity that provides a warning?" Emergency managers, assuming this and thinking all they need to do is keep a hotline to the experts, are seriously misguided. The question, however, should be, will a warning based on some degree of precursory activity have been issued in time for evacuation of the area at risk to have occurred? A corollary question is, will the public and its institutions actually evacuate or facilitate the evacuation? Of course, the answers are likely "no" or "depends . . . ," and the reason for an event-warning system is made clear. With *tendenko*, at least you will have a chance to save yourself.

At Mount Rainier, the event-warning system defends large populations in lahar pathways, but those populations must be continually supportive of the system. To cost-conscious skeptics we can say, well, we don't complain about paying for fire insurance when we don't have a fire, so why should we complain of taxes that support

A "Black Swan" refers to a totally unexpected event. The birds are exhibited in a Beijing, China, zoo. They were migrating to Mongolia and Siberia when this photo was taken.

the event-warning system and its linkage to more than twenty sirens, even when there is no lahar?

The story of the lahar-warning system at Mount Rainier began with USGS glacial geologist Dwight "Rocky" Crandell. Rainier has an unusual personality—a history of huge collapses and less eruptive activity than Mount St. Helens, and yet it is currently the most dangerous volcano in America. I take pride in my role in the conception of the event-warning system. It is a story with a lot of luck and has involved many laypeople and scientists.

§

Most people were sleeping late that quiet Sunday morning of May 18, 1980, in the cities and towns along the Cowlitz River, draining Mount St. Helens above its confluence with the Columbia, the great river of the Pacific Northwest. Although the volcano was increasingly restless, there was no reason for any downstream alert or evacuation plan beyond the existing hazard zones. But only geological circumstance would allow thousands living along the Cowlitz River, and even beyond its confluence with the Columbia River, to escape death.

What could have happened was not in the playbook of any emergency manager. At 8:32 A.M. Pacific Time, 2.8 cu km (0.67 cu mi) of Mount St. Helens failed as a rockslide and debris avalanche, what geologists call a sector collapse. Harry Truman, the elderly curmudgeon and friend of Supreme Court Justice William O. Douglas, lived at the base of the mountain. He was instantly buried beneath about 200 m (more than 600 ft) of blocks and mud. Harry owned the lodge on the shore of Spirit Lake, several kilometers north of the volcano, and he had been the iconic figure on the nightly news who "knew the volcano," unlike "Chicken Little" government scientists. "What the hell did they know, anyway?" Quite a bit actually. They knew that the over-steepened north flank of the volcano reflected the steady interior growth of a cryptodome, a bulbous mass of molten magma.

The failed north flank of the mountain ran out as a blocky, high-velocity avalanche 27 km (17 mi) down the North Fork of the Toutle River but then stopped dead. Several hours later the upper part of the stalled, dewatering deposit would flow off to become a lahar. The lahar, although relatively small, traveled over 85 km (53 mi) down the Toutle and Cowlitz rivers. I would spend several years studying it and the many older lahars in the river system. The unique sedimentology and extraordinary behavior of the largest of the ancient flows, with a flow rate similar to that of the Amazon River at flood stage, would cause President Reagan to order the Corps of Engineers to accelerate a huge mitigation project. My monograph would receive the Kirk Bryan Award of the Geological Society of America. I had joined the renaissance in volcano science triggered by the 1980 eruption, and the Cascades Volcano Observatory (CVO) in Vancouver, Washington, was the place to be. We were in the trenches of defining hazard risks and expanding ways to detect hazard size and probability, both for volcanoes of the Cascade Range and, progressively, around the world.

Rarely did I look north 80 km (50 mi) to the next volcano in the Cascade Range, massive Mount Rainier. There, much like Mount St. Helens in 1980, the top 3 cu km (0.72 cu mi) had failed, except that this time, 5,700 years ago, the failed mass immediately transformed to a huge lahar. The deposit had first been seen as a glacial till, but in a scientific detective story, my colleague Rocky Crandell would trace it to the tip of the cleaver known as Steamboat Prow on the east flank, and to a realization: This was not glacial till, but evidence of a lahar.

Mount St. Helens in winter, 1980–81, looking due north with Spirit Lake at right. The lake's level was 60 m (200 ft) higher than before the eruption of May 18. The lake was dammed by the debris avalanche that flowed north before most of it turned down the North Fork Toutle River.

He wrote about his epiphany in a letter to his wife and daughter, dated January 15, 1970: "The idea of a mudflow came to me one evening in the summer of 1953 . . . I had been mapping this peculiar formation [the Osceola mudflow] around Enumclaw for several weeks without understanding how it got there. The light suddenly dawned on me as I was thinking about it, and it was as if a light did literally go on in my brain."

The Osceola mudflow had begun as a sector collapse (a landslide involving the volcano summit) of the top 600 m (more than 1,900 ft) of the volcano, which then flowed as a volcanic mudflow around the north side, dumping a cubic kilometer of its volume into Puget Sound at Tacoma. With Rocky's report, the volcanic mudflows long known as lahars were recognized as a major volcanic hazard in the Western Hemisphere. Rocky received the Kirk Bryan Award for his monograph.

If the 1980 sector collapse at St. Helens had behaved like the one at Rainier, *and like many if not most of them do*, large parts of cities and towns along the Cowlitz and Columbia rivers would have been crushed like Harry Truman beneath a rapidly moving wall of rock and mud. The gigantic lahar could have transformed *directly* from the 1980 debris avalanche and then flowed part of the way down the Columbia toward the Pacific Ocean. It may well have had enough volume to reach upstream in the Columbia, and given the low channel gradient, to approach the outskirts of Portland, Oregon.

This hypothetical lahar would have been a "Black Swan" in 1980. Now, we could deal with that hypothetical possibility, but won't need to until St. Helens restores its beautiful pre-1980 cone in the next several centuries. From 2004–08, the volcano began that process by replacing 6 percent of the volume lost in 1980.

Dwight "Rocky" Crandell (Knox College)

§

I first met Rocky Crandell in 1965 when I joined University of Texas geomorphologist Ken Fahnestock in measuring the 1963 debris avalanche on Emmons Glacier at Mount Rainier. Rocky had returned to the volcano to place the ashes of his son Tom in Glacier Basin on Rainier's east flank. Glacier Basin is located below Steamboat Prow, where Rocky had his epiphany about the origin of the Osceola. Years later, Rocky expressed admiration for our two 1995 reports on Rainier, one of which was an atlas showing lahar inundation areas. Our philosophies coincided, and our minor disagreements on Mount St. Helens history were reconciled in the field.

Rocky, with greater experience and cachet, was more vocal in stating that "the answers are not on the volcano," as opposed to what he then saw as "crater-focused" efforts, the repetitive focus on what is happening around the active crater. These are events for nightly news but less so for science. By "answers," Rocky referred to volcano behavior over time, the insight needed for long-term planning. Rocky believed that he and Don Mullineaux had offered the necessary insight in their stunning 1975–76 prediction, which appeared in a *Science* magazine article and in a USGS press release.

The prediction: Mount St. Helens would erupt by the end of the twentieth century. This was a dramatic, then-unparalleled statement derived only from the volcano's history.

The field work that Rocky and I did, and I continue to do, can be compared to what viewers see in television series such as *Forensic Files* and *New Detectives*. These are stories of investigators analyzing cold cases and solving crimes using forensic evidence such as DNA. To forensically examine the history of volcanoes, we twist a principle of geology: uniformitarianism. Uniformitarianism is an idea conceived by an obscure Edinburgh physician and farmer during the Scottish Enlightenment of the late eighteenth century. It states that "the present is the key to the past," a product of the then-recent recognition of "deep" geologic time to suggest that the landscapes of the earth's surface were formed by the same processes we see today. It also points us to the inference that the past is the key to the future, simply stating that what has happened over recent millennia is likely to continue. Thus, catastrophes such as eruptions have occurred and can be expected at somewhat similar frequencies.

Adjacent volcanoes like St. Helens and Rainier have markedly different histories (and thus probable futures) that are consistent through postglacial time. We read these different volcano personalities from the "forensic" layers of airfall, flood, debris flow, and collapse deposits around the volcano; they record past events and serve both as pages in the archives of volcanic history and as circumstantial evidence for long-term planning to save lives.

§

A small summit eruption of Nevado del Ruiz in Colombia melted enough ice and snow to entrain (bulk) sediment to form a lahar. Why on earth had the city of Armero, Colombia, been constructed exactly where towns had already been twice obliterated by lahars (this is the incredible part) in historic time? It had happened in 1595 and 1845. Unbelievable? With lahars once again snaking down the flanks of the majestic volcano in 1985, officials and a priest had asked people to stay in their homes, the standard mantra for emergencies. Mostly they did and remained there to die. More than 20,000 people—70 percent of the population, were killed.

Thoughts flow when you walk the deserted, silent streets of destroyed towns and villages. *What had these people thought as the wave of mud and rock approached? Had the shaking ground been a warning?* I pondered these questions in 1998 as a colleague and I walked where streets had once been in the towns of El Porvenir and

Rolando Rodriguez, Nicaragua. The villages and nearly all of their 2,500 residents, many now represented by tiny piles of cremation ash, had disappeared beneath a wall of flowing debris from collapse of the flank of a small, long-dormant volcano named Casita. Rainfall from a dying hurricane had been the trigger and had kept the populace in their homes to die rather than at work in the fields.

Walking the silent main street of Toez, Colombia, in 1994, I marveled that the street had been buried by a meter (3 ft) of mud. The wave of mud had followed an earthquake by only several minutes. Thousands of synchronous failures of the soil mantle had mobilized and then coalesced into the gigantic lahar known as *La Avalancha*. So fast was the wave that in one tourist video, the flow front was completely plastered to the valley side by centrifugal force in a curve. Crashing boulders in the oncoming flow created ground tremor that some would think was an earthquake aftershock.[3]

The idea of compiling a collection of case histories crystallized as I walked the deserted streets of Beichuan, China. Rubble from the 2008 Sichuan earthquake had entombed 15,000 bodies beneath me, never to be recovered. Hundreds of dusty cars in parking lots waited for their owners. Several months later, the city would be declared a disaster museum, both a memorial and a lesson in where to *not* build a city—a valley incising the front of the Tibetan Plateau.

Tens of thousands killed at Armero, El Porvenir, Rolando Rodriguez, Toez, and Beichuan—if I did not tell their stories, who would?

NOTES:

1. I use the terms "post-glacial" or Recent throughout these accounts. They refer to the most recent interval of geologic time, the Holocene, originally identified as the last 10,000 years, the time since withdrawal of the last continental ice sheet and a final spasm of alpine glacier advance, the Younger Dryas (YD). The period of 10,000 years was based on early radiocarbon dating and that interval is widely used today, although we now know that 10,000 radiocarbon years are actually 11,700 "calendar" years.

2. "Black Swan" is a metaphor for the totally unexpected coined by Nassim Taleb, NYU Professor of Risk Engineering. It refers to the black swans first seen in the Southern Hemisphere. His book of that title is hard to put down: Taleb, N. N. *The Black Swan*. New York: Random House, 2007.

3. The masonry and bamboo homes in Toez had readily collapsed before much of the town was overrun by *La Avalancha* minutes later. It appeared there was no systematic approach to integrating the bamboo to enhance the stability of the masonry. Some had clearly died from the masonry collapsing independently from any frame. Why not standardize a plan in which bamboo serves as seismic reinforcement? Not an original idea, but it bears repeating.

"Bayonet trees" were created following the St. Helen eruption of 1980, when the debris flow in the South Fork of the Toutle River sharpened these trees to needle points.

Chapter 2

Pyroclastic Density Currents and Lahars: Agents of Death and Destruction

Volcanic flow hazards are categorized as either hot and dry or cold and wet. Either one is a killer. The hot-and-dry types are known as pyroclastic density currents or pyroclastic flows (PFs), while the flows that are cold and wet are called lahars (volcanic debris flows) and debris avalanches. You know the first if you've ever seen a portrayal of Pompeii overwhelmed by clouds of glowing ash. The second type looks like flowing concrete. It may begin as a landslide that then mobilizes to coarse, block-laden debris flows. Or it may begin as a water surge formed when a volcanic eruption melts ice and snow, and the surge entrains sediment to become a lahar.

Both lahars and debris avalanches are debris flows, slurries in which the sediment moves the water. Debris flows differ from floods, in which the water moves the sediment. In the case of debris avalanches, I like to think of them as blocky slurries, rafting pieces of the mountain that protrude from their surfaces as hummocks or mounds.

The "poster volcano" for those hot, dry pyroclastic flows is the backdrop for Naples—Mount Vesuvius in Campania Province, Italy. Cities like Pompeii and Herculaneum are "disaster museums," cities or towns that have been obliterated, although not publicized as such. History gives the impression that these ancient cities were devastated and buried with little warning in 79 CE. Actually, there was enough time, over a day in fact, for many inhabitants to escape. A great many—probably most—did leave. The Spanish Viceroy commissioned stone warning signs a year after visiting Naples during a smaller, later eruption of Vesuvius, in 1631 CE. His billboards warned the populace to forget their possessions and evacuate immediately when the volcano rumbled. One of them still stands, and its "evacuate now" advice is even more appropriate.

The "poster volcano" for lahars is Mount Rainier. There are no disaster museums for lahars there because the last large flow, which Rocky Crandell named the Electron, occurred about 500 years ago, dated by retired Centralia College Professor Pat Pringle from tree rings. The best disaster museums are the newly created parks such as those where once existed the cities of Armero in Colombia, and El Porvenir and Rolando Rodriguez in Nicaragua.

How does Mount St. Helens compare with these poster volcanoes? Just 50 mi (80 km) away from Rainier, it is the exact opposite in behavior. While Rainier has a history of huge collapses but relatively small explosive eruptions, St. Helens is more of a mini-Vesuvius, with a history of explosive eruptions producing widespread ashfalls. These layers of ash (tephras) from past eruptions, when dated, become excellent markers that can greatly reduce radiocarbon-dating costs. One of the best known markers in the Pacific Northwest is Layer O, named by Don Mullineaux for its eye-catching orange color. We immediately know that every layer stratigraphically above it is younger than 7630 years BP,[1] the date of the powerful explosion of Mount Mazama in southern Oregon. The erupting magma became Layer O, and the remaining edifice collapsed, creating a caldera. Visible today is the sparkling lake that fills that caldera—Crater Lake, the centerpiece of a national park.

The city of Beichuan, China, was declared an official disaster museum after its destruction by the great Sichuan earthquake of 2008. Over 15,000 bodies lie unrecovered in the rubble. Other "unofficial" disaster museums may be found in Italy, Mexico, Colombia, and Nicaragua.

Explosive heat or fast-moving debris flows—which of these two hazards has proved the more dangerous in recent decades is debatable, but the popular conception of volcanic risk generally involves only the first, pyroclastic density currents.

Most people, scientists included, are more familiar with pyroclastic flows. They account for the majority of the fifty-seven fatalities at Mount St. Helens in 1980, and overall throughout history have produced far more fatalities. History has been written by the climate change initiated by huge explosive eruptions. Two of the largest, both in Indonesia, include Tambora in 1815, and Toba, a gigantic eruption about 60,000 BP to 70,000 BP in radiocarbon years.[1] The latter may even have threatened the human race. Similarly, the eruption of the Campanian Ignimbrite in Italy about 40,000 years ago may have caused the extinction of the Neanderthals.[2]

Death by Pyroclastic Flow

These hot, dry clouds of initially incandescent ash cover a flowing basal avalanche of coarser particles that are disintegrating into ash. The most recent terminology favors the term pyroclastic density currents, with two subdivisions—pyroclastic flows and pyroclastic surges. The latter are faster and more violent.

An image from the 1991 disaster at Mount Unzen, Japan, appears in signage near the elementary school. It was among the buildings overrun by the pyroclastic flow of June 3. In December 2007, a new armored observatory stood at left. Behind it, vents at the dome were still producing small steam emissions.

The first inhalation of a pyroclastic flow probably can be survived, as the lungs begin to fill with fluid; the second cannot. Fluid and ash create a searing, wet cement. By the third, hopefully you are losing consciousness. Autopsy film of victims shows airways, packed with cemented ash, being chiseled open. Peter Baxter, the well-known Cambridge physician specializing in volcano-eruption injuries, describes 106 burn victims from two eruptions at Merapi volcano in Java.[3] To prevent future such catastrophes, Peter and his colleagues prescribe effective warnings, adequate evacuation measures, and the political will to accomplish them. One of my colleagues carries cans of pressurized air in his field pack, thinking he might bury himself and breathe from the cans if he were overrun by a pyroclastic flow. The strategy seems to make sense, but it has every hallmark of a really bad idea.

§

The Japanese know how to design memorials—simple, but elegant. In southern Japan, a nearly flawless white granite monument was dedicated at the base of Mount Unzen during the 2007 Cities on Volcanoes meeting (COV5). It remembers June 3, 1991, the terrible day when some forty Japanese media members, policemen and taxi drivers, along with three scientists, lost their lives. I had been near this site in 1993 as flows were still forming, when pieces of the growing dome were breaking off and exploding into clouds of incandescent pyroclasts every few minutes. Finally, by 1995, the eruptions ceased.

The COV5 meeting held in Shimabara, the city with outskirts directly impacted by the flows from Mount Unzen, was a festival of survival. We visited schools and spoke to students who told us their parents' stories of survival between 1991 and 1995, the period of dome growth and pyroclastic flows. In giving a thank-you speech for our group, I was too enthusiastic—the translator's versions were getting shorter. For me, it was hard to realize that it had not all taken place yesterday. I was shocked when I realized the students were telling stories from another generation, whereas I was recalling experiences that seemed so fresh. I flashed back to a similar welcome at an elementary school in Portici, Italy, on the flanks of Mount Vesuvius, the world's poster volcano for risk from pyroclastic flows. Reaching out to parents via their children and their teachers is one that we, especially colleague Carolyn Driedger, employ at CVO.

Consider the volcanologists who died while sampling gas in the crater of Galeras, Colombia, in 1993. A sudden small explosion killed six of them and three tourists.

Galeras is an active volcano where pressure is not released by frequent gravitational collapse. At a volcano workshop in 1993, a gas-focused field trip led by Stan Williams, Arizona State professor, had entered that crater. Following the deadly explosion, Williams received the blame and nearly paid with his life. Dr. Peter Baxter, the acknowledged expert on volcano death, joined another physician in treating Williams and putting him on a private jet to Arizona.

Dueling book tours later paired a book that Williams wrote titled *Surviving Galeras*, which justified his actions,[4] and one that was critical of his safety measures, titled *No Apparent Danger*.[5] When both authors visited Powell's, Portland, Oregon's, iconic bookstore, about two weeks apart, I was surprised at the small turnouts in spite of national reporting of the controversy in the likes of *Time* and *Outside* magazines. The Galeras tragedy just did not resonate with the public, at least to the extent the publishers were hoping. Unexpectedly, I found my practical sympathies leaning toward Williams, in contrast to how I knew many of my experienced "crater-focused" and "hot-rock" colleagues felt. Still, in spite of the pressure on Stan to sample the crater fumaroles, there is also probably no way they should have been there, based simply on recent Galeras history and the chance of an explosive eruption[6] A map of the Galeras crater inside the cover of Stan's book shows the crater geometry and the body locations.

No USGS scientists were at the Galeras workshop—the State Department had denied official permission to attend because of kidnapping risk by the FARC (Revolutionary Armed Forces of Colombia). Their lives could have been saved by State, but for the wrong reason. But it would be the right reason that would keep me from certain FARC kidnapping, and an approximate 50 percent probability of death, at another Colombian volcano years later. I did not like Stan's statement that the USGS scientists had "backed out," implying cowardice. If the decision had been theirs, they would have been there and one or more could have died. So, a thank you to the State Department in both cases. However, one or more of the people that State kept away from Colombia might well have prevented the tragedy by asserting the risk. Norm Banks, my outspoken colleague at CVO, may well have filled that role.

A senior volcanologist notes that, in his opinion, the summary judgment of Stan Williams is largely based on his personality that some found abrasive, as well as the "ego-driven," after-the-fact promotion of the evidence from seismic signals at Galeras. The same scientist notes that a lot of the criticism came from people who had seldom entered a crater systematically to do monitoring work. We who ventured into the active St. Helens crater in 1980–81 had faced similar risks.

Death by Lahar

Time after time, hearing the stories of survivors and seeing the pitiful fragments of crushed homes, the endless ash piles of cremated bodies, I cannot help but picture those who could only watch as a roaring wall of mud came at them. What did they experience in their final moments? Some, like a father in Barranca Grande, Mexico, would recognize the speed and force of the surging mass and drop the hands of the two small sons he was leading and then run to save himself. How many citizens of Toez, Colombia, had been sitting on the row of open-air toilets above the town as the huge lahar that would be known as *La Avalancha* flashed by below them at nearly 50 mph, taking half their town and many of their children and relatives?

Stationed at Clark Air Base in the weeks after the Pinatubo eruption in the Philippines, we were working like dogs. Dick Janda and I were exhausted, in Dick's case because he was fatally ill. Normally I am mild-mannered, but I had confronted Dick, backing him into a corner and yelled at him to take it f…n' easier. He had hired

Lahars were incising still-hot pyroclastic flow deposits in the Sacobia River valley after the cataclysmic 1991 eruption of Mount Pinatubo, Philippines. The event closed nearby Clark Air Force Base, once a strategic military facility built atop older pyroclastic flow deposits.

me in 1980 as his second-in-command of the Water Resources Division part of the nascent CVO. Before the cataclysmic eruption of June 15, 1991, Clark housing for some 30,000 personnel had been situated on a broad interfluve, now covered by ash. The Sacobia River cut its valley just to the north, a few kilometers above the Japanese prison camp that was the end of the Bataan Death March in World War II. Huge pyroclastic flows had descended the valley, mobilizing hot lahars that came down the channel every few minutes. My colleagues had prepared a pre-eruption hazard map based on previous pyroclastic flows, and it was nearly dead on.

It was relaxing in the evenings to climb down from the new Pinatubo Volcano Observatory at Clark, stroll across the Sacobia valley bottom, and watch the flows steam by in the incised channel. Today, Dick had not joined us; I hoped he was resting, but knew he was not. A volcanologist from the Philippine Institute of Volcanology (Phivolcs) and I descended into the valley as dusk set quickly, as it does at low latitude. The ground shook, and upstream, a freight train of mud suddenly appeared, swinging up the outside of curves. It was a lahar, probably an order of magnitude larger than the previous channelized flows. We both stood, rooted to the ground. There was literally no time to think as the train came at us and then flew by, swinging and sloshing.

I had been stunned like this before. In 1957, working summers at the Naval Ordnance Test Station in the Mojave Desert, coworkers and I spent weekends horsing around in the Sierras. At probably 4:00 A.M. on July 5, unable to sleep, pitch dark, I was hiking solo by flashlight, nearly at the summit of Mount Whitney, 14,495-foot elevation. Instantaneously it was brighter than noon—my first thought was that the sun had exploded. The crests of the Sierra summits marching away to the north glowed, and the entire sky seemed alight. *Could it be an asteroid strike?* No. But it was a preview of the end of the world. Barely a hundred miles east at the Nevada Test Site, the fireball of the largest above-ground nuclear test, 74 kilotons, was fading.

So that was the answer. You simply did not have time for rational thought, regrets, or even for fear. You would either be killed or you wouldn't. Below Pinatubo volcano, the sight of the lahar roaring by us was so awesome and unexpected, it took our breath away. And for us, it was not really such a close shave. That outlier surge had been out of the incised Sacobia River channel, but, in terms of horizontal distance, it was not dangerously close. But we could not know that as it approached. We had seen and felt what tens of thousands have experienced as their last moments alive. Time just stopped. That seemed comforting.

In working with older lahar deposits, like the gigantic Osceola or Electron mudflows from Mount Rainier, I wonder why we do not find more human remains. They are certainly there, especially in the case of the Electron, only five hundred years ago. I think I found the answer to this question at Casita, a small volcano in Nicaragua that yielded a hurricane-triggered collapse that mobilized into a lahar that killed 2,500 souls. The bodies float to the top of the flow and are distributed along the sides; they are not generally buried in or beneath it.

If we compare the recent numbers of fatalities from both categories of hazards, total deaths from cold, wet flows greatly exceed those from pyroclastic flows, the classical way people die, as at Pompeii and Herculaneum in 79 CE. This reflects the disaster at a Colombian volcano, Nevado del Ruiz, where over 23,000 died from lahars, mainly in a single city, Armero, which had been destroyed by lahars twice previously. No example better illustrates the portrayal of the future from the past, and that is the most basic theme of this book.

History is a great teacher, but its students do not live long enough to put the lessons fully into practice. Even today, however, the 79 CE eruption of Vesuvius and the destruction of Pompeii and Herculaneum by pyroclastic flows are much better known than the destruction of Armero by lahars. Why? Probably only because death from a hot boiling cloud is more dramatic than that from a river of mud. Much better television. The lessons from Armero are more useful, however, if saving lives is our goal. Certain actions could have saved most of those who died there, even as the roaring fronts of mud and boulders approached, even after hearing a popular radio personality repeat the mantra, "Stay safe in your homes." The citizens surrounding Mount Vesuvius, on the other hand, had no historical record to look back on and learn from, as well as no media to mislead them. Most citizens of Pompeii and many in Herculaneum actually escaped the scorching surges that finally buried their cities. With this knowledge, an even higher percentage could escape today after onset of a comparable eruption. The citizens of modern Naples have a very instructive history, but are discouraged by Italian politics and religion from putting the lessons into practice.

Memorials like the white granite sculpture at Unzen volcano in Japan are beautiful, but the best tribute to those who died is the educational video, *Understanding Volcanic Hazards*, created by CVO's Chris Newhall and Steve Brantley. The film is a compilation of footage made by Maurice and Katia Krafft, the husband-and-wife photographer team who perished at Unzen on June 3, 1991.[7] I have shown the video to groups countless times, and always, at the end, there is complete silence for several seconds. Then, it seems, nearly everybody wants to ask a question.

NOTES:

1. Dates cited here are in the format of the original research. Dates may be radiocarbon dates, commonly cited in scientific papers as ^{14}C years BP, or if calibrated (converted to calendar years), as cal yrs BP. The difference between radiocarbon years and calendar years is caused by variation in atmospheric radiocarbon.
2. The Campanian Ignimbrite was erupted about 40,000 years ago from the caldera west of Naples known as Campi Flegrei (Phlegrean Fields). Naples is located midway between the caldera and Mount Vesuvius.
3. Baxter, P. J., Jenkins, S., Seswandhana, R., Komorowski, J.-C., Dunn, K., Purser, D., Voight, B., and Shelley, I. 2017. Human survival in volcanic eruptions: Thermal injuries in pyroclastic surges, their causes, prognosis and emergency management. *Burns* 43:1054–69.
4. *Surviving Galeras* (Houghton Mifflin, 2001) by Stanley Williams and Pulitzer-finalist writer Fen Montague. Makes the case that the explosion was unpredictable, and essentially just bad luck. Reading both the Williams and the Bruce books reveals the conflict and competition between use of gas composition versus long-period seismic signals, then just being proposed by USGS researcher Bernard Chouet, for short-term forecasting, The degree to which long-period signals were known, appreciated, or evident at Galeras (or could have been radioed to the field group) is a major point of the controversy, and some colleagues whom I need to keep anonymous think this was Stan's fatal error (not regularly assessing the seismicity). Williams, quoted in *Outside Magazine*, says, "Everything in volcanology is so nasty. You learn the most after the fact."
5. *No Apparent Danger* (Harper Collins, 2001) by Victoria Bruce integrates some of the personalities at Galeras in 1993 with those involved with the 1985 disaster at Nevado del Ruiz in 1985. Williams also describes that tragedy. Much of the best and truest retrospectives of Ruiz, however, are the journal articles by Barry Voight that I summarize in that chapter. Bruce's book focuses on Williams's graduate student, petite Marta Calvache, who played a valiant role in hauling him out of the crater and back to Pasto, the city 8 km east of Galeras that was the site of the workshop meetings. She, a native of Pasto, has become a distinguished researcher. In summary, Bruce does a fine job of elucidating the character flaws and ego clashes that are routine in science at the cutting edge.
6. An experienced volcanologist tells me, "Stan may believe it was bad luck, but I feel the tragedy related to the fact that Stan had no real experience with active volcanism and led his group irresponsibly into danger without establishing a radio relay system back to Pasto's seismic monitors, requiring hard hats to at least acknowledge risk, and not briefing visitors about the danger. If USGS pros had been there and not been denied travel by State Department bureaucrats, the outcome might have been very different."

   Voight, B., and Calvache, M. 2013. Galeras Volcano, Colombia, in *Encyclopedia of Natural Hazards*. Bobrowsky, P. T., ed. Springer Science+Business Media.

   Aspinal, W. P., Woo, G., Voight, B., and Baxter, P. J. 2003. Evidence-based volcanology: Application to eruption crises. *Journal of Volcanology and Geothermal Resources* 128:273–285.
7. The video was replaced in 2009 by a DVD, *Understanding volcanic hazards and reducing volcanic risk*, produced by IAVCEI and United Nations Educational Scientific and Cultural Organization (UNESCO); distributed by Volcano Video Productions. See www.volcanovideo.com.

Photographer W. A. Hesse made moving pictures of Katmai volcano just one year after an eruption covered many miles of the Alaska Peninsula, and beyond, with ash, wiping out villages, wildlife, and vegetation. (Photo by M. Hohner, General Photo File; Anchorage Museum, B1991.043.4)

UNITED STATES

Chapter 3

Mount Katmai (Novarupta), Alaska

My introduction to volcanoes came in a strange way—meeting a survivor of the twentieth century's largest eruption, the 1912 eruption of Novarupta. Incredibly, the eruption did not directly kill a single person, even though four Native Alaskan villages in the region were buried in ash. At Katmai village, residents were evacuated and moved far down the peninsula to an uninhabited site they named Perryville. But that site was near another dangerous volcano, one of many active volcanoes of the Alaska Peninsula and the Aleutian Islands. In my first job as a geologist, with Richfield Oil, I met one of the last survivors.

We pioneered use of Korean War-vintage helicopters in the most dangerous terrain imaginable. We felt like lab rats, given that wind velocities could be greater than that of the helicopter with the drag of its inflated rubber floats. Did we enjoy it? When not terrified, we loved it, and I was introduced to the field geology of volcanoes. Mount St. Helens would be in my future.

The 1912 eruption was the largest in the world since Tambora, Indonesia, in 1815. The eruption of "Mount Katmai" began June 6, 1912, and lasted for sixty hours, but was not even of that volcano. Not until decades later was the actual vent recognized as Novarupta, a lava dome 10 km west of Mount Katmai. Katmai itself had collapsed, forming a 3-km-wide crater-like caldera resulting from subterranean movement of magma from Mount Katmai to Novarupta. The eruption of Krakatoa in 1883 was less powerful than Katmai as we now measure eruptions, but it took 36,000 lives, mainly from tsunamis.

In 1912, much of the sparsely inhabited region opposite Kodiak Island on the Alaska Peninsula was buried in ash. During the occupation of Russian sea otter hunters in the previous century, Katmai village was an important trading site. Alaska had only been a U.S. possession for forty-five years when Novarupta filled the sky with ash.

The Alutiiq and Unangan (Aleut) people had coexisted with active volcanoes for at least nine centuries, and well knew the dangers. Some villagers had already departed for seasonal work when severe volcanic tremors began late on May 31. Many hurriedly fled, and the last two families left on June 4.

With the cachet of the National Geographic Society, botanist Robert Griggs began a campaign to preserve the area with his naming of the Valley of Ten Thousand Smokes in 1916.[1] He said later that he could have called it the Valley of a Million Smokes. The "Smokes" were fumaroles from the thick pyroclastic flow deposit, cooling and consolidating, still steaming and consisting of about 10 cu km of ash flow from the Novarupta vent into the downstream river valley to depths more than 200 m. They would die out in the 1920s.

The Katmai cluster of twenty volcanic cones and vents is a volcanic group USGS colleagues Wes Hildreth and Judy Fierstein have described in, so far, nearly forty papers. Their synthesis monograph, USGS Professional Paper 1791, is the penultimate example of this prestigious publication series.[2]

As the eruption began, the 200-ft, steel-hulled U.S. Revenue Cutter *Manning* and its captain, Kirtland W. Perry, were in Kodiak, the main town on the island of that name. The captain was standing on the town dock during a coaling stop when the eruption began. He thought at first that snow was falling. With floating pumice accumulating in harbor, he may even have thought of the fate of Pliny the Elder, the Roman navy commander in 79 CE. Pliny and his rescue fleet of four-decker quadriremes (galleys) had been forced away from the coast below erupting Mount Vesuvius by a reef of floating pumice.

The *Manning* departed to gather survivors from ash-devastated fishing camps east of Katmai. They huddled in *barabaras*, traditional semi-subterranean homes with doors in the roof. An ash-blinded bird flopped into one dwelling and the children washed its eyes. It survived. Millions of other birds and even grizzlies perished in the ash. When the rain of ash stopped, nine young men in three skin-covered *bidarkas* (kayaks) were chosen to cross the pumice-clogged Shelikof Strait to summon help. A tug boat responded, taking them to Afognak on the island of that name north of Kodiak Island. They would later leave on the *Manning* when Captain Reynolds of the Bering Sea Revenue Cutter Service decided they would be moved to a remote site far to the southwest.

The new Katmai village was 400 km down the storm-raked and cliff-embayed Pacific side of the Alaska Peninsula. It would become Perryville in honor of the *Manning*'s captain, and it would survive, never again making national news until

An ash-covered crew of the U.S. Coast Guard Revenue Cutter *Manning* sailed from Kodiak to the Alaska Peninsula to pick up survivors from fish camps and Alaska Native villages, some of whom are pictured with their rescuers. (Alaska State Library Place File, ASL-P01-1532)

2010 when its schoolteacher, Candice Berner of Slippery Rock, Pennsylvania, was brought down and eaten by wolves while running on a road for exercise. It was the first documented killing of a human by a wolf in United States history.

Katmai National Park, including the site of Katmai village, is now an area of expanding tourism, modestly reforesting a century after the eruption. The area has been recently in the public eye for animals killing and eating people, two by a grizzly

A Landsat image shows the Mount Katmai Caldera, Novarupta Dome (the 1912 eruption site), and the Valley of Ten Thousand Smokes. (USGS)

in 2003. The area is so popular that tourists compete by lottery to watch bears catch salmon. A "bear cam" at Brooks Falls is widely viewed, and if bears are not there fishing, highlight clips are shown.

In June 1912 the idea was simply to get out of a desert of drifting ash. At the new site, far down the Peninsula, the survivors unloaded their *bidarkas* from the *Manning*'s deck. They probably were not paying much attention to the scenery. On clear days, they could have seen the top of a giant stratovolcano, with its then-ice-filled summit caldera 5- to 7-km wide, only 25 kms to the north. None of the exhausted villagers had, on clear days, ever been out of sight of a volcano. But few volcanoes were even close to the size of this one, including those of the Katmai volcanic cluster. What the volcanoes in the 25-km-long Katmai cluster might lack in size, however, they made up in eruption frequency. At least fifteen eruptions yielding ash clouds are recorded by ash layers in Holocene (postglacial) time, the last 10,000 years. Most of the risk from Alaska Peninsula volcanoes is the potential for ash impacts to aircraft crossing the Pacific on great circle routes.

§

The first thing I remember about the Katmai village survivor sitting across from me in her Perryville *barabara* was her teeth or, more accurately, black stumps.[3] During a subsequent fifty-plus years of field geology, I would see worse in developing countries around the Pacific Rim, but not by much. Her proud husband, the eager young man who had grabbed me with hospitable possessiveness, obviously held her in great respect. He clearly wanted to show her off, and I was honored. We had stopped to take a break from long days mapping the Alaska Peninsula south of Katmai for Richfield Oil. Paul, our pilot, had flared to land at one side of the village, then quickly diverted to the other to avoid the crowd. On landing, I felt like a celebrity alien, as otherworldly as Hernán Cortés may have felt in 1519 as he cantered astride his "giant deer" down a lake causeway into Tenochtitlán, capital of the Aztec empire. Another giant stratovolcano, Popocatépetl, had dominated that landscape. In Alaska, we were literally visitors from outer space, but our spacecraft was only an older B series of the dragonfly-like Bell helicopters in the television series *MASH*, the adventures of Korean War medics.

Our ground speed of 70 to 80 mph was routinely exceeded by the wind velocity on the Alaska Peninsula, when we could find ourselves flying backwards in wind-tunnel passes. Our inflated rubber floats were an aerodynamic disaster, now long replaced by "pop-out" floats that explosively inflate from CO_2 cartridges for a water landing. Floats would be needed a lot less frequently with modern jet turbines than with the chugging, 6-cylinder engines of the old Bells, in spite of their two spark plugs per cylinder. Our flying was in terrain and along coasts with minimal autorotation options. Paul promised me that in the event of a ditching in any sea that prevented the craft from remaining upright on its floats (which would be all of them), I could count on my side going in first, and I would be his "step" as he bailed out his upright side.

Fatigue and serious overloading were the reasons we left our brand-new D series Bell in pieces at the bottom of a canyon. It was a clear day, after many such, and in long Alaska summer days, you work twelve to fourteen hours a day. We were exhausted, and Paul opted to shortcut us to our survey site by flying directly up a canyon; suddenly we did not have power to proceed, nor room to turn, and we hit the side wall and spun to the valley bottom. I got my head in my lap below the whipping steel rod at the center of the balsa-wood blade splintering explosively from the "Jesus nut" (when it fails, you meet Jesus). I then became Creighton Burk's no. 2 in Richfield Oil's mapping of the Peninsula, a project that would become his doctoral thesis at Princeton and lead to fame in the field of marine crustal structure.

That summer, a rig was drilling not far south of Katmai. We visited the site, high in barren terrain, offering fresh salmon but actually to get a read on the drilling. They weren't talking, of course, and the bit was grinding optimistically through thousands of feet of Naknek Formation, a textbook lithology for an unlikely oil-reservoir —impermeable rock, hopelessly "tight" to an oil geologist, but now possible with horizontal drilling and fracking. It had what sedimentologists call "poor sorting," with a large range in grain sizes so that little grains filled the spaces between the larger ones, leaving little space for oil, as well as restricting its permeability—its ability to migrate through the rock. The Naknek consisted of angular detritus shed from an active volcanic chain into muddy, clam-infested water.

Perryville when I saw it had reverted from the original tents, frame buildings in 1912, to a nineteenth-century Aleut village of mainly below-ground *barabaras*. Life above ground level was cold and unsustainable. Visitors in 1975 noted that only three of the above-ground frame buildings built for them in 1912–13 had not been replaced by barabaras. I could not remember any from our earlier visit.

I had started that summer as field assistant on a party with two career Richfield geologists. We lost one after the helicopter crash, and hence my battlefield commission. Creighton Burk had discovered two oil fields for Richfield in Wyoming, and he would go on to serve as director of the Texas Marine Science Institute, the Scripps of the Gulf Coast.

My usual day was to get set down on some barren ridge top and start describing the completely exposed section. Keeping a lookout for bears, of course, but a single wolverine was the only wildlife I encountered on the ridge tops. This left Creighton free to map structural geology all day with a minimally weighted helicopter, with fuel caches from a monohull Grumman Widgeon. Creighton integrated his structure and my stratigraphy in Geological Society of America Memoir 99, *Geology of the Alaska Peninsula*. His acknowledgment of my work "through many tribulations," he said later, was intended understatement.

A version of what happened after the helicopter crash that I definitely do not recognize is a chapter in our cook's (Carl Dunrud) autobiography, *Let's Go!* I admit only that large bears were involved. I did not know it then, but our cook was already legendary. Creighton had met Carl while doing field work in Wyoming. The ultimate model of a cowboy; with his heels together, you could run a good-size calf between his legs. He had been a friend of aviator Amelia Earhart and her publisher husband George Putnam. A famous photograph shows him cutting Amelia's hair at his dude ranch in Wyoming. A skilled roper, in the 1920s Carl had gone to Greenland on a Putnam-financed expedition and lassoed polar bears for the Bronx Zoo, as well as musk oxen and walruses.

§

Teacher Candice Berner's senses, jogging after class that cold day in early March 2010, were lulled by music from her iPod earbuds. She did not see or hear the wolves tracking her on the road to Chignik airport. Chignik was the nearest village to Perryville, where Candice was based. She would not have been glancing back to see the animals, desperately hungry in early March, getting up their nerve and certainly attacking from behind, unlike the grizzlies that she would encounter face to face. Without her iPod she could have heard the wolves' final charge on the gravel-covered road. She would have had only to turn and face them down, unholstering her pepper spray. I did just that in the 1970s, during three summers of work on river channel behavior in permafrost along the route of the Alaska Pipeline. My wolves were not very hungry, and were just begging, being well but illegally fed by pipeline workers. One had lost his face when offering a wolf a sandwich from his mouth. According to the State wildlife biologist, the wolves Candice encountered, maybe only two, were young and in the process of forming a pack.

Several weeks after Alaska pipeline completion (the "Golden Weld") in 1977, I walked by shops on 4th Avenue in Anchorage crammed with wolf-fur coats. The wolf packs, tamed essentially into dogs, had been killed *en masse* along the previously secured road from the Yukon River to the Arctic coast. They had readily approached any vehicle on the pipeline road, hoping for sandwiches, but were shot down like dogs.

§

In 1912, Captain Perry did not make any recorded comment on Mount Veniaminof, the massive volcano visible north of Perryville. One of the largest on the Alaska Peninsula, the volcano was named for Ivan Veniaminov, a strapping, brilliant Russian missionary who first brought the Russian Orthodox faith to Unalaska Island in 1822.

It stands more than 8,000 ft high and 40 km wide at its base, a large stratovolcanic edifice with a young but complex history.[4] Veniaminof was not active at the time, and the steep-walled 5- to 7-km-wide crater, similar in size to Crater Lake in Oregon, was a sea of ice when Paul nursed our old Bell zigzag up the glacier on the west side. Had Captain Perry moved his charges from a fire to a future frying pan?

The captain went beyond the call of duty. President Taft would honor him and the officers of the *Manning*. He had discharged (I want to say "dumped") the villagers 25 km from the base of Veniaminof, evicted far from their former homes. Katmai village had been a similar distance directly south of Mount Katmai and Novarupta.

§

I received permission from UCLA to work into October. Our last camp of the season was on the north shore of Meshick Lake on the south side of the Aniakchak Caldera. Directly on a bear trail, as we found out when darkness came. We built a fire and I semi-volunteered to stay up, armed with a can of Jet Fuel A and a drinking cup. I could hear them coming, grunting with each massive step, but the first sign was the odor of rotten meat. They would not divert from the trail until I threw a cup of gas on the fire, creating an impressive explosion. They would rear up and roar, bathed in a red glow. After one and a half such nights, the novelty of this performance wore off, and I said the hell with it and went to sleep.

After a total of seven field seasons in grizzly country, I dare to offer a bit of advice, given to my student advisees—keep your bear spray in a holster, not your pack, and rehearse a "quick draw." And no iPods. At the end of the field season, discharge it to see the distance of the spray, and get a new one next year. Grizzlies can come out of nowhere in forested or brushy terrain, suddenly and with bad intentions. I confess—I am scared stiff. Researching stream behavior in permafrost on the treeless North Slope, I would have to summon courage for solo access to my study sites, trekking without a firearm across swales, any one of which could contain a "barren-ground" grizzly mother with cubs.

Firearms were not permitted during pipeline construction. Grizzlies are irresistible theater. During summers at pipeline construction camps on the North Slope, I could stand a few feet away, in the middle of the housing, watching them open the plastic baggies holding extra sandwiches that had been thrown away. The bears used a single claw to slit the bag and remove the sandwich as a surgeon uses a scalpel.

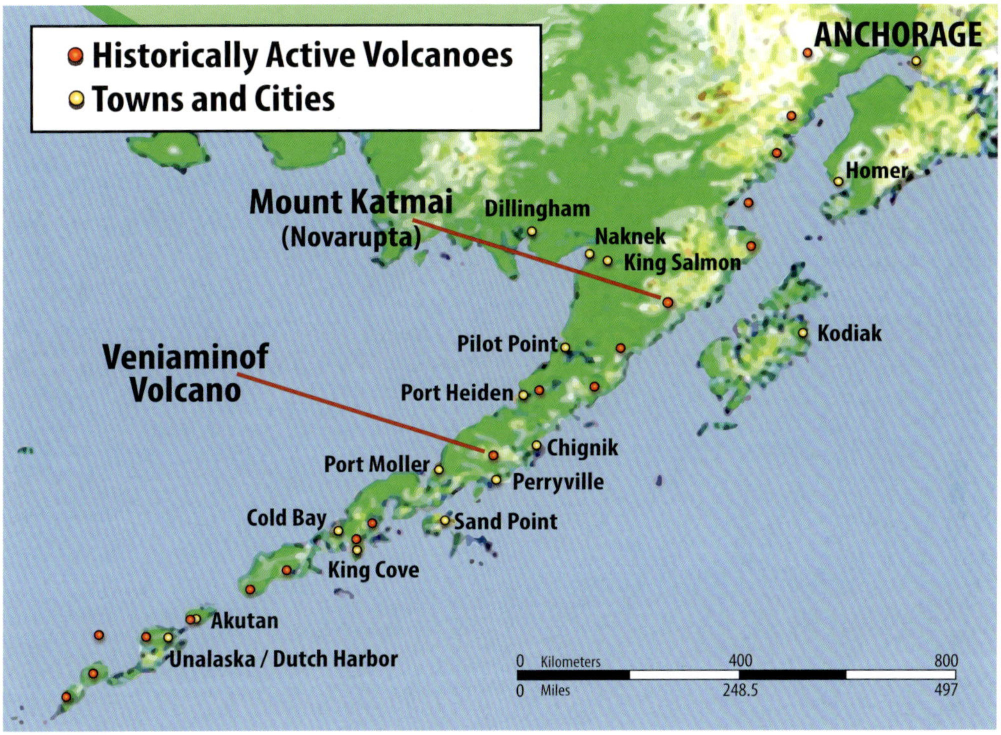

A map of the Alaska Peninsula shows Mount Katmai and Veniaminof Volcano. Evacuated Katmai village was due south of Mount Katmai on the coast. In 2018, Veniaminof remained active, routinely releasing minor ash emissions. (C. L. Nye, Alaska Volcano Observatory)

§

Might Perryville residents consider returning to their ancestral homeland? You look at their group picture on the *Manning*'s deck, and you think, did these trusting souls really have to get dumped way down there? Reading the Park Service's excellent summary, *Witness: Firsthand Accounts of the Largest Eruption of the 20th Century*, one wonders if any in Perryville are thinking about returning to Katmai.[5] Candice's blogs described a totally different Perryville than the one I saw (she was planning a book, *Adventures of an Alaskan Bush Teacher*). My Perryville hostess would now be flown to Anchorage for dentures, no expense spared.

Perhaps the Perryville elders might think about moving by studying the AVO website, the prevailing wind direction, and the compelling Katmai scenery as seen in the eight cable episodes of *Grizzly Man*, compiled from self-appointed bear-protector Timothy Treadwell's videos. If I were an adventurous age twenty-six (the Perryville median age), I might jump at the chance. Family ties are all-powerful; it would probably take a critical mass of a family group. Perryville is far different today—regular air service, a school with a basketball court, four-wheelers, most modern amenities. While Perryville may consider the issue, the Alaska Volcano Observatory keeps the rest of us up to date with a webcam in Perryville trained on Veniaminof.[6] People there just look north.

Can 1912 happen again? Judy Fierstein and Wes Hildreth note that within 500 mi of Anchorage, seven deposits of volcanic ash younger than 4,000 years equal or exceed the volume of the 1912 Novarupta ash, and that at least ten volcanoes in southwestern Alaska are capable of a 1912-scale eruption.

NOTES:

1. Griggs, R. F., 1922. *The Valley of Ten Thousand Smokes.* Washington, D.C.: National Geographic Society. A picture of the crowded deck of the *Manning* shows that "suffering caused by overcrowding was far worse than that due to the eruption."
2. Hildreth, W., and Fierstein, J. 2012. The Novarupta–Katmai eruption: Largest eruption of the twentieth century; Centennial perspectives. U.S. Geological Survey Professional Paper 1791. This Professional Paper is a model of the series.
3. Her original home at Katmai village is an inference, but highly probable; she may have come from another, similarly ash-devastated village. Captain Perry, in the Annual Report of the United States Revenue Cutter Service for 1913, reports that the 78 who embarked in his cutter at Afognak were from both Katmai and Cape Douglas.
4. Bacon, C. R., Sisson, T. W., Calvert, A. T., and Nye, C. J. 2009. Geologic map and eruptive history of Veniaminof record Aleutian Arc processing of mantle-derived melts (abs): American Geophysical Union Meeting, San Francisco, Abstract No. V51A-1652. I hope Charlie and Tom are planning a comprehensive report.
5. Hussey, J. A. 1971. *Embattled Katmai; a history of Katmai National Monument.* Washington, D.C.: Office of History and Historic Architecture, National Park Service. For events around Katmai village, see p. 336–65.
6. Visit www.usgs.gov/AVO. As of 2017, the webcam is operated by the FAA because of the risk of ash to aircraft.

Chapter 4

Mount St. Helens, Washington

We remember the Sunday morning of May 18, 1980, as the day our lives changed. In Oban, Scotland, I was returning from a day trip to the island of Iona after visiting former colleagues at the University of Edinburgh. My bed-and-breakfast landlady wordlessly grabbed my jacket and pulled me toward their "telly." She knew I was a geologist and she had an odd look on her face. It was about 8:00 P.M. in Scotland, and the first overflights of the Mount St. Helens blast zone were being shown live on the BBC. We stared at the bleak gray landscape. The blast had occurred at 8:32 A.M. local time that morning. I was not a volcanologist, per se, but I was viewed as someone who knew something about dangerous surficial processes. As we watched, nobody spoke. I knew that my life had changed, and so had that of many others, far beyond the amazingly low total of only fifty-seven fatalities.

Colleague Richard Waitt, more the studious professor, has chronicled the events before, during, and immediately after May 18 in his book *In the Path of Destruction*, recording the drama that had begun with the first earthquakes centered beneath the cone in March. An excellent addition to the story, especially the convoluted machinations involving the hazard zones, is *Eruption, The Untold Story of Mount St. Helens* by Steve Olson. My story is what came later and of what was to become a renaissance of volcano-related science around the Pacific Rim. It began with the interpretation of deposits of that historic eruption.

Rocky Crandell and Don Mullineaux were geologists who had devoted their lives to the histories of Mount St. Helens and Mount Rainier. Rocky was an artillery commander during WW II's Battle of the Bulge; Don was more mild-mannered and would find himself, almost by default, in the breech as the USGS spokesperson following the eruption. They would have been surprised that morning but probably only at the nature of the eruption—the ground-hugging lateral blast knocked down

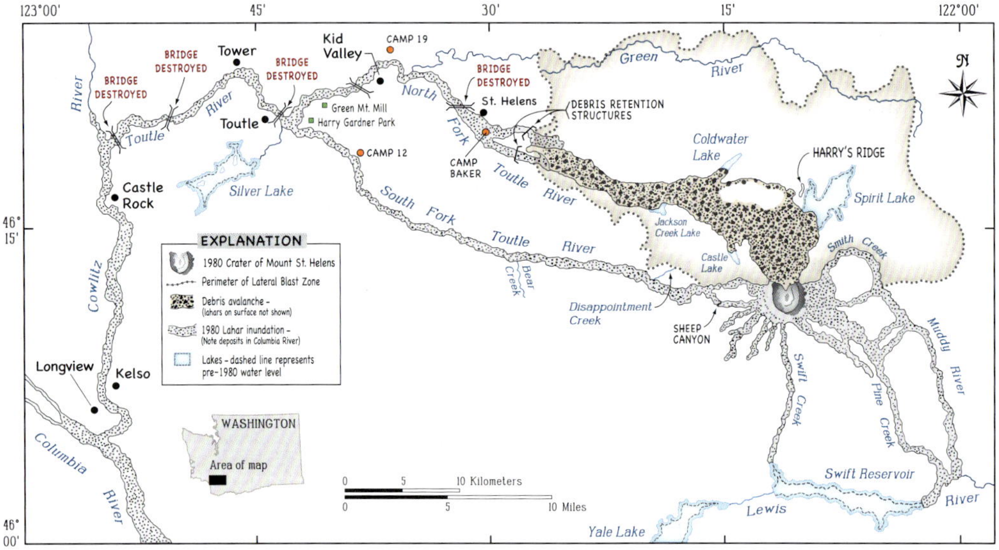

A detailed index map shows the blast zone, debris avalanche, and routes of lahars in the Toutle River system. (After USGS Professional Paper 1447-A)

nearly 600 sq km (230 sq mi) of forest. Their dramatic 1975–76 forecast of a major eruption by the end of the century had only needed four years.[1] They would only have been surprised if the eruption had not occurred by 2000. You could not blame them for feeling a bit of exultation at seeing their life's work so astoundingly validated, especially with such a low number of fatalities.

Spirit Lake Lodge owner Harry Truman should have been surprised but probably was not, only because he may not have had time to turn his head before he was crushed by the debris avalanche. The crusty old gentleman "knew the volcano." He would stay come hell or high water. Those who talked to him shortly before the eruption thought he was getting worried, but he simply could not retreat from his know-it-all appearances on the national news. Others had promised to helicopter in and pick him up when the eruption alert was issued. That, of course, would be a false promise. He could look up and see and hear rock falling from the growing bulge above him. Magma was rapidly intruding the edifice, and the north flank was becoming more over-steepened by the minute. Had he condescended to read the 1978 history of the volcano compiled by Rocky and Don? They outlined a long history of dangerous explosive activity that put the location of his lodge at risk even without the north flank inching toward failure. Once he elected to stay, there would be, and there could be, almost no chance of a warning.

The Lateral Blast

The north flank of St. Helens failed as three successive blocks that flowed down the North Fork Toutle River as the debris avalanche. Two modest earthquakes were either the cause or the result of the failure. Inside the north flank, a hidden, expanding mass of magma was suddenly exposed, causing it to instantly depressurize as the flank collapsed. It exploded northward, blasting through the sliding avalanche as a huge, ground-hugging pyroclastic density current. Awesome in its violence, it boiled northward at about 130 m/s (300 mph), flattening old-growth forests as if, as one survivor said, "they were instantly slapped down by a giant hand." People died in their campsites outside the red zone, crushed by the falling trees.

The future-CVO staff had watched the growing "bulge" on the north flank with concern, but the resulting "red and blue zones" were not adjusted to account for a laterally directed blast. I would later hear one of our most senior staff wonder if the proportion of on-site scientists with predominantly Hawaiian experience might account for the lack of a blast prediction. But even if this were so, it would have been tough. The hazard zone boundaries were closest to the volcano on the north, where the effects of the blast would be the greatest, but this had been largely the result of lobbying by the huge Weyerhauser Timber Company, which owned most of the land around the volcano, as well as bureaucratic confusion at the state level. Governor Dixie Lee Ray was busy at a rhododendron festival on the critical weekend when she could have extended the "blue zone" and saved some of those who died Sunday morning. Weyerhauser dodged a bullet—hundreds of loggers working in the blast zone would have been killed had the blast occurred on a weekday. A blue-gray chunk of the "blast dacite"—a piece of the cryptodome that blasted northward—sits on my desk as a reminder.

Weyerhauser has a lot of clout. In grad school at Wisconsin I received a confidential map of their holdings in Washington and Oregon. Their land-grid sections were shown in red, and there was a lot of red. I had been asked by UW's famous professor Stan Tyler to devote a summer to preparing what ended up as a 2-inch-thick bound volume, *Mineral Resources of Weyerhauser Timber Co. Lands in Washington and Oregon.* Calling their Tacoma HQ recently about a Rainier issue, I found they now have a seven-person office devoted to that subject. My effort is still in their files, I think as an historical curiosity.

A close parallel of St. Helens in 1980 was Bezymianny, a volcano in Kamchatka, Russia, that erupted in 1956 with a sector collapse and lateral blast, it would later be noted repeatedly. Professor Barry Voight flew out from Pennsylvania State, camped in

An aerial view above the crater rim of Mount St. Helens, looking north to Mount Rainier, 80 km (50 mi) away. Spirit Lake is pictured in the foreground, covered with blown-down trees. Its outlet to the west via the North Fork Toutle River is blocked by the debris avalanche. Near lower center, Harry Truman is buried at a depth of about 180 m (600 ft). (USGS photo by Lyn Topinka, CVO)

view of the bulge, and brought up the case of Bezymianny in the morning conferences of the scientific staff.

The year 1980 marked a divide between the time when USGS staff had little international study and the years that followed, when opportunities for foreign collaborations and disaster responses opened regularly. I benefitted from this trend as much as anybody. It was triggered in part by the deluge of visitors, domestic and foreign, that began to arrive and encourage reciprocal visits. Many collaborations would be born in the next several years.

Recent Stanford graduate Harry Glicken was surprised, but also greatly saddened. Later, as we shared an office, we never spoke of that morning. He had been assigned to man the observation post recently established atop the ridge now memorialized as Johnston Ridge. Harry must have felt guilty about being replaced by scientist David Johnston, who died the next morning instead of him. Senior scientist Don Swanson unknowingly dodged the same bullet. He had asked David to fill in for him just between Harry's Saturday-night departure and Sunday afternoon. He needed to see a visitor off on a Sunday flight. Harry departed the evening of May 17 to meet with one of his Ph.D. advisors, R. V. Fisher, of the University of California-Santa Barbara. David Johnston would be the one who died, moments after sending the now-famous message, "Vancouver, Vancouver, this is it!" Blown off the ridge by the lateral blast, his body was never found. Years later, during road construction, pieces of his trailer were located in the valley north of the observation post. Harry Glicken eventually would die on a mountain, killed by another pyroclastic flow, eleven years and fifteen days later on Mount Unzen. He had been on borrowed time, literally and figuratively.

Long-time colleague Carolyn Driedger and her Canadian meteorologist friend Mindy Brugman also visited David Johnston on May 17 at the new observation site atop the ridge now named for him. Carolyn and Mindy would have stayed the night and died the next morning had not David advised otherwise. Carolyn today recalls how aware David was of the risk. Harry departed in an old pickup and, with both his and its reputations for being accident prone, drove out through a large area of what would be blasted the next morning. Had the vehicle broken down, as was its regular habit, Harry could have joined David, Carolyn, and Mindy in death the following morning had the women elected to stay.

Back in southern California, I got the expected phone call and was soon on the way to the embryonic Cascade Volcano Observatory (CVO) in Vancouver, Washington. I acted as Dick Janda's second-in-command of the Water Resources Division (WRD) part of the operation. We worked with our colleagues in the Geologic Division (GD), with only occasional visits by the now-legendary Rocky Crandell and Don Mullineaux, who had retained their duty stations in Denver and would shortly retire. I would be fortunate to overlap with them for some crucial field investigations. Dick assigned me to study the lahars and their flow down the Toutle and Cowlitz rivers and into the Columbia. I began with the two 1980 flows and then transitioned to the ancient examples. Harry Glicken had the debris avalanche as his thesis topic, supervised by R. V. Fisher of the University of California and Barry Voight of Pennsylvania State.

The road system around the volcano had only locally survived, as on the south flank that was unaffected by the lateral blast. The volcano's post-eruption flanks would be accessed by helicopter, and safety practices and helicopter reliability had changed radically since my accident in Alaska. Helmets, fitted for each researcher and wired for intercom, complemented flying suits and gloves of fire-resistant Nomex. My post-crash comment about helmets, doubtless added to many others, had now resonated to the extent that not wearing them can be a firing offense.

The Debris Avalanche—Why Did It Stop?

The top 2.8 cu km (0.67 cu mi) of Mount St. Helens became the debris avalanche that traveled 27 km (17 mi) west down the North Fork Toutle River. Harry Truman and his many cats were instantly buried on the shore of Spirit Lake by debris traveling nearly 70 m/s (160 mph). In the same moments, the gigantic flow displaced Spirit Lake, forming a tsunami running up over 250 m (800 ft) on the ridge that would later be named Johnston Ridge. It raised the lake level slightly over 60 m (200 ft). With the lake outlet blocked, the water level continued to rise. Initially, the freeboard on the blockage was sufficient to withstand overtopping until 1983. But it could have failed from what engineers call "piping" or from an earthquake. Harry Glicken filled our files with memos on the blockage composition and stability, which he saw as a logical extension of his thesis and improvement of his chances for a permanent USGS position.

About five hours later, the surface deposits of the avalanche slumped and flowed off as a lahar that was small compared to the debris avalanche. Still, it was large enough to travel more than 85 km downstream to block the Columbia River shipping channel to the port of Portland, Oregon. It would remain blocked for four days. If the entire debris avalanche had not stopped, if it had continued as a lahar, as many do, the Washington state cities of Kelso and Longview might have been, as we in the volcano business like to say figuratively, toast. That term works best when pyroclastic flows are the hazard.

Why did the Mount St. Helens debris avalanche run out only 27 km, in contrast to the much larger mobility of other large volcano collapses, like those at Mount Rainier? And why did fatalities in five figures *not* occur in the Toutle–Cowlitz–Columbia River system on May 18, 1980?

Questions about the St. Helens debris avalanche nagged me and my former CVO colleague, Ed Wolfe, who like me indefatigably labors on as an emeritus. Nobody has spent more time mapping St. Helens geologically and knows it better than Dr. Wolfe. We discussed the 1980 event topic many times during our field trips to plan for the Acoustic Flow Monitors of the lahar-warning system on Mount Rainer. Our conclusion: low clay content, referring to sediment size, produced by hot acid water percolating through the volcano. Mount St. Helens is simply a very young volcano (< ca. 50,000 years), thus having less time for hydrothermal weathering to act than Mount Rainier, much of which is most of a million years in age. Ed verified my thinking on why tens of thousands did not die in 1980 throughout the Toutle, Cowlitz, and Columbia River systems.

North Fork lahar, 12 km downstream from Mount St. Helens, mobilized by dewatering of the 1980 debris avalanche five hours after its emplacement. Shear lines crease the lahar surface. Flow is toward the viewer. The barren hummocks beyond are the debris avalanche; forest blow-down on valley-side slopes records the lateral blast from the upstream volcano.

Scientists were impressed by the photogenic hummocks on the 1980 debris avalanche, as well as the horseshoe-shaped crater formed by the sector collapse. The hummocks are the surface expressions of coherent megablocks—chunks of the mountain rafted buoyantly by the flow. Scientists, including Lee Siebert of the Smithsonian Institution, would quickly extrapolate this morphology to identify more than two hundred other examples around the world.

The runout distance of the Mount St. Helens avalanche was only ten times its vertical fall distance. Could channelized volcanic debris avalanches be limited in their mobility, like, but much less so, than their less-mobile alpine debris avalanches? The 1980 flow became the archetypal example of how the risks from this volcanic hazard might be restricted to "zones." However, with time, as we really started looking at the extent of debris avalanches, including those at the far-larger volcano visible 80 km (50 mi) north of Mount St. Helens on clear days, we saw the danger of this assumption. That volcano, of course, was Mount Rainier. There, the debris avalanches kept flowing, megablocks breaking into smaller pieces or buoyantly rafting into backwater areas. What had been the interblock matrix now became the entire flow, a lahar for all intents and purposes. The downstream parts of these lahars that transformed from debris avalanches had few if any hummocks, the evidence many early investigators had relied upon both for identification as well as for the extent of debris avalanches. Because of this, runout distances of many prehistoric volcanic debris avalanches were, and can still be, underestimated.

Two Types of Lahars with Different Texture—A Key to Volcano History

A lahar swept down each fork of the Toutle River valley on May 18, 1980, hours apart and each with a completely different origin and behavior. Their differences would provide important clues to the way lahar deposits reveal a volcano's history.

The first was the South Fork lahar that began with the eruption at 8:32 A.M. It formed when ejected debris, some of it hot, melted snow and glacial ice. As this water surge flowed, it entrained surface detritus on the volcano's west flank from which the clay[2] had previously been washed away. After ingesting enough coarse sediment, it became a lahar, but total clay in the deposits of the South Fork lahar was less than 1 percent. This lahar proceeded downstream to the confluence of the Toutle and Cowlitz rivers, and the flow wave underwent a profound change along the way—it was no longer a debris flow. Instead, it became a hyperconcentrated flow (HF).[3]

The second flow was the North Fork lahar that formed when the increasingly watery surface of the debris avalanche slid away. It began as a debris flow, and it retained all its original clay (3 to 5 percent) that had originated when the rocks were "cooked" by hot water in the volcano's hydrothermal plumbing system. It remained a debris flow to the end, far downstream. Dick Janda would bug me, "Are you really sure it didn't change, too?" Yes, I was sure, and I had sampled it in the last place it could be seen, at the junction of the Cowlitz and Columbia rivers as it flowed into the latter's channel.

This recognition of two different behaviors related to sediment content was first made by two Russian workers in an obscure translation journal. They called them cohesive, with more clay, and noncohesive, with less clay. Because those terms apply strictly only to the deposits, and not the flows themselves, the preferred terms now are "muddy" and "granular," respectively. *As seen around the world, this difference proves to be one of the most useful criteria for looking at deposits and interpreting volcano history.*

The most important thing about the two types is that one type, granular or noncohesive, transforms downstream to hyperconcentrated flow (HF). This is flow that has a sediment concentration intermediate between upstream debris flow and downstream flood flow. Its deposits are unique and easily recognized in the stratigraphic record.

Hyperconcentrated Flow (HF) and its Deposits—Missing Link Discovered

Another amazing discovery especially excites volcaniclastic stratigraphers who are deciphering volcano history from deposits.

Mixtures of water and sediment can range, obviously, from 0 to 100 percent of water to sediment, or of 0 to 100 percent of sediment to water.[4,5] Typically, floods contain *as much as* 20 percent sediment, and debris flows can contain *as little as* 30 percent sediment (both as measured by weight).

Okay, so there is a gap of 50 percent in the sediment concentrations of water-mobilized flows known from the Earth's surface. Do they exist? Where are their deposits? Why do we know nothing about them?

It is astounding that middle segment of sediment-water concentrations remained unrecognized for so long. The first clue in this mystery emerged from the routine sampling of stream flows in the arid Southwest. There, hydrologists found that very small stream flows, essentially trickles, contained a concentration of more than 20 percent sediment. The suspended sediment was almost entirely mud, the term for the total of

In the summer of 1980, just months after Mount St. Helens erupted, Dick Janda works on the volcano's flank at the headwaters of the South Fork Toutle River.

Dick Janda photographs the "spool locality." The bottom 40 percent of the cable spool, once a picnic table, was inundated with HF deposits of the South Fork lahar, holding it in its pre-lahar position. Five to ten hours later, the top 60 percent was buried by the North Fork lahar. Right of the spool, the dark lower part of exposure is the sandy HF deposit, beneath the lighter-colored, pebble-rich and muddy debris flow deposit.

clay- and silt-size sediment. The hydrologists who first analyzed the data described these flows as hyperconcentrated flow (HF). And there the matter stood until the winter of 1980–81, when I found a partly buried cable spool that had been used as a picnic table.

That winter, I routinely reviewed my field work on the Toutle River lahars with Dick Janda every week or so, and I escorted him and interested colleagues to places I found interesting. While traversing the route of the larger North Fork lahar, I met a man logging his riverbank property of its lahar-killed trees. We got to chatting, and he led me to a cut bank where a wooden cable spool stood on end, partially buried in sediment. This, he said, had been his family's picnic table and it was sitting exactly where they had last used it. Furthermore, he said, he could still see it during the five-hour period *between* the first (South Fork) and second (North Fork) lahars. That was after the deposits of the first flow had buried only the spool's bottom half, thereby pinning it in place. It would be buried by the much bigger and muddier second lahar

Hyperconcentrated flow deposit transitional from the National lahar at Mount Rainier. The dish structure was formed by dewatering of the en masse-emplaced deposit. The "dishes" are concentrations of fine sediment left behind by waves of upward-moving water.

The transition facies of a noncohesive lahar in North Fork Toutle River, March 18 and 19, 1982. This deposit is in the transition zone from debris flow to HF, characterized by debris flow deposits at top, transitional from hyperconcentrated flow deposits below.

five to ten hours later. Finally, later in the winter of 1980–81, bank erosion would uncover it, and the property owner would show it to me. It was his testimony that he had seen it in the time interval between the two lahars that was crucial.

I knew Dick would love to see what would become legendary, at least to us, as the "spool locality." Here, documented by the owner's story, were the deposits of the low-clay South Fork lahar that were directly overlain by deposits of the relatively high-clay North Fork lahar. Everything—timing, stratigraphy, texture—was documented. We went there together several days later, and Dick was duly impressed. The South Fork deposits were granular, concentrated within the range of what sedimentologists define as sand-size material. I described to Dick how I had seen the same material in the South Fork of the Toutle River and how downstream it had gradually replaced the typical debris flow deposits of the South Fork lahar. He looked at me and said, "Well, these have to be hyperconcentrated flow deposits, right?" I agreed, but it was Dick who first connected the dots.

HF deposits had not been described from the geologic record at the time of our discovery. Now they are among the most diagnostic features of volcanic terrains. They have a distinctive texture, with sorting (standard deviation of grain size) intermediate between that of debris flow and streamflow, and one that volcano stratigraphers can easily recognize.

HF deposits stand out in the stratigraphic record because of two features: lack of obvious stratification and dish structure. Visible evidence of those two characteristics prove the sediment was deposited *en masse* and nearly instantaneously.

Prior to the discovery at the "spool locality," HF deposits were reported as fluvial in origin. The most diagnostic feature of HF deposits is sorting in the range between the sorting of a flood deposit we would want to call "sand," and that of a debris flow deposit that has a distinctly bimodal texture (like a plum pudding) of coarse sediment [pebbles (the plums), 4-64 mm and larger], dispersed in a matrix (pudding) of < 4 mm material. USGS hydrologists directly sampled the small lahar of March 18 and 19, 1982, and Tom Pierson and I described the runout-HF textures of that lahar in our 1985 paper published in *Water Resources Research*.[6]

§

When you find the HF runout deposit of a lahar in your stratigraphy, you can infer an upstream lahar beginning as a water surge from snowmelt melted by the heat of an eruption. *Thus you have identified and can date past volcanic activity.* The other possible source of a water surge is a lake breakout, from a crater lake or one formed by damming by a debris avalanche.

The reason many experimenters do not admit to the real-world importance of fine sediment content is because it is *a scale effect*. That is, the transformation of granular debris flow to hyperconcentrated flow commonly occurs over a channel distance measured in kilometers and cannot be seen in a flume. The effect of little clay (< 1 percent typically) is to minimize cohesion (particle stickiness) below the level needed to remain a debris flow. When the clay content is 3 to 5 percent or more in a cohesive debris flow, the grains stick together and *the flow does not transform*.

Greater than the Amazon River in Flood

This section describes what I think is an amazing case history—one deciphered only on the features of the lahar deposits.

The 1980 North Fork lahar had flowed back up the channel of the South Fork Toutle River for a short distance. At that time, there was a wayside called Harry Gardner Park at the South Fork highway bridge. There the upstream-flowing North Fork lahar had stopped. Over the coming months we showed visiting geologists the two lahar deposits that overlay the asphalt of the pre-1980 highway. We liked to point out a mobile home, completely intact, floated atop the North Fork lahar below the

How "bulking" occurs: the egg-shaped mass had just been entrained in the first huge flow from the ancient breakout of Spirit Lake. Bank height was 9 m (30 ft). Overlying lahars came from the same source.

bridge. It had been gently buoyed upward by the slowly upstream-flowing lahar, and not even the floor had gotten wet. It was later moved and re-inhabited.

Harry Gardner Park was a regular stop on our guided trips, and the "floating" mobile home was a popular photo-op. Mount St. Helens was now famous, and we could not turn down requests from fellow academics and the media. This had been going on for some time when Dick and I were at the Park with a visiting group of Chinese. He asked me to identify the larger bank of older material in the background. Frankly, I had never really focused on it, as I normally concentrated on the 1980 deposits. But now I did, and what I saw led to an amazing story. The vertical bank was about 5 to 6 m high and consisted of pebbles (4 to 64 mm) and cobbles (64 to 256 mm) dispersed in a sandy matrix with very little clay.[7] A 2-m blue megablock of altered dacite from a debris avalanche was entrained in the deposit, which was clearly that of a huge lahar. And the odd thing was—*the clasts were rounded!* That was a problem. It was evidence they could not have come directly from the volcano and must have been rounded by river transport *before* being incorporated in the lahar. And the miniscule amount of clay in the lahar meant that fine material had been washed from the sediment during that river transport, described as "selective sorting."

About 30 meters above level of North Fork Toutle at Kid Valley, we see the base of the ancient lake-breakout lahar.

If the clasts are rounded, it must mean one thing—they were entrained ("bulked" to sedimentologists) into a surge of water that transformed to a lahar. The rounding must have been caused by earlier stream transport. The lahar had originated from sudden melting of snow and ice, creating a surge of water that bulked rounded clasts from the river valley leading from the volcano. There was, however, a second possibility for the origin of the water surge, which was obvious in this case, and that was a breakout of an ancestral Spirit Lake when its outlet had been dammed by a debris avalanche from the north side of the volcano. Followed by blockage failure or overtopping and release of a huge flood wave—just exactly what had happened 2,500 radiocarbon years ago and *would happen again after 1980 if the blockage failed!* That was the only possible source of a surge of water large enough to form the huge lahar. That the blockage had been another debris avalanche was deduced from the fact that the gigantic lahar deposit contained many megablocks of hydrothermally altered bedrock from the interior of the volcano.

Deposits of the ancient lake-breakout lahar dominate the North Fork Toutle River valley. I published a summary article[8] on the characteristics and hydraulics of the huge flow, leading to its recognition as one of the world's largest floods.[9]

I obtained several radiocarbon dates from the outer rings of stumps of old-growth trees at the base of the deposit. These were uniformly about 2,500 radiocarbon years in age. No debris avalanche of that age was known from Mount St. Helens, but several years later, one was discovered by an academic colleague on the north side of the volcano, exactly where it should be based on the evidence. Everything just fell into place. But Rocky disagreed. He remembered finding Mount St. Helens tephra Y (for its yellow color), with a radiocarbon age of 3400 years BP. Rocky had found it in terrain where the lake-blocking avalanche or the breakout surge should have covered or removed it according to my hypothesis. So, Rocky, Dick, interested colleagues, and I went to look at the lahar's deposits upstream, where they contained even more and larger clasts of the debris avalanche. Finally Rocky was thoroughly convinced by the field evidence.

What if Spirit Lake's 1980 Blockage Failed?

On May 18, 1980, Spirit Lake was raised vertically just over 200 ft (60 m) by the debris avalanche. A tsunami of lake water sloshed up the south side of Johnson Ridge over 800 ft (240 m) and fell back into the raised lake. The lake's pre-May 18 outlet, the North Fork Toutle River, was buried and blocked by the debris avalanche. So, there was no outlet for the lake, and it would progressively fill with runoff from throughout the blast zone. The Corps of Engineers calculated that by 1983, the lake level would rise to the low point on the new blockage. At that point a huge flood surge would be released. The Washington District of the USGS Water Resources Division used dam-break and flood-routing models to predict its downstream course *as a flood only*. They publicized the results in 1980,[10] and such was the interest in St. Helens issues that it made national front-page news. The risk was clear—the blockage must fail or be overtopped. But the potential "flood" was far larger than our Washington District hydrologists had calculated. And their next actions did not speak well for their ethics.

Dick Janda and I quickly mapped the inundation area of the ancient lahar, shown by large clasts of pumice marking its "high-water mark." The map and flow description were approved for publication. District hydrologists, having learned from us that the flood would certainly be a "mudflow," quickly recalculated their model. However, they made no mention of their 1980 "flood" results, they arranged to delete funding for our report, and they made no mention of how they concluded in their 1983 report that the hazard from a Spirit Lake breakout had changed from a flood to a much larger debris flow.[11,12] Our report was listed as unpublished in their bibliography, but not mentioned or cited in the text itself.[13]

The implications of the evidence at Harry Gardner Park were clear. Because the breakout of the ancient Spirit Lake had transformed to a huge debris flow, the modern repetition of the same thing would create another debris flow, *not a water flood*. The more than 20 km of highly erodible debris avalanche and the abundant alluvium and lahar deposits in the North Fork channel, all abundant sources of the sediment for a debris flow, made it a certainty.

Here, in a nutshell, is the evidence for debris flows, not floods, and their probable synchroneity seen in downstream lahar deposits:

1. The dominance of rounded clasts in the PC lahar deposits proved they were formed by entrainment of alluvium rounded by stream transport, not from erupted broken fragments directly from the volcano.

2. The lahar deposits contained megablocks composed of pink and blue dacite. They are uncontestably from a debris avalanche. Brian Hausback, a professor at Sacramento State College, would later find deposits of two pre-1980 debris avalanches on the north flank. His dates overlapped with confidence limits of the lahar ages.
3. The size of the PC lahars indicated that the only possible source of the necessary volumes of water was Spirit Lake. There are four nearly synchronous lahars, labeled PC1 through PC4 because of their occurrence in the Pine Creek eruptive period.
4. Vertical tree molds extend at least from the base of PC1 through the top of PC3. The bark pattern for even small trees is identical throughout individual molds. Thus, the flows were nearly synchronous. For the 1980-dammed Spirit Lake to fail or be overtopped, the volume(s) of the flow(s) released would increase by at least three times that of the volume of a water flood. Let me explain how.

Jim Blodgett stands in at the mold of a small tree (forming a "tree well") in backwater area of deposition of lahars PC1 and PC3. His shovel marks the flow contact. Lahar PC2 is not present.

For the 1980-dammed Spirit Lake to fail or be overtopped, the volume(s) of the flow(s) released would increase by at least three times that of the volume of a water flood. Here's how: Think of streamflow as water moving sediment, generally only several percent, and of a debris flow as sediment moving water, with a sediment content of about 30 to 40 percent by volume. Because debris flows are about one-third water and two-thirds sediment, *the volume of the debris flow (versus the volume of water released when the blockage was overtopped) must increase by at least three times.*

At the same time several geologists, including Harry Glicken, were investigating the stability of the blockage material and expressing concerns that it could fail with an earthquake or weakening by piping, in addition to the eventual overtopping. Either way, the result would have been a debris flow extending upstream in the Columbia River to Portland and downstream to the Pacific Ocean.

The tunnel through which Spirit Lake had drained successfully for thirty years was threatened by deformation in 2015. With the tunnel's closure, the rising lake level could once again renew the risk of a lahar with a peak discharge the size of the Amazon River in flood. By early 2016, the tunnel cross-section was repaired for $3 million.

What Comes Next?

Mount St. Helens began to restore its classical Mount Fuji shape in 2004 with lava extrusion into the 1980 crater. That episode ended in 2008, with 6 percent of the volcano replaced. So, when does the stratigraphic record tell us the next dangerous explosive eruption is probable? In 1990, Rocky Crandell predicted that there was "...a high probability of a major explosive eruption . . . within the next sixty years." His (and Don Mullineaux's) earlier prediction of the 1980 eruption was based on the record of the last 4,500 years. Re-examination of more recent periods of activity led Rocky to conclude the more probable future should be based on the 150-year period preceding 1857. Rocky predicted, "Mount St. Helens is a young volcano and seems to be still growing. There is no reason to think its past eruptive periods are unique. I'm certain they will continue."

NOTES:

1. The two reports: Crandell, D. R., Mullineaux, D. R., and Rubin, M. 1975. Mount St. Helens volcano: recent and future behavior. *Science* 187:438–41. Crandell, D. R., and Mullineaux, D. R. 1976. USGS press release.
2. Clay can refer to the layer-lattice silicates known as clay minerals, or to clay-size sediment defined as particles < 0.004 mm in diameter. Here, I use it only as a size term.
3. Hyperconcentrated flow is the medial portion of the spectrum of sediment concentrations:

   Sediment content by weight percent:

   Streamflow — Hyperconcentrated flow — Debris flow

   0% ——— < 20% > ——— < 80% > ——— < 100%

   See later discussion in this chapter for its recognition at Mount St. Helens.

4. From Scott, K. M., Macías, J. L., Naranjo, J. A., Rodriguez, S., and McGeehin, J. P., 2002. Catastrophic debris flows transformed from landslides in volcanic terrains: Mobility, hazard assessment, and mitigation strategies. USGS Professional Paper 1630.
5. Tom Pierson has compiled an updated and more sophisticated analysis of hyperconcentrated flow: Pierson, T. C. 2005. Hyperconcentrated flow—transitional between water flow and debris flow *in* Jakob, M., and Hungr, O., eds. *Debris-flow hazards and related phenomena*. Berlin: Springer-Verlag, 159-196.

   The two seminal papers:

   Pierson, T. C., and Scott, K. M. 1985. Downstream dilution of a lahar: Transition from debris flow to hyperconcentrated streamflow. *Water Resources Research* 21:1511-1524.

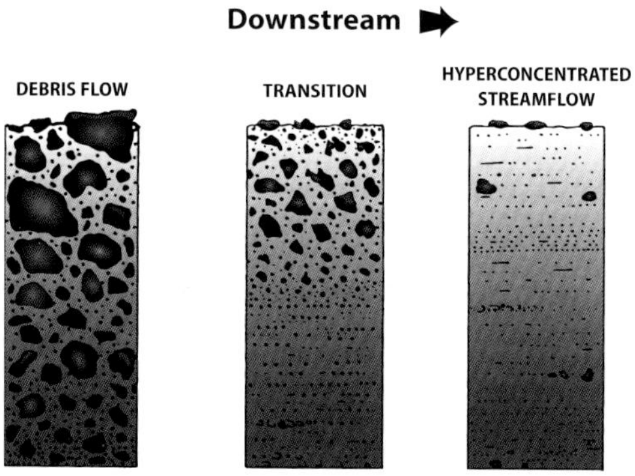

A granular or noncohesive lahar transforms as it moves downstream, forming a transition facies, where it is transforming from debris flow to hyperconcentrated flow. (After Pierson and Scott 1985 article in *Water Resources Research*)

   Scott, K. M. 1988. Origins, behavior, and sedimentology of lahar-runout flows in the Toutle–Cowlitz River system. U.S. Geological Survey Professional Paper 1447-A.

6. Names and size fractions of sediment particles:

Name	Range in mm	Range in inches (approx)
Boulder	> 256	> 10
Cobble	64–256	2.6–10
Pebble	4–64	1/6–2.6
Granule	2–4	1/12–1/6
Sand	0.0625–2	–
Silt	0.004–0.0625	–
Clay	< 0.004	–

7. Scott, K. M. 1988. Origin, behavior, and sedimentology of prehistoric lahars at Mount St. Helens, Washington. Boulder, CO: Geological Society of America Special Paper 229, 23-36.
8. O'Connor, J. E., and Costa, J. E. 2004. The world's largest floods, past and present: their causes and magnitudes. U.S. Geological Survey Circular 1254.
9. The "flood" report, the results of which were released in 1980, was finally published as Kresh, D. L. 1985. Spirit Lake dam-failure flood routing assessment. U.S. Geological Survey Open-File Report 82-770.
10. Swift, C. H., III, and Kresch, D. L. 1983. Mudflow hazards along the Toutle and Cowlitz Rivers from a hypothetical failure of Spirit Lake blockage. U.S. Geological Survey Water Resources Report 82-4125.
11. Ten years after 1982, the Washington District was still trying to cover up its ethical lapses with this too-little, too-late report: Kresch, D. L. 1992. Development and routing of mudflow resulting from hypothetical failure of Spirit Lake debris dam, Washington. U.S. Geological Survey Water Resources Investigations Report 91-4028.
12. Scott, K. M., and Janda, R. J. 1982. Preliminary map of lahar inundation during the Pine Creek eruptive period, Toutle–Cowlitz River system, Mount St. Helens, Washington. Water Resources Report 82-4067. This is the approved report that the Washington District of the Water Resources Division prevented from being published.

CHINA

Chapter 5

Natural Dams: Volcanic and Coseismic

Natural dams have a variety of origins in addition to volcanic debris avalanches like those blocking drainages as at Mount St. Helens both in 1980 and 2,500 radiocarbon years ago. The blockage is commonly a landslide, in many cases triggered by an earthquake. We call those dams coseismic. The debris avalanche blockage of Spirit Lake in 1980 was triggered either of two ways: by earthquakes at the time of the north flank collapse, or simply by the continuing intrusion of magma.

Examining the failures of both constructed and natural dams and their circumstances has lessons for students of volcanic hazards.[1,2] Constructed dams downstream may fail or be overtopped by water displaced by lahars, or they may completely block the lahars if drawn down in response to a warning of an eruption that produces lahars. Natural dams formed on or near volcanoes include failures of rims blocking crater lakes, moraine dams on volcano flanks, ice dams and glacier outbursts, and those formed by debris avalanches and lahars ramping up adjacent valley sides and blocking tributary valleys. Both the modern and ancient blockages of Spirit Lake illustrate the latter case.

Visiting Tibet with my Chinese colleagues in 2010, the Min River canyon was down-cutting through the eastern edge of the Tibetan Plateau. A weathering, hand-painted sign in a roadside pullout seemed to be reporting the statistics of the long lake that filled the Min River valley to about 30 m below us. This was the most upstream of three lakes that were created when the 7.5 M Diexi earthquake of August 25, 1933, triggered landslides. The lakes would then merge into a single lake called the Diexi Sea. The combined lake finally overtopped the downstream landslide blockage forty-five days later.

I bugged my colleagues to decipher the sign, as nearby, a white yak stood forlornly, saddled and waiting for tourists that did not come. He was tethered to a cement block, with no place to lie down but more cement. At least he was not burdened with the

Of the three landslide-dammed lakes on the Min River, this one is the furthest upstream. In 2004, a tourist yak rests in the view overlook, while signs offer details about the lake.

elaborate robes of most tourist yaks. I wished I could have bought him an hour in the grassy shade. However, he was well cared-for—he had a good food supply, and his temperament seemed cheerful. At this trivial 7,000-ft altitude, the yak needed but a few of his three-times-normal number of red blood cells. I, on the other hand, already felt an altitude headache coming on. It would not be serious until we got well over 10,000 ft.

In 2004, this uppermost lake measured 3,500 by 300 m in area; at its deepest point, it was 80 m, with the average depth of 42 m. The Red Army had passed this way, traveling up the Min River, over halfway around their clockwise Long March from Guanxi Province in southern China to the famous caves of Yan'an in Shaanxi Province in the hills of the north. There, I recall, was where a busty Shanghai actress would seduce Mao, leading to her own pretensions as the next empress, and the hideous deaths of thousands occurred, including teachers and artists beaten to death by their students or escaping by suicide. What fun for some adolescent students during the actress-led Cultural Revolution—no school, permission to torture teachers, free travel to destroy anything "old." That ended with Mao's death in 1976.

In 1935, Mao, riding in a litter and well fed, had traveled by the lake, his cadres pausing long enough to record that it was then 5,000 by 450 m, 40 m deep, at an elevation of 2,390 m. Since the partial draining of the Diexi Sea, the outlet has been gradually downcutting during the intervening seventy-five years.

A bathtub line of yellow silt appeared about 80 m above the level of the present upper lake. That line is evidence of a gigantic landslide dam, I argue to my skeptical colleagues. Judging from the several tens of meters of deposits on the uphill side of the road, it had lasted awhile. I tracked down an article in *Earth Science Frontiers*, a translation journal like those that brought Soviet earth science to the West beginning in the 1960s. It described a lake reported as 30,000 to 40,000 years in age based on three radiocarbon dates. A 67-m section of its deposits had been described from a downstream site.

The middle 1933 landslide was the most spectacular, leaving huge rubbly levees on each side, one with the small temple I had hiked to when I visited on my way to eastern Tibet in 2000. It was built to commemorate the quake deaths. In 2010, a new Chiang watchtower memorialized those killed by the June 2008 quake. Bedding planes in the blocks of Triassic sandstone in the landslide glistened in the sun.

The largest and lowest of the three 1933 landslides really did the damage. We stopped and let a local beekeeper point us to where my partner Professor Ge Yonggang was tracking about in the undergrowth. He found the old city gates to the original Diexi Town, supposedly consisting of 9,000 souls, none of whom survived. The gates are precisely on the lip of a landslide scar measuring about a kilometer wide, looking downslope toward the buried town in the far distance. When the Min River runs clear, you can see the remains.

At the Dadu River site of the 1786 natural dam that killed about 100,000 people, light-hearted tourists recall another somber time in history. Visitors re-enact the famous crossing of the chain bridge by Mao's troops, who in 1935 lobbed hand grenades into nationalist machine-gun emplacements.

How many died when the Diexi Sea breached its dam? No good statistics exist, but probably more than a few thousand lives were lost, especially far downstream. I can picture the surge roaring past the gigantic Leshan Buddha, carved from the riverbank cliffs at the junction of the Min and the Dadu. Those are two of the major drainages that pour off the Tibetan Plateau, what some call the Third Pole. At least 4,000 bodies were found along the flood's downstream course.

Perhaps a very large-capacity siphon could be at the ready that, with helicopter transport, could buy time for creation of an armored sluiceway before a naturally dammed lake overtops. This worked for the Spirit Lake blockage at Mount St. Helens, albeit with pumps. Time can be of the essence, illustrated by a 1786 landslide dam farther south that reportedly failed only nine days (yes, nine days) after a huge earthquake.[3] That failure is ascribed to a large aftershock, and the death toll is conservatively estimated at 100,000, the world's largest from failure of a landslide dam. Nine days is not enough time for an engineered breaching. For example, it took most of a month to helicopter men and machinery to cut a sluiceway in the largest 2008 coseimic dam, 3 km upstream of Beichuan, for a planned, engineered breaching.

We looked for the site of the 1786 landslide dam near the 1701 iron-link bridge that crossed the ferociously roaring Dadu River, a bridge that is now legendary in Chinese history. In 1935, about twenty brave PLA Long Marchers fought their way hand by hand across only the sixteen iron chains, from which the footway boards had been stripped, to lob hand grenades into the Kuomintang machine guns of Chiang Kai Shek. Today, however, several Chinese women clung to me for balance as the wobbly bridge swayed. They giggled charmingly. At the far end, Chinese tourists rented army costumes and posed with wooden weapons. I learned later that the story is mainly fiction. The defenders were actually semi-sympathetic warlords who may not have been defending as enthusiastically as Chiang would have wanted.

In summary, natural dams, volcanic and coseismic, vary greatly in their potential danger. The risk can be greatly reduced with engineering measures such as portable siphons. Magnitude of the hazard will depend on the volume of water to fill the reservoir behind the dam and lead to overtopping, the slope of the dammed channel, as well as the discharge of the dammed river.

NOTES:

1. Comprehensive summaries of natural dams and the circumstances leading to their failure are:

   Costa, J. E. 1985. Floods from dam failures. U.S. Geological Survey Open-File Report 85-560.

   Costa, J. E., and Schuster, R. L. 1991. Documented historical landslide dams from around the world. U.S. Geological Survey Open-File Report 91-239.

2. Sources for 1933 information in Chinese:

   Sichuan Seismological Bureau. 1983. *The 1933 Diexi Earthquake*. Chengdu, Sichuan: Sichuan Science and Technology Press.

   Chai, H. J., Liu, H. C., and Zhang, Z. Y. The catalog of Chinese landslide dam events. *Journal of Geological Hazards and Environmental Preservation* 6, no. 4 (1995):1-9.

3. Dai, F. C., Lee, C. F., Deng, J. H., and Tham, L. G. 2005. The 1786 earthquake-triggered landslide dam and subsequent dam-break flood on the Dadu River, southwestern China. *Geomorphology*, 205–21. Article also describes the 1933 coseismic dams on the Min River.

Chapter 6

Nevado del Ruiz: Day of Reckoning

The Nevado del Ruiz lahar disaster motivates us beyond all others. Ruiz is the northernmost active volcano of the Colombian Cordillera Central—volcanic massif seems a more appropriate term—5,389 m (17,680 ft) in altitude. In papers by Barry Voight, he called November 13, 1985, the "Day of Reckoning."[1] And that it was.

A Wall of Tractors

One stunning survivor account recorded by Jack Lockwood gives an idea of the power of lahars inundating Armero, Colombia. It was later reported by Barry Voight and appeared in the textbook *Volcanoes—a Planetary Perspective*,[2] by Jack Lockwood and Rick Hazlett.

"We went back in the hotel . . . a three-story building of cement," the survivor stated. ". . . suddenly I felt blows . . . towards the rear of the hotel I saw . . . [a wall of] mud approaching, . . . and it started crushing walls . . . and then the ceiling. I thought [the hotel] would resist, but it [mud and boulders] was coming in such an overwhelming way, like a wall of tractors, razing the city, razing everything . . . "

With a volcano-wide death toll of 23,000, Nevado del Ruiz in 1985 was the fourth worst volcanic disaster in recorded history and the worst caused by lahars. During the preceding year, the volcano had shown increasing restlessness with episodes of seismicity and increasing steam emissions. Yet the realization of a possible natural disaster unfolded in a slow, byzantine manner. Barry Voight had the patience to reveal the painful details and wrote three seminal papers on the events.[1] With the wisdom of hindsight, we can wonder at the excuses that warnings, potential evacuations, and, indeed, the hazard map itself, would frighten or panic the citizenry. Barry mused that the officials, at least, were not frightened enough. I believe a simple approach could have saved lives: self-warning from the ground tremor of approaching lahars.

Nevado del Ruiz is so high that it's nearly always obscured by clouds. (iStock.com / Natycubillos)

This could have reduced fatalities by half as estimated by Jack Lockwood, who interviewed numerous survivors.

The final reckoning at Ruiz began shortly after 9:00 P.M. on November 13, with a relatively small eruption of enough pyroclastic material to melt snow and ice, creating slushy surges that entrained sediment as they transformed to lahars on their way down the flanks of the Nevado. In documenting the formation and dynamics of the flows, Tom Pierson and colleagues found that their volume increased as much as four times during descent.[3]

Picture the rumbling, boulder-rich slurry in the Rio Lagunillas as it hit Armero like a "wall of tractors." In the lahar wave, crashing boulders and finer sediment moved the water (not the reverse as in a flood) with several times the impact force of a flood surge. The tractor analogy was very apt.

This was not the first time. *It was entirely predictable.* Twice before in recorded history, large lahars had come surging off the Nevado to devastate previous incarnations of Armero. Many had already died in the exact place where 21,000 died in 1985. A population center reformed again in both historic cases. And still the people stayed in place.

On the day of the 1985 disaster, authorities procrastinated into the afternoon and evening, spreading the standard mantra of "do not panic, remain in your homes." A priest said the rosary on the public address system and claimed that the alarm was not warranted. The mayor was on HAM radio, telling people to stay in their homes. Suddenly he interjected, "Wait a minute . . . " and was heard no more. Radio Armero was playing cheerful music when the transmitter went dark.

In one of Barry Voight's papers, he offered this account by a Colombian naturalist: "Descending along the Lagunillas from its sources in the Nevado del Ruiz, came an immense flood of thick mud which . . . covered or swept away the trees and houses, burying men and animals. The entire population perished in the upper part . . . of the Lagunillas valley . . . The depth of the mud layer varies greatly and is much greater toward the upper part of the deposit where it reaches 5 to 6 m."

The account is not from 1985, but from 140 years earlier, 1845, when about a thousand people perished. That same layer of mud would have been visible to modern forensic geologists, but unfortunately none studied the site before 1985, and the 1845 town slowly developed again as memories faded, and because the site was ideal as a regional agricultural center.

'It is astonishing . . . '

In a 1850 letter to a French geologist, Joaquin Acosta wrote, "It is astonishing that none of the inhabitants of these villages, built on the solidified mud of old mass movements, has even suspected the origin of this vast terrain . . . although ancient traditions testify to the frequent mudflows in these regions." Among those ancient traditions was one recounted by a Spanish priest, Father Pedro Simón. He arrived in the New Kingdom of Granada in 1604 and recounted an eruption of 1595 when the Lagunillas River "ran so full of ash that it looked more like cinders than like water. . . . the land [was] so devastated that for many years afterwards it produced nothing but small weeds."

A flood erodes its banks, removes some vegetation, leaves a thin layer of overbank deposits, and the terrain recovers relatively quickly. Some deposits of ancient floods can survive, but paleohydrologists seeking long-term flood frequency are frustrated by their scarcity. Lahars, however, leave thick deposits on flood plains and in backwater areas and can be preserved for thousands of years and integrated into an accurate record. Their layers, in which the texture reveals the behavior and origin, remain as easily recognized testimony to disaster. The Ruiz lahars had a granular, noncohesive texture, revealing their origin as meltwater surges entraining (bulking) sediment, thereby increasing in volume and transforming from water or slush to debris flows as they traveled. We can expect that the two historic lahar deposits also have the identical texture, revealing their probably identical origin.

Classic Case of the 'False-Alarm Problem'

Today we are more saddened than astonished by the lack of recognition of those old "mud layers," as well as by the lack of timely appreciation of the two historical accounts. Do the same blinders linger on authorities at volcanic centers around the world? Hopefully not, in large part a tribute to those who died at Ruiz. Barry noted that, presumably even with the known evidence of the earlier lahars, ". . . the failure was to wait until the last possible minute. Evacuation cannot be accomplished at that time scale, but such last-minute warnings are what the public seems to demand." Hence the reluctance of authorities to risk a false-alarm. They want to be sure that a catastrophe impends. Then it's too late, of course. Disaster odds are increasing with every tick of the clock. The appropriate lesson here is that the emergency manager who makes the wrong call by *not* warning of a hazard that then actually occurs should, in Japanese tradition, commit *hara-kiri* (ritual disembowelment). Waiting too long must also qualify.

After 9:00 P.M. local time on November 13, about 23,000 were to die below Ruiz, beginning with the first and largest lahar wave that arrived in Armero at about 11:30 P.M. People died simultaneously as buildings were crushed, or they died slowly over several days, immobilized in an escape-proof crypt of sticky mud. Although the texture of the deposits was granular (noncohesive), they contained just enough mud-size sediment to make them look muddy. Those of 1845 also appeared as mud to Joaquin Acosta, in large part due to the rapid dewatering that occurred once the flows ceased. The sand- and gravel-dominated deposit settled in place, forcing silt and clay toward the surface of the deposit.

By noon on November 14, only sixty-five of the 1,000 to 2,000 people still visibly trapped in Armero "mud" had been rescued. In all, 70 percent of Armero's citizens were killed, encrypted in mud and many died very slowly.

The eruption was a relatively small one, yet it melted enough ice and snow to start the flood wave that progressively entrained detritus on the volcano's flank to form the flow that Tom Pierson and others report traveled the 72 km to Armero at velocities of 8 to 10 m/s (18 to 22 mph). The flow took nearly two hours to make the trip, seemingly plenty of time for many to evacuate. *El Tiempo*, the Bogota newspaper had reported on the front page that Armero would have a two-hour warning. But they actually had none. But during this two-hour travel time, however, within minutes of the end, there was still one more chance. The ground was shaking.

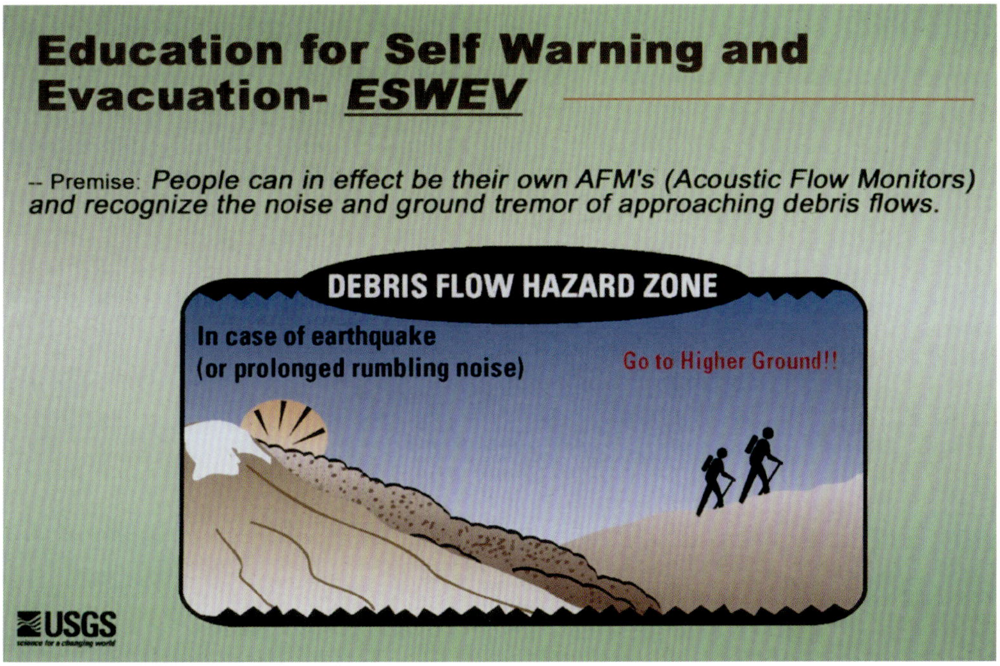

Life-saving signs like these were created following the Nevado del Ruiz tragedy in Colombia. (Lisa Faust, USGS)

'Strong vibration'

A final epitaph to all the failed human attempts to mitigate the catastrophe is the fact that "Strong vibration was felt several kilometers from the river."[1] Boulders clashing at the base of a lahar created powerful ground tremor that was felt for considerable distances. This is the case history that, thanks to Jack Lockwood, inspired us with the self-warning idea. By email, Jack wrote me that most of those who died at Ruiz need not have done so, if they had only recognized the meaning of the ground tremor as the flows approached.

We now incorporate this concept in suggesting warning signs where lahars are likely. Graphic individuals are shown hiking up a valley as a lahar approaches, with the warning, "In case of earthquake (or prolonged rumbling noise), go to high ground." It is a potentially useful strategy in cases like Armero, an illustration of the decline in awareness that occurs when the hazard has not occurred recently. The signs can also remind people of the distances that lahars can reach and prove lethal.

A subtext of this book is the influence of spiritual and political leaders in volcanic hazard response. In addition to the Armero priest telling people to remain in their homes on the evening of the 13th, in the preceding month the Archbishop had criticized the media for "volcanic terrorism" in even describing the risks. The Bogotá newspaper *La Patria* was concerned that publication of the volcanic-risk map, finally presented at a press conference on October 7, would cause real estate devaluation.[1] The mayor of Armero claimed that the residents found the map and the information so confusing that they did not know whether to stay or leave, and that they "have commended their fate to God." God knows, the mayor certainly added to the confusion. But there is always strong resistance when emergency-management authorities and scientists do what they think is the right thing, with red zones, "strongly encouraged" evacuations, and land-use restrictions. In the case of Ruiz, however, rarely has a volcanic crisis evolved to such a "dog's breakfast" of bureaucratic rivalries, politics, and foot-dragging.

Incidentally, excusing a lack of response on a "confusing" map or on "technical" jargon should not be taken seriously. The real reason, I suspect, is the fear and inertia inherent in the false-alarm issue. You fear looking like a fool if nothing happens, and you have depreciated property values. Your past experiences in a bureaucracy probably have shown you that delay and obstruction work in your favor. If not, you blame others.

Again, we see the failure of the local players, and the media and public in general, to fully recognize the power and mobility of lahars entombing people far from the volcano, versus the classical picture of a "blowing" volcano. Pompeii, for example, was only 9 km (5 mi) from the Vesuvius summit. Marta Calvache of the Servicio Geológico Colombiano (the Colombian USGS) told me in 2017 that Nevado del Ruiz was not visible from Armero, thus eliminating the volcano as a visible reminder of its hazards. Volcano education still needs to focus effectively on the ability of volcanoes to kill and destroy at distances of tens to more than 300 km (in the case of a lahar from Cotopaxi in Ecuador), in numbers greater than those actually "on" most volcanoes during an eruption.

Everybody in this business, even those of us involved in the long-term issues, should study Barry's three papers. Then, let's consider exactly what the Colombian naturalist Joaquin Acosta had wondered 135 years earlier—why had they rebuilt here despite obvious historical and geological evidence (multiple deposits of "mud")?

A volcanic stratigrapher, if assigned to study Ruiz in detail, would have identified the overwhelming risk in short order. My colleagues and I would both love and hate to have been the first to work out the size and frequency of the lahars inundating the

In Armero, more than 20,000 fatalities occurred from lahars that flowed down the massive Nevado del Ruiz on November 13, 1985. This shot was taken just weeks later, and outlines of destroyed city blocks are still visible. This was the third time the city had been wiped out in exactly the same way. Previous incarnations of Armero were destroyed in 1595 and 1845. (Richard Janda)

site of Armero, but then to have the obligation to make authorities and the public aware of the risk. The latter would have involved numerous confrontations with authority. Many foreign experts came, warned, and went. Ideally, having warned, you are obligated to see that the appropriate response is made and that evacuation is planned or begun, and to even risk your career to do it.

The failure at Ruiz to predict the tragedy in Armero was not one of technology. There were no neglected seismic signals, as possibly at Galeras in 1993. Summarizing results from a scientist who made a comprehensive review of the data from Ruiz, Barry notes that "neither cumulative earthquake energy, tremor energies, nor low-frequency earthquake or tremor patterns would have been recognized as short-term precursors prior to November 13.

"The depressing conclusion is correct regarding the lack of seismicity contributing to the catastrophe," Barry noted. ". . . in this case there was to be no recognizable short-term warning." The failure, in both Barry's and my views, was the lack of warning well within the time frame (days to weeks) for evacuation, based simply on the increasingly active volcano and the lessons easily read from the layers of mud, especially those of 1595 and 1845, when the death tolls were 636 and at least 1,000, respectively. Of course, that would have involved the risk of a false alarm. One can see from the official statements about the impending risk just how difficult evacuation would have been.

The lahars that would kill more than 21,000 in Armero and more than 2,000 in other drainages of Ruiz, began with a small eruption, just large enough to melt snow and ice in the summit ice cap that measured 4 sq km by 20 m, a seemingly minor circumstance in creating such a death toll. This meltwater would be the beginnings of granular, noncohesive lahars entraining sediment progressively and growing in size as they entered the headwaters of the rivers draining the volcano. They probably surpassed the 4.2-times increase in volume that we documented for the 1998 Casita lahar in Nicaragua. This growth in volume, even after many lahars leave the volcano and travel onward, is one of their unique characteristics that make them so dangerous.

This is the only disaster I discuss in detail in which I have been only a technical reviewer. I have not studied it directly, nor was I among the responding scientists. However, Nevado del Huila is the next huge edifice to the south in the Cordillera Central of central Colombia and a near twin of Ruiz. Consequently, I like to think I know Ruiz well, thanks to the retrospectives by Barry Voight, (the "smart one" in the Voight family according to actor/brother Jon Voight), as well as the technical work of colleague Tom Pierson and of now-retired Colombian geologist Hector Cepeda.

Hector prepared the map that accurately predicted the outlines of the area of what was to be one of almost complete fatal ground. It just wasn't seen by anybody brave enough to act. The fear of inciting fear in others, incidentally, would prove a well-trodden excuse for not acting on the part of multiple authorities and journalists throughout the late stages of the crisis.

"In a nutshell," Barry summarized, "the government on the whole acted responsibly, but was not willing to bear the economic or political costs of early evacuation or a false alarm. Science accurately foresaw the hazards but was insufficiently precise to render reliable warning of the crucial event at the last possible minute. . . . Thus the catastrophe was not caused by technological ineffectiveness or defectiveness, nor by an overwhelming eruption, or by an improbable run of bad luck, but by *cumulative human error*—by misjudgment, indecision, and bureaucratic shortsightedness. Armero could have produced no victims, and therein dwells its immense tragedy."

Ruiz has since become active, beginning sporadically in 2010. Apparently, the recent eruptions have been either phreatic or phreatomagmatic (steam or water-magma interaction) in character, but there have been no significant lahars. In 2015, CVO hosted a talk by Milton Ordoñez of the Manizales Volcanological Observatory, located northwest of the volcano. After his talk, we speculated on why there had been no lahars. I think it's simply a lack of pyroclastic flows. More recently, Marta Calvache told me about a dome that's now growing in the crater. Clearly the stage is being set. Certainly lahars will come again, and fortunately, the site of Armero is now a nature park. A new museum in nearby New Armero/Guayaquil commemorates the lives lost and is named for one of the tragedy's well-known victims, Omaya Sanchez.

Japan: Studying the Past and Teaching Tendenko

The issues that plagued Ruiz continue elsewhere today, only becoming clear when each arrives at its own day of reckoning. This one, however, did not involve a complex of well-meaning international and domestic agencies. But it was entirely similar in ignoring a known history. For a short period, the nation of Japan was at serious risk in two important ways:

1. Six nuclear reactors of the Fukushima Daiichi complex were constructed on the eastern coast of Japan, north of Tokyo, and
2. For more than ten years, protective seawalls were not raised even after experiencing tsunamis that were larger than those for which the seawalls were designed.

On May 22, 2011, the reactor complex was overrun by tsunamis following the 9.0 M Great East Japan Earthquake. Three of the six reactors in the complex suffered meltdowns within days. The clean-up will take decades if not a century. Further south another 10 km at the Fukushima Daini complex, four reactors owned by the Tokyo Electric Power Company (TEPCO) were overrun by waves three times the height of those expected. Meltdown was approached there but did not occur because of excellent management.[4]

The total of dead and missing was about 18,500, with more than 200,000 left homeless. Official and unofficial analyses attributed the disaster to TEPCO. Several days after the tsunami, the Prime Minister was considering the possibility of evacuating 50 million people, including Tokyo, possibly for decades, had the pools of spent fuel rods been exposed. Japan had truly been to the brink. Obvious lessons from the past had simply been ignored. Why? Possibly the cachet of esoteric engineering models? Again, as at Ruiz, "it is astounding . . . "

The Associated Press (AP) investigation later that month showed that TEPCO engineers designing the reactor had relied on a computer program instead of studying Japan's documented tsunami histories and the heights of those tsunamis based on the heights of their deposits. According to the AP, the TEPCO engineers began their work by eliminating earthquake data before 1896, citing unreliable data or data-collection techniques. This left them to create tsunami-earthquake models based on the short, modern record of accurate data that covered only the previous 70 to 80 years. In contrast, some planners in the United States apply 11,700 years (10,000 radiocarbon years) as a recurrence interval of a reactor-threatening disaster. That is the time since the final withdrawal of the continental ice sheet.

Apparently, the beginning of the TEPCO tsunami-earthquake record was the 1896 Sanriko Earthquake, measured at 8.5 M. It generated tsunamis that affected much of the same coast as the 2011 tsunamis, but were much larger than would be expected from a quake of that size. This anomaly led to recognition of a category of quakes described as tsunami earthquakes. The 1896 quake apparently was included in TEPCO's modeling, but the model still yielded unrealistically low tsunami heights.

There is no excuse to ignore the tsunami stratigraphy. TEPCO excluded the Jogan tsunami from the year 869 CE, which had created 26-ft waves near the reactor complex. Their modeling approach allowed them to construct the Daiichi reactors on a small bluff from 14 to 23 ft above sea level. Part of this liberal interpretation may have been the convenience of such a low site. While the utility company predicted a maximum wave height of 18 ft, the tsunami wave that disabled much of the complex exceeded 27 ft. The 2011 waves disabled backup power generators, located in basements or on ground floors, imperiling the nuclear reactors and nearby spent fuel pools.

After the reactor construction in the late 1960s and early 70s, evidence from 2001 had documented the deposits of two additional large tsunamis in the last 3,000 years, not including the Jogan tsunami. There was plenty of time—from 2002 to 2011—to construct a higher seawall. You'd expect such a project following the 2004 "Boxing Day" tsunamis that killed 230,000 people in Indonesia and Southeast Asia.

Although the death toll from the 2011 tsunamis was moderately less than the total from the 1985 Colombian lahars, the example is as egregious if ignorance of the geologic record and the evidence of some 300 "tsunami stones" are considered. The "stones" are stella marking the inundation heights, with accompanying warnings, of past tsunamis, including that of 869 CE. The utility company defense—that geological tsunami deposits constitute unreliable data, or that the simple measurements of the deposit heights are unreliable, seem a sad excuse. I think we can be sure that the "tsunami stones" are accurate and reliable. Evidence is lost in the mists of time, but the crucial TEPCO error may have been simply in not involving geologists and tsunami-deposit stratigraphers in the original site-planning process. Those areas of expertise were not well developed in the 1960s, but anybody worried about tsunami hazards should have known about the stones. The motive of the people erecting and engraving the stones was to preserve a record of tsunami disasters that transcended three generations, the time that Japanese tradition says it takes for the memories of a disaster to disappear and for the stage to be set for the next one.

Japan's building codes are the world's most widely and strictly applied. So the earthquake death toll was much less than the 140,000 who died in Japan in the early twentieth century following a 7.9 M quake. In 2011, a warning network of a thousand seismometers reportedly gave about a minute's warning to Tokyo (based on telemetered warnings versus the slower seismic waves), and many lives were saved. In 2011, most perished from the tsunamis. The seawall at Taro, a fishing town of 4,400, is Japan's longest and strongest. The government and media called it the "Great Wall of China"—2.4 km (1.5 mi) long, consisting of two walls, the second 10.4 m (34 ft) high. Construction began in 1933 after a tsunami decimated the Taro population, and some believed it gave a false sense of security. It was reinforced and expanded during the era of Japan's economic ascendency. A local saying is that people born in Taro will encounter a tsunami twice in their lives. That is their fate.

From the top of the second wall, residents were swept to their deaths in 2011 as the first wave poured over it to destroy most of the city

A noteworthy national tradition in Japan is the advice to volcano emergency managers who make the wrong call to commit *hara-kiri*. In regard to tsunamis, the Japanese conceived the self-warning concept long ago—it originated with the deaths of complete families, restrained by their slowest member, attempting to flee a tsunami as a group. Tendenko evolved after killer tsunamis from subduction-zone quakes in 1896 and 1933. Tendenko directs residents under tsunami threat to immediately go uphill and save yourself—just like the self-warning for lahars around volcanoes.[6] The term translates loosely as "tsunami scattering." Like the tsunami warnings along sections of America's and Canada's west coasts, it emphasizes speed and immediacy, because the tsunami-generating quake may have originated only a short distance offshore, and only minutes may elapse before a tsunami arrives.

At the time of the 1896 Sanriku earthquake, family members delayed to help each other, but ended up dead from the tsunami that destroyed the entire coastal region. That same year, in Kamaishi, in the Taro region of Iwate Prefecture, only 36 of 1,859 residents survived.

A front-page story in Japan, shortly after the tsunami of March 2011, credited tendenko for saving thousands of lives. The philosophy includes these points for coastal towns and cities:

1. Proceed uphill independently without pause. Forget about protection from the seawalls. Many were overtopped in 2011.
2. Trust your family to be doing the same thing. Large numbers perished, especially in 1896, by focusing on rescuing their families, in the Japanese tradition of strong family ties.
3. Assist others as you proceed to high ground (as with older students helping the younger during a school evacuation).
4. Integrate tendenko with route planning, trail and route signs, and designated "muster points."

Professor Toshitada Takada of Gunma University in Maebashi city teaches tendenko at fourteen local primary and middle schools. His classes include lessons on the ethics of saving yourself (trust that others far from you have been evacuated, and concentrate your aid on those nearby), as well as calculations of the power and velocity of tsunami waves, and pre-disaster planning of routes to the high ground you will try to reach after an earthquake. At a local school, at which the tsunami reached the third-floor of the school, older students had grabbed the hands of younger ones and led them to safety in 2011.

§

As the fifth anniversary of the tsunami earthquake neared, on March 1, 2016, the *New York Times* reported that three TEPCO ex-executives had been charged with criminal negligence for their failures to prevent or even to admit the Daichi meltdowns. They included TEPCO's chairman and two former heads of its nuclear division. As evidence of much higher historic and theoretical tsunami waves had accumulated, critics pressed for a higher seawall and for backup electrical generators to be placed in higher locations. Prosecutors initially refused to bring charges, citing a lack of criminal wrongdoing. However, a rarely used feature of Japanese law allows committees of citizens to examine prosecutorial decisions and order them reversed. Two such committees looked at the Fukushima case and both called for criminal indictments. Prosecutors in Japan rarely lose (99 percent guilty verdicts), except for those forced on them by citizen-review panels, where acquittals are the norm.

Shockingly, on March 17, 2017, a district court north of Tokyo ruled that both TEPCO and the government were liable for trauma to 137 plaintiffs fleeing radiation from the Daichi meltdowns. Other courts had awarded damages in other cases, but this was the first time the government was found liable. Court decisions aside, we can be sure that TEPCO and the government are totally to blame. The tsunami stones speak and reveal their guilt.

NOTES:

1. Barry's seminal papers:

   Voight, B. 1988. Countdown to catastrophe. Pennsylvania University College of Earth and Mineral Sciences 42:17-30.

   ---. 1990. *Journal of Volcanology and Geothermal Research* 42:151-188.

   ---. 1996. The management of volcano emergencies, *in* Scarpa, R., and Tilling, R. I., eds. *Monitoring and Mitigation of Volcano Hazards*. Berlin: Springer-Verlag, 719-769.

2. Lockwood, J. P., and Hazlett, R. W. 2010. *Volcanoes; Global Perspectives*. New York: Wiley-Blackwell. A wonderful textbook.

3. Pierson, T. C., Janda, R. J., Thouret, J. C., and Borrero, C. A. 1990. Perturbation and melting of snow and ice by the 13 November 1985 eruption of Nevado del Ruiz, Colombia, and consequent mobilization, flow and deposition of lahars. *Journal of Volcanology and Geothermal Research*, 41:17-66. This paper documents the enlargement of the flows by bulking.

4. The drama surrounding potential meltdowns at the Daini complex: Ranjay, G., Casto, C., Krontiris, C. How the other Fukushima plant survived. *Harvard Business Review*, July–August 2014 issue.

5. *Daily Yomuiri* online. An article reports that on March 11, 2011, in the city of Kamaishi, repeatedly hit by tsunamis throughout history, nearly all 2,900 school children were saved by tsunami tendenko; five that perished did not go to school that day. About 1,200 others in the city were killed by the 2011 tsunami.

Nevado del Huila in December 2008. (Martin Roca; CC by-3.0)

Chapter 7

Nevado del Huila: *La Avalancha*

South of Colombia's Nevado del Ruiz lies another active stratovolcano, the highest, most snow-covered in that country: Nevado del Huila. Almost perpetual clouds hide the summit, so its exact height is poorly known. Like its neighbor, this "nevado" (snow-covered massif) was the scene of a "day of terror" on June 6, 1994. That horrific day began with a tectonic earthquake of 6.4 M, centered several kilometers southwest of the volcano's base. The quake was a non-magmatic trigger of multiple small landslides that coalesced to form the single gigantic lahar remembered as *La Avalancha*.[1] Because residents mistook the ground tremor for an aftershock, and not an approaching lahar, about 1,600 people were killed. Like the 1985 disaster at Nevado del Ruiz, significantly fewer would have died if they had understood and acted on the signs of an approaching lahar.

At first, the earthquake devastated the communities of Toez, Irlanda, and others along the Río Páez, the river that drains the entire volcano. Stunned residents who had not been crushed by collapsing masonry staggered from their homes. Within minutes the ground began to shake a second time, but this time it was not an earthquake. A rumbling 15-m-high front of cascading trees and boulders appeared from upstream. This leading edge of the lahar raced toward them faster than any vehicle could travel on the area's primitive road system. At that point, there was no escape for most in its path.

Scientists of the U.S. Geological Survey—Tom Casadevall, Bob Schuster, and I—would later walk in abandoned villages among the structures that had been above the peak of the flow. I realized that lives could only have been saved by the immediate recognition that the second "earthquake" was the ground tremor of the approaching lahar. In fact, nearly all the people engulfed by the flow could easily have reached high ground in time had they known of that possibility.

A map showing Nevado del Huila and vicinity showing the route of *La Avalancha*.

The channel of Río Páez at Irlanda, Colombia, can be seen at bottom in the photo, with the flow from right to left. (Tom Casadevall)

More than 3,000 landslides, shallow failures of a saturated regolith, were synchronously triggered by the earthquake from the flanks of Nevado del Huila and the surrounding terrain. As they mobilized and flowed into channels, they entrained additional material and joined other flows, finally coalescing in the Río Páez to produce the single gigantic lahar: *La Avalancha*.

In one amateur video, an unbelieving visitor continuously exclaimed, "Dios Mio!" while footage showed the sudden arrival, a well-defined peak, and a smooth recession of the flow wave. *Can there now ever be a disaster unrecorded by videocam or iPhone?*

It is difficult to get out of range of cameras, and a nationally compiled video soon appeared showing the awesomely fast *avalancha*. One sequence shows the flow flying by, littered with forest debris and bodies that are mainly animals. Another shows centrifugal force literally plastering the entire flow in the bend like a race car on a banked track.

At Belalcazar, a larger town 30 km farther downstream, a Red Cross team of six was attempting to cross the river to render aid just a half-hour after the earthquake when they were buried by the flow. They become national heroes. Tracing the flow downstream, we would eventually follow its course more than 100 km downstream to a large reservoir. Belacazar was the last community seriously damaged.

Upstream, although it is the heart of FARC country (Fuerzas Armadas Revolucionarias de Colombia), we landed at the villages of Irlanda and Toez.[2] Fear of the FARC dominated the area. Our vehicle driver had a holstered pistol tied to the gear shift. Leather and clothing stores featured numerous models of holsters in their windows. In spite of rumors of a possible declared truce in the area, our helicopter tried to maintain a 3,000-ft altitude. Even Philippine terrorists declared a mutual truce in 1991 after Pinatubo, and I did not hear of its violation during the lengthy time I was there.

Our Colombian pilot believed we had lost one of our two engines to ground fire during our return to the city of Popoyan. People were still being evacuated as we landed, and we watched as a load of survivors arrived in an old Russian helicopter. A 100-m ring of armed soldiers was posted around the landing pad.

Upstream, the village of Irlanda (probably named by a homesick Irish priest) stood on the terrace surface of a previous debris avalanche. A surviving dog was chasing surviving domestic animals, and chaser and chasees were all getting desperate. An unrecovered body in a red shirt floated in a pool dammed by one of the small slope failures, and for the moment, the water protected it from would-be predators. Our pilot was warned not to fly any farther upstream, toward the town of Dublin; this is the inner sanctum of the FARC.

Walking the remainder of the Toez main street, silence reigned. High above, on the surface of an older and much larger avalanche, we saw smoke from a small group of refugees. The flow was just high enough to hit a stone animal barn, an international aid project that almost withstood the force, but finally yielded to the flow. Survivors at Toez had been evacuated by the time we arrived, but not before one had painted "valley of the forgotten" below the image of a skull on the side of a house. The spelling was poor, and Bob and I argued over the meaning—he thinks it could mean "wave of death," referring to the flow. The smell of decaying bodies was ample evidence of either translation. Our immediate appraisal was similarly bleak—the deposits and terraces of ancient flows inset throughout the valley of the Río Páez were a warning that catastrophic flows had happened before 1994 and could certainly happen again. Future risk had not been reduced by the many, but small and surficial, 1994 slope failures.

The event is an example of a hazard linked simply to volcanoes as constructional landforms and not directly to volcanic activity, in this case a tectonic seismic trigger of surficial failures in tropical soils with slip planes of tephra. Here, most of the failures were not located on the flank of the volcano, but in the surrounding terrain. No single failure was large enough to continue for a significant distance in the main river channel. The key to the magnitude of the disaster was the synchroneity of the failures with the seismic trigger, and thus their coalescence into a single huge wave. Had the same number of flows been successively triggered by rainfall in this sparsely populated region, probably fewer people would have died.

Volcanic activity played no part in the 1994 disaster of *La Avalancha*. But we did not have long to wait. Barely fourteen years, in fact. In February and April 2007, and in November 2008, flank eruptions melted sufficient glacial ice to form granular, noncohesive lahars with sediment entrained by the meltwater surges. The 2008 lahar took twelve lives and was larger than *La Avalancha*.

The most recent previous volcanic activity at Nevado del Huila is dated at 3000 years BP, but more intense study in this inaccessible and FARC-dominated area will probably show more recent activity. The 2007–08 activity was a mini-version of the 1985 meltwater disaster at Nevado del Ruiz, similarly producing noncohesive lahars like the 1994 *La Avalancha*. A lahar-warning system, using the system of Acoustic Flow Monitors (AFMs) developed by the CVO and Rick LaHusen worked perfectly, but it sent a signal only to the observatory in Popoyan. The key to these installations is direct transmission to those at risk via sirens, reverse 911, etc. That is the expensive part and will take time and funding wherever AFMs are installed. What kept fatalities to only twelve in 2008 was not the warning system but the lessons learned from the 1994 lahar. Toez, I can see from recent air photos, had been relocated to higher ground. Better late than never.

As we walked by collapsed house after collapsed house, I wondered why these structures have collapsed in spite of the reinforcing of their masonry with the strongest material available, bamboo. To me, some enterprising and socially concerned engineer needs to design a bamboo framework that would be both a construction design and a seismic retrofit.

§

Bernardo Pulgarín, a young Colombian geologist, was with us on the 1994 reponse, and later received funding from INGEOMINAS to get a master's degree at UNAM under my long-time partner José Luis Macías.[2,3] His subject, one that José Luis and I encouraged, was study of the large older debris avalanches forming the terraces in the valley of the Río Páez. That valley was a particularly interesting case history because, among other reasons, it was the course of a single river system that drained the entire Huila edifice, and thus contained the complete record of all types of flows. I was invited to accompany the field check of Bernardo's work and quickly agreed. I was just as quickly sobered up. Assistant Secretary of State Eagleton sent me this message: "We simply cannot believe

This stone animal barn at Toez could not withstand *La Avalancha*. In this image, the flow direction was right to left. (Tom Casadevall)

Toez was overrun by *La Avalancha*, and its main street, at center, disappeared beneath flow deposits. The direction of flow here was left to right; an arrow indicates the location of a stone barn. Note the high terrace from large, older debris avalanches. (Tom Casadevall)

anyone would want to go to this part of Colombia." With that, thus denying me official permission, he could well have saved my life. The odds of a U.S. citizen getting out alive from FARC kidnapping were then approximately 50 percent, and at this time they were at the apex of their influence, with the inroads to their power to come with the recovery of Presidential candidate Ingrid Betancourt in 2008.[4] Yes, José Luis's now-gringoless field party did encounter and was confronted by a FARC unit. The leader, who had apparently taken a geology course, quizzed them about continental drift to establish their credentials. My kidnapping would have been a certainty and my ransomed release, as a U.S. federal employee, unlikely.

NOTES:

1. Other earthquake-triggered collapses or landslides described herein are those in 1933 on the Min River in China, 1920 at Citlaltéptl in Mexico, 1785 on the Dadu River in China.
2. Pulgarín, B., and 13 others. 2015. Erupcionas Recientes del Volcán Nevado del Huila: Lahares, Asociados y Cambios Morfológicos del Glaciar. *Boletín Geológicas* 43:75-87.
3. Undated online article by Worni, R., Pulgarin, B., Stoffel, M., Schneider, D., and Huggel, C. Volcano-glacier interactions and related hazards during the 2007 and 2008 eruptive crisis at Nevado del Huila, Colombia. INGEOMINAS (Institute of Geology and Mines), 2009(?).
4. Ingrid Betancourt was rescued in 2008 with fourteen other hostages, including three American military contractors and eleven policemen, after 2,321 days of imprisonment. She had been campaigning as a Green for the Colombian presidency in 2002 and had entered rebel-controlled areas of the country against the advice of the government.

Citlaltépetl and Barranca Grande lie at the east end of the Trans-Mexican Volcanic Belt (TMVB). (iStock.com / Mirko Oleg Tiburcio Gomez)

Chapter 8

Citlaltépetl and the Trans-Mexican Volcanic Belt

In 1920 a father hurriedly led two small sons away from a rumbling, earthquake-triggered lahar as it came into sight. The boys couldn't run fast enough, and the father dropped their hands and raced up the valley-side slope to save himself. At least five minutes earlier, the lahar had caused ground tremor and noise that alarmed the people of Barranca Grande, who probably thought it was another earthquake. The lahar took them by surprise.

Citlaltépetl ("star mountain" in the Nahuatl language), also known as Pico de Orizaba, marks the eastern end of the Trans-Mexican Volcanic Belt, or the TMVB. The volcano has an extensive record of debris avalanches and block-and-ash flows.[1] It is the highest mountain in Mexico (5,636 m; 18,491 ft) and the third-highest in North America. On the north flank of Citlaltépetl, the Río Huitzilápan drains the Las Cumbres volcanic complex. In 1920 it conveyed a huge debris flow that destroyed the town of Barranca Grande and several other villages. Like the event of *La Avalancha* at Nevado del Huila in Colombia, it was triggered by a tectonic earthquake of about 6.5 to 7.0 in magnitude. The 1920 lahar on Citlaltépetl was largely unnoted until Claus Siebe and his colleagues mentioned it some sixty years later.[1]

University of Mexico Professor Sergio Rodríguez and I visited Barranca Grande in 1996. The mountain is described as a "slide-and-die" peak by mountaineers like my Mount Baker research partner Dave Tucker, meaning, should you slip and then fail at self-arrest, that's it. Dave is a retired alpine guide who used to help recover bodies on the mountain. He retired from the profession after suffering high-altitude edema above 4,000 m in the Andes. The only treatment is to descend as quickly as possible,

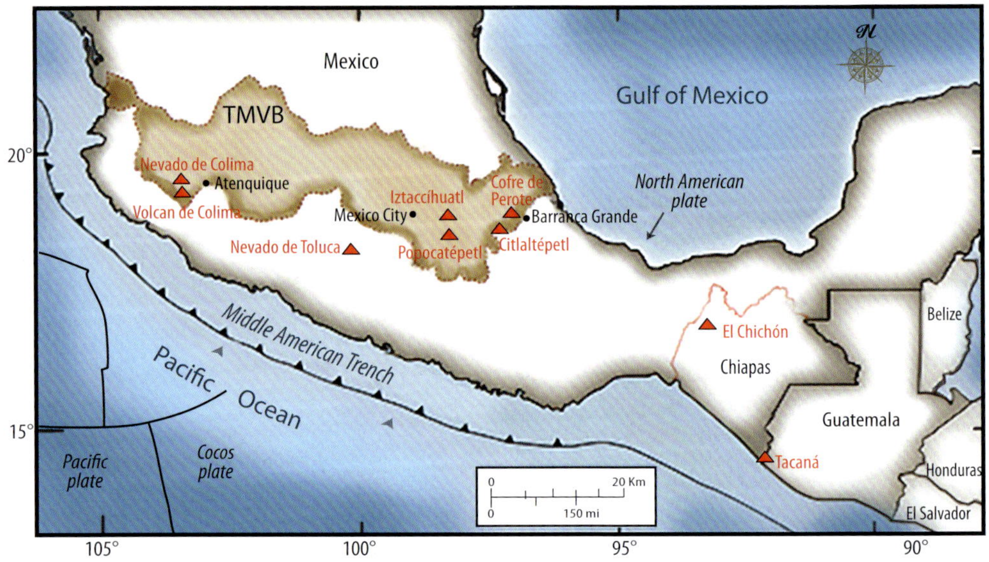

The TMVB literally girdles the country, where townspeople uneasily live with volcanoes as neighbors.

and Dave's life was saved by two of his clients that day, husband-and-wife physicians who diagnosed his condition and supervised the remedy.

"Slide-and-die" peaks are deceptive in not looking very deadly. In profile, this mountain looks like a stroll to the summit, albeit steep. I recall Mount Egmont (now known as Mount Taranaki), a classically shaped volcano in New Zealand that was reported in newspapers to have taken its fiftieth life while I was there. The most recent tally is more than eighty victims, many of whom slid and died. In 1953, six died on a single rope, and the last sound heard by fellow climbers was the scraping of the leader's ice axe as he attempted arrest.

The valley flat where the main part of Barranca Grande had been is now vacant pasture. Parts of the area are planted in coffee with banana trees as shade. The 1920 population was approximately 900. All but about 30 perished. The main part of the existing town has been rebuilt above the level of the 1920 lahar. At the time of our visit in 1996, only two elderly women remained who were girls at the time of the flow and remembered it in person. Another resident recalled accounts of three successive waves as much as 40 to 65 m deep. Photographs show multiple hillslope failures that must have coalesced to form the first large flow that hit the town, with successive waves from the more-distant parts of the watershed. The shallow

At left, a map of the Rio Huitzilápan drainage indicates the isoseismals, the areas of uniform shaking, in the 1920 earthquake. Right, the 1998 view of the Barranca Grande site on a valley flat shows how the town was reconstructed above the level of the 1920 lahar.

failure scars are now completely overgrown, so will not serve as future evidence of the event. That evidence will come from the deposits of the lahar that are preserved along the river channel.

The event is well described in a 1922 monograph, a masterpiece before its time, by the Instituto de Geológico de Mexico.[2] It was a replay of what must have happened downstream from volcanoes many times previously. Likewise, it was a forerunner of what would happen again at Chile in 1960 with the historic 9.2 M earthquake,[2] at Nevado del Huila in Colombia in 1994, and other places. The common factor is volcanic terrain where tephras have accumulated in significant thicknesses that will readily mobilize in response to an earthquake, with the probability increased by recent rainfall. Such an infrequent hazard probably wouldn't require mitigation in itself, but it is yet another reason to avoid locating critical facilities (schools and hospitals) in the valleys below volcanoes. The same can probably be said of landslides triggered by rainfall, like Casita in 1998. Those, or course, are not triggered simultaneously, so they're unlikely to coalesce with others to form even larger flows.

Earthquake triggering of long-runout landslides—mainly debris flows transformed from rockslides mixed with snow and ice—are a genuine hazard in the volcanic zones of Central and South America.[3] The textbook flow was the 1970 failure from Huascarán, the highest peak in Peru, but not a volcano. That flow was triggered by an earthquake estimated at 7.8 M.[4] An avalanche of snow, ice, and rock approached a velocity of more than 300 km per hour (about 200 mph) as it took more than 18,000 lives in the towns of Yungay and Ranrahirca.

A nonseismogenic avalanche runout killed more than 4,000 people in Ranrahirca in 1962. Surviving residents said they normally had about thirty minutes between hearing the failure and seeing the avalanche. However, in 1962, the flow needed only seven minutes to reach the town, leaving little time to escape to high ground. The 1970 flow had needed only three minutes to reach Ranrahirca, sending house-size boulders flying and bounding in front, with awesome dents of their impacts preserved in the landscape.

NOTES:

1. E.g., Siebe, C., Abrams, M., and Sheridan, M. F. 1993. Major Holocene block-and-ash fan at the western slope of ice-capped Pico de Orizaba volcano, Mexico: Implications for future hazards. *Journal of Volcanology and Geothermal Research* 59:1-33.

2. Instituto Geológico de México. 1922. Memoria relativa al terremoto del 3 de enero de 1920. *Boletín Numero 38*. These two parts of *Bulletin 38* are particularly interesting:

   A. Flores, T. 1922. Efectos geológicas. Chapter IV, Primera Parte, 27-29.

   B. Camacho, H. 1922. Efectos del temblor sobre el terrano. Chapter V, Tercera Parte, 89-94.

3. The 1960 example: Wright, C., and Mella, A. 1963. Modifications to the soil pattern of South-Central Chile resulting from seismic and associated phenomena during the period May to August 1960. *Seismological Society of America Bulletin* 53, 6:1367-1402.

   The 1987 example: Schuster, R. L., Nieto, A. S., and O'Rourke, T. D., Crespo, E., and Plaza-Nieto, G. 1996. Mass wasting triggered by 5 March 1987 Equador earthquakes. *Engineering Geology* 42:1-23.

4. The classic paper: Plafker, G., and Ericksen, G. E. 1975. Nevados Huascarán avalanches, *in* Voight, B., ed. Rockslides and avalanches. *Natural Phenomena* 1:277-314. Amsterdam: Elsevier.

MEXICO

Chapter 9

Popocatépetl and the Eagle Warriors

This giant stratocone looms (stratovolcanoes always loom) over a metropolitan concentration somewhere in excess of 30 million people, including Mexico City. It is here, in the trenches of periodically threatening volcanoes like Popocatéptl and Colima that the conflicts will be resolved between the government and the indigenous people whose lives the government wants to save. To evacuate or not? How many? How far? These are questions that seem eternal. And without a clear end to well-defined activity, when to allow moving back?

Do the decision-makers base their answers on case histories of past eruptions, computer simulations, pragmatism? Results are not promising. At Fuego de Colima (the active "Fire of Colima"), a huge volcano like Popocatépetl, but near the other end of the TMVB, the inhabitants of at least one village say they fear the scientists more than the volcano.

I first looked at Popocatépetl as a geologist peering down from the window of a commercial jet. As a member of the most frequent of the frequent-flyer classes, in Los Angeles, I had been personally escorted by a stewardess from the Red Carpet lounge to the plane. There the pilot welcomed me to my first-class seat. This was the golden age of commercial aviation for international flyers—first-class upgrades, flight lounges, gourmet cuisine. *Sic transit gloria*. While waiting to board, I had seen television reports that the recently revived dome in Popo's crater had exploded, killing everybody on the volcano, a party of five mountaineers blown off the rim. It was April 30, 1996, and I was arriving to give a talk at UNAM, the gigantic main campus of the National Autonomous University of Mexico. This was the home of the most dedicated, personable and socially motivated volcanology group I knew anywhere—what I like to think of as the incarnation of the Aztec "Eagle Warriors," whom I have come to know less pretentiously as "Los Guys."

Mike Sheridan of New York State University at Buffalo was the Ph.D. advisor to several of the Guys. They in turn were responsible for involving me and other scientists, known as "names," to work in the TMVB. Mike is primarily known for his life's work on Vesuvius. He is credited for what another colleague, Roberto Santacroce of the University of Pisa, told me is the "golden age" of reconstructing Italian volcanic history from deposits. That age was mainly the 1980s and '90s, inspired by Mount St. Helens.

The volcano-studded eastern half of the TMVB reeks of drama and history. In 1519, Hernán Cortés and his band of conquistadors were taking an unexpected course to a fabled city in a lake, Tenochtitlán, on the site of modern Mexico City, reached finally by causeways in Lake Texcoco. The Aztec emperor Montezuma and his advisors were doing everything possible to discourage him, but Cortés had enlisted the strongest of their enemies, the tribute-weary Tlaxcalans. From Tlaxcala, east of Popocatépetl, he headed west toward the volcano, uphill via Cholula to the 13,000-ft-high col between two volcanoes. Active Popocatépetl was to the south, with inactive Ixtaccíhuatl to the north, separated by what would become the *Paso de Cortés*. The band was a fearful sight to the "Mexica," as the Aztecs would be known to scholars. Their horses, described as "giant deer," were "high as rooftops." And the war dogs, huge, described as ". . . spotted like ocelots, great hanging jowls, blazing yellow eyes . . . ." Their ferocious barking added a supernatural touch; the tiny Mexican dogs raised mainly for food only yapped, later to become "purse dogs" of heiresses.[1]

Montezuma had informants at the col. They were awestruck as the column wound its way upward toward them. As described in *Conquest*, by Hugh Thomas, "Their iron lances glistened . . . , their iron swords moved in a wavy line as if they were a water course . . . gleaming . . . , they caused astonishment."[2] As they approached the pass, the dogs went ahead . . . "at the vanguard they came, in the lead . . . panting," their nostrils distended, foam dripping. The war dogs are overlooked in most accounts of the conquest, but they were long remembered by the defeated. Horses, however, got and deserved most of the credit. Even though horses had evolved in North America, they had become extinct there; had they not, of course, the Mexica may well have been sailing east toward Europe. "Next to God, we owed our victory to the horse," Cortés once said. Later, the conquistadors on horseback would have to fight their way out of Tenochtitlán, barely surviving a near-slaughter on the arrow-showered causeways during *la noche triste*, the tragic night. Most of the quilt-armored mastiffs also escaped and it was said, "with what fury the dogs had fought," even turning the tide of one battle as Cortés and his soldiers retreated to the coast.[3]

Popocatéptl, south flank, December 2, 2008. (José Luis Macías)

Today the ruins of the Great Pyramid (*Templo Mayor*) of Tenochtitlán, once running red with the blood of sacrifices, have been discovered and reconstructed next to the Zócalo, the main plaza of Mexico City. Orders of Mexica knights were headquartered within two corners of the pyramid—the warrior-sorcerers of the eagle and of the jaguar. The site of investiture in the orders (confirmed by images of both creatures) is a magical place in the mountains above Malinalco, southwest of Mexico City. For me, it was a pilgrimage.

Los Guys and I ascended to a small temple quarried in the rock. We climbed on low-angle strata of late-Tertiary volcaniclastics, the detritus of ancient volcanoes. Jaws of serpents formed the entrance to the citadel where warriors learned the ways of the gods. In 1519, they would be severely tested by the small band of foreigners approaching their island fortress from between the two volcanic massifs to the east. Their custom of capturing enemies for later sacrifice, rather than killing them in battle, would be a fatal mistake.

Headed west from Tlaxcala toward the golden city in the lake, the Spanish could see Popocatépetl, meaning "smoking mountain" in the Nahuatl language. "Popo" was then emitting a vigorous fumarolic plume. It had erupted several times in preceding years, the last time in 1509.[3] Cortés sent Diego de Ordaz with a ten-man scouting party. They approached the summit and were driven back by smoke and hot ballistics. On Cortés's second trip, a lieutenant climbed the volcano and lowered himself by a chain to obtain sulfur, making an important contribution to their gunpowder supply. He was not the first to summit, however; the volcano had been climbed by the Mexica.

Of the two other stratovolcanoes that threaten the metropolis—Nevado de Toluca to the southwest and Jocotitlán to the northwest—only once has there been a Plinian eruption in the Holocene. Popocatéptl, however, has had at least four Plinian eruptions in recent time, ca. 8000, 5000, 2100, and 1100 cal yrs BP. The last two Plinian eruptions destroyed human settlements in the Basin of Puebla, evidenced by pottery shards and other artifacts covered by Plinian pumice falls and lahars east and northeast of the volcano. The largest-known eruption was recently dated by Claus Siebe, José Luis Macías, and their colleagues as 27,800 cal yrs BP. It produced a debris avalanche extending to the southwest for 72 km, covering 1,200 sq km, with a volume of more than 10 cu km. The horseshoe-shaped crater has been almost refilled subsequently.

The work of Claus and José Luis documents that the last two eruptions destroyed human settlements in the Basin of Puebla on the east. The great pyramid of Cholula, supposedly the world's largest by mass, was temporarily abandoned about 822–23 CE because of an eruption from Popocatépetl. The pyramid was surrounded by lahar deposits, but Claus found anthropologists and archaeologists were not convinced. The lahars were not necessarily syneruptive (occurring with eruptions) and likely were triggered by later rain on fresh ash. The evidence that the pyramid had been surrounded by lahars was clear; at a nearby location, we found a site with a lahar exposure covered with weathered-out artifacts, pottery shards, scrapers, obsidian flakes, and a white quartz arrowhead-flaking tool, perfectly faceted to fit a human hand. I heard Claus on his cell, telling a colleague it was the most artifact-rich lahar exposure he has ever seen. The tool is now a paperweight.

In the United States, Cinco de Mayo is an excuse to party. But here it honors the May 5, 1862, Battle of Puebla, not far to the northeast, in which outnumbered Mexicans defeated the French. The city was now the site of a Volkswagen assembly line that's the length of forty-seven football fields. By chance, we stayed in Cholula on a May 5, and I looked forward to an authentic celebration of the Mexican victory.

I wandered out in the evening but there was nobody outside and silence reigned. A tumbleweed rolled through the deserted town square.

The 822–23 CE eruption of Popo occurred close to the time of the Classic Maya Collapse. That eruption, along with possible eruptions of El Chichón, probably triggered drought that significantly accelerated, if not the main cause of, the final disintegration of Maya culture. Reasons for the decline and fall of a civilization, with which Mesoamerican historians pass the time, fall away if we focus simply on the correlation of eruptions and severe climatic effects. Claus and his colleagues selected the year-specific date of 822–23 CE based on an otherwise uncorrelated Greenland ice core, which recorded a sulphuric acid peak from a volcanic eruption. That year is centered in the range of radiocarbon dates obtained from the main airfall deposit.

Popocatépetl and the Maya collapse are a classic case of the impact of volcanic activity on civilization with climate change.[4] A view that volcanism can explain the Ice Ages has lost favor, and one focus, with the onset of global warming, has shifted toward analysis of climate-forcing by a variety of geological hazards, including volcanism. A 2009 discussion section with a colloquium on that subject was appropriately titled, "Volcanism and climate: chicken and egg (or vice versa?)"[5] Volcanic systems unloaded of their glacial cover may become more active, and what has happened in Iceland is persuasive. Unloading may also increase the instability and collapse potential of stratovolcanoes. Meltwater seepage within the edifice may weaken the structure. Thus global warming may seem to increase risk to those living on the edifice, but on the other hand the longer-term risk of eruption-related meltwater lahars is decreased. There is plenty of material for future colloquia.

Our story here, however, is the recent evacuations, and attempted evacuations, in response to unrest at the volcano. The potential is for sector collapse and huge debris avalanches, either transforming like the Osceola Mudflow from Mount Rainier, or not transforming, like the 1980 collapse and debris avalanche at Mount St. Helens. Either one will kill thousands, if not many more in the first case. Plinian fallout has the potential to shut down the economic, cultural, and political heart of Mexico for many months. At greatest risk, of course, are the towns and villages on the edifice flanks. Their citizens need to leave when the volcano gods begin to murmur seismically.

Will they? Or must they be forced? Or should they be allowed to do what they wish? Scientists believe, of course, that if those living on the volcano truly understood the danger, as well as the scientists do, they would be profusely grateful for their advice. Unfortunately, that supposition is not true. Some living on the volcano seem to prefer to make pilgrimages to a dark-colored outcrop, the "bellybutton,"

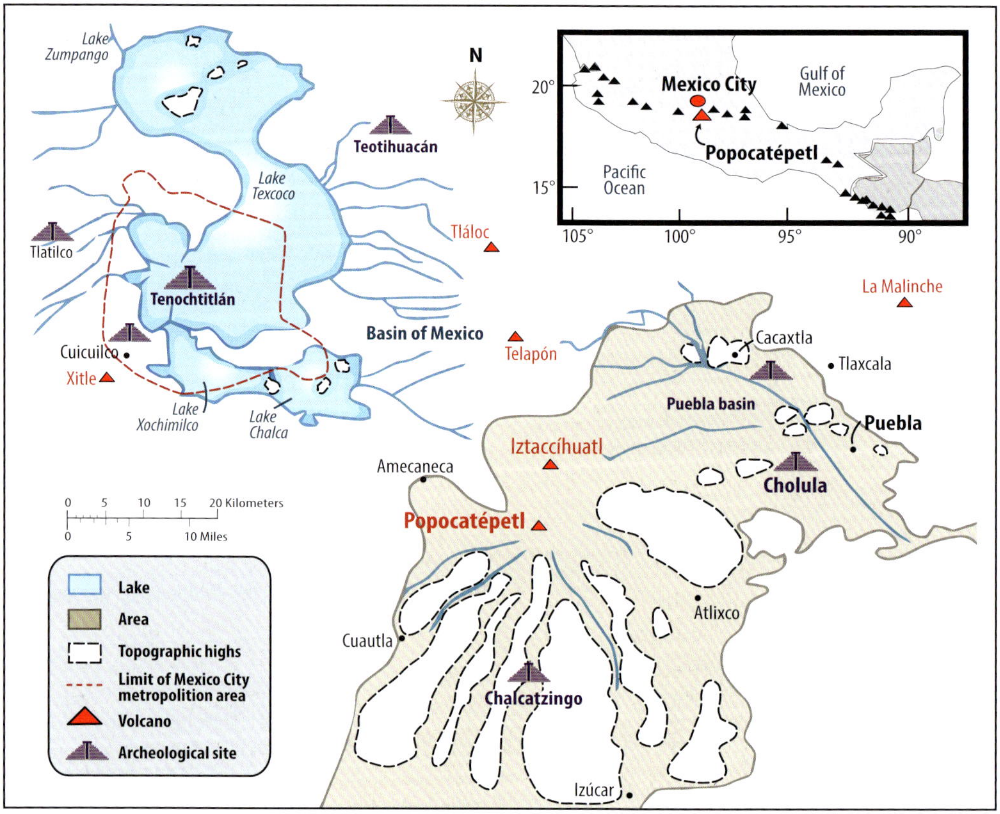

Lahar flow routes are visible on this map of Popocatépetl and surrounding cities, with Tenochtitlán to west and Tlaxcala to east. (After Siebe and Macías, 2004)

to pay homage to Don Goyo, the volcano's affectionate and respectful nickname for Don Gregorio. They seek the peak's benign calm as well as its continued water supply from springs and from rainfall runoff. Only the shrunken remnants of alpine glaciers now remain, and their melting is not an important source of surface water.

The great stratovolcano is difficult to read in terms of just how serious it is when tremor begins. A small dome has formed and exploded in the crater many times in recent history, and that is what killed the climbers when I first arrived. But these small, common events are unlikely to trigger a sector collapse.

In 1996, I joined Claus and other colleagues on a helicopter overflight. Later, while driving east over the Paso de Cortés, we stopped at San Nicolas de los Ranchos, the first small community we encountered, and Los Guys climbed on the roof of a medical station to search for primary ejecta. Just how large an evacuation is needed as seismicity continues? It looks like an unavoidable "government crying wolf again" mindset may be developing as the government gets more serious about protecting its citizens by getting them out of harm's way as these crises arrive. Mexico in 1996 had an excellent FEMA-like agency, CENAPRED, the National Center for Disaster Prevention.

In 2000, forty villages, including Xalizintla, all within 12 km of the volcano, were ordered to evacuate. Many villagers were hesitant, but eventually several tens of thousands were crowding the roads leading away. The people had abandoned their crops and animals, essentially their only assets and possessions.

Taking personal charge of the situation, President Vicente Fox sent 2,400 troops to force remaining villagers to depart and to take care of the dog problem. Considerable ill-feeling resulted, and nearly all the communities were reoccupied within about a week after the crisis diminished.

The 2000 episode of explosive dome growth resonated throughout Mexico's media. Claus wrote me an email and shared some of what he witnessed at Xalizintla. When the people refused to evacuate, the government modified the order. Those who chose to remain would be required to "sign a paper absolving authority in case of injury or death . . . ," Claus wrote. "Lawyers told me that this was illegal because the State has sole responsibility for the welfare of its citizens, and they cannot sign that away. So, about half left, half stayed . . .

". . . the media installed telephoto cameras just outside town," Claus continued, "which came to look like a gypsy camp of RVs and TV trucks. They would mainly shoot at night, making the explosively growing dome appear far more dangerous than it really was—spectacular, but with the telephoto effect creating a greatly distorted picture of reality. Commentators dramatized the scene as if it was a soccer game. During the day, bored TV crews roamed the town looking for drama, which arrived in the form of a convoy of army trucks.

"Hundreds of abandoned and hungry dogs had begun to chase turkeys and chickens. The army had received orders to remove this threat, humanely if possible, thus ruling out automatic weapons. The soldiers decided to lasso the dogs, which then, panicked, could only be controlled by swinging them around centrifugally by their necks, hoping to flip them, unstrangled, into the trucks. The sport was not a pretty sight."

The "dog-affaire," as Claus termed it, was widely viewed and did not inspire citizens' confidence in their military. It may have ended with dispatching the dogs away from the cameras, and most of Mexico probably suspected that. Street dogs are a common problem throughout the country, and poison baits may be spread throughout entire municipalities. I met a dog owner who had lost her beloved pet as a result. Some of the lassoed dogs in Xalizintla were probably pets, not street dogs. I tried to not incur the wrath of small restaurant owners when I sailed tortillas out their open fronts to grateful *perros del camino*. I embarrassed Los Guys, but they put up with me.

In their 2004 retrospective of the situation, Claus and José Luis noted that of the 40,000 people who were ordered to evacuate, "hardly more than 20,000" actually reached an evacuation center.[6] Claus and José Luis implied that the number ordered to evacuate was too large given the expected circumstances. They hoped that "after all these contradictory experiences, the people will . . . still follow mandatory instructions to evacuate their homes." Claus added, "There are doubts about this, with existing potential for a tragic situation." This is yet another version of the "false-alarm problem."

Control of population density, or growth management, has not been much of an option for Mexico, similar to the circumstances on the flanks of Vesuvius or in the lahar pathways at Mount Rainier. Population pressure finds a way, incrementally in the case of Greater Naples, and probably with palms crossed with silver. In Mexico City, growth has occurred when large areas were rapidly filled with squatters. In response, the government called in bulldozers to plow through the ad hoc structures and create a street grid. In the case of the flanks of the volcano, well, the difficulties are clear.

A Popo-specific analysis of risks versus the effects of emergency evacuation[7] emphasizes the need for three things:

- clearly understanding the hazards and associated risks,
- treating individuals as parts of family units, and
- assuring care for animals (commonly their only possessions) left behind during the evacuation.

Each is more difficult than it seems. We preach volcano hazard education endlessly; the family-unit issue is obvious but impractical at times of crisis. With regard to animals—even at Pinatubo in the Philippines, when nearly 15,000 people were evacuated from Clark Air Force Base, the U.S. Air Force told the people to leave their animals behind with several days of food and water, suspecting if not knowing that their owners would not be returning. Crises create their own microclimates of necessary ethical compromises. Who can or will stay to guard animals, and then not themselves flee as the threat escalates? The obvious answer: only their owners.

During our 2004 return to Mexico, we looked at some ancient debris avalanche deposits in a canyon on the east side of Ixtaccíhuatl. We passed a village as poor as any I have seen, with hovels constructed of unsawed timbers. Here death for every life form seemed close. A starving dog cowered. I took a sandwich from my pack and laid it on the ground and she groveled toward it. My companions followed my lead.

When evacuation is necessary, we can promise that property and animals will be guarded, but the citizenry knows what may happen. Officials probably think that, should an eruption actually occur, these considerations would appear trivial. As the continuing cycle of dome growth and small eruptions at Popocatéptl continues in the twenty-first century, a policy to allow small numbers to return and feed their animals is being refined.

NOTES:

1. "Dogs of war" were specially bred mastiffs, in the case of those with Cortés having been used to track down and probably kill native peoples in Cuba and throughout the Caribbean. They were common in European battles. Henry VIII had sent 400 dogs, some with armor, to Charles V of Spain for use against the French. A dog named Mohama fought so valiantly against the Moors at Granada that he was awarded a horseman's share of the spoils.
2. Quotations from Thomas, H. 1993. *Conquest*. New York: Touchstone. An extremely readable and dramatic history of one of the most memorable episodes of human history.
3. I saw a descendant of these ferocious mastiffs guarding a yard in Cienfuegos, Cuba, in 2017. Exactly as described by the Aztec scribe, "with great hanging jowls," it was the size of a Great Dane, but with twice the mass. It may have weighed over 250 pounds.
4. Bernal Diaz, writing in the 1550s.
5. Gill, R. B. 2000. *The Great Maya Droughts*. Albuquerque: University of New Mexico Press.
6. McGuire, B. 2010. Climatic forcing of geological and geomorphological hazards. *Philosophical Transactions of the Royal Society* A 368:2311–15. Summary of colloquium held at University College London in 2009. Preface of theme issue.
7. Siebe, C., and Macías, J. L. 2004. Volcanic hazards in the Mexico City metropolitan area from eruptions at Popocatépetl, Nevado de Toluca, and Jocotitlán stratovolcanoes and monogenetic scoria cones in the Sierra Chichinautzin Volcanic Field. *Field Guide for field trip with the Penrose Conference, Neogene-Quaternary Continental Margin Volcanism*, Geological Society of America. Other relevant references by Los Guys include:

   Siebe, C., Abrams, M., Macías, J. L., and Obenholzner, J. 1996a. Repeated volcanic disasters in Prehispanic time at Popocatépetl, central Mexico: past key to future? *Geology* 24:399-402.

   Siebe, C., Macías, J. L., Abrams, M., and Obenholzner, J. 1996b. La destrucción de Cacaxtla y Cholula: un suceso en la historia eruptive del Popocatépetl. *Ciencias* 41:36-45. Cacaxtla is a Mayan temple of strikingly well-preserved murals not discovered until the 1970s.
8. Tobin, G. A., Whiteford, L. M., Jones, E. C., and Murphy, A. D. 2007. Chronic hazard: weighing risk versus the effects of emergency evacuation from Popocatépetl, Mexico. *Proceedings of Applied Geography Conference*.

MEXICO

Chapter 10

Volcanes de Colima: Debris Avalanches

Continuing west along the Trans-Mexican Volcanic Belt, we encounter three other massive volcanic complexes, first, *Nevado de Toluca*, and at the westernmost end of the belt, *Nevado de Colima* and *Fuego de Colima*. Each is unique.

Nevado de Toluca is known for huge pyroclastic density currents and the blocky varieties known as block-and-ash flows. Both *volcánes de Colima* are known for huge collapses, the largest of which ran to the Pacific Ocean.

A volcano with a high potential to cause a catastrophe is *Fuego (Fire) de Colima*, or more commonly, *Volcán de Colima*. It is one of a pair with the name Colima. The other is *Nevado (Snow) de Colima*. They comprise the Colima Volcanic Complex (CVC), along with an older, poorly known volcano north of *Nevado de Colima*.

Fuego or *Volcán de Colima* is the active, younger, slightly lower, and more southerly of the two major volcanoes. Their geometry, at the west end of the TMVB, reflects the migration of magma generation toward the Middle American Trench, 100 km off the coast. To its north, apparently left behind, is the inactive *Nevado*. This geometry is the same as seen near the other end of the TMVB with the inactive Ixtaccíhuatl in relation to the southerly, active Popocatépetl. At the extreme east end of the TMVB are the less active *Cofre de Perote* and the southerly, more active *Citlaltépetl*.

The Smithsonian Institution's James Luhr, the distinguished student of the complex, once labeled *Fuego or Volcán de Colima* as "the most active volcano in North America"[1,2] This is based on 10,000 years of volcanic stratigraphy, plus the extensive record of historic activity which, surprisingly, is represented by only a single known tephra. Thus only one of the fifty-seven eruptions recorded by the Smithsonian's Global Volcanism Network from reports since 1519 CE was large enough to record geologically. This is discouraging for stratigraphers wishing to analyze a tephra-based history at Colima and elsewhere, but encouraging for risk analysts at Colima in that, of the numerous magmatic eruptions,

Fuego de Colima, lava flow and ash plume, December 17, 1998. (José Luis Macías)

only one was large enough, and its eruption dangerous enough, to leave a tephra record.

Luhr's findings left me wondering how many eruptions that my Mount Baker partner, Dave Tucker, and I have missed, even as we searched for the smallest tephras. Night sightings of glowing pyroclastic and lava flows establish that most of the Colima eruptions were magmatic, including that of 2015. CNN's broadcasts showed glowing material cascading down both sides of Fuego.

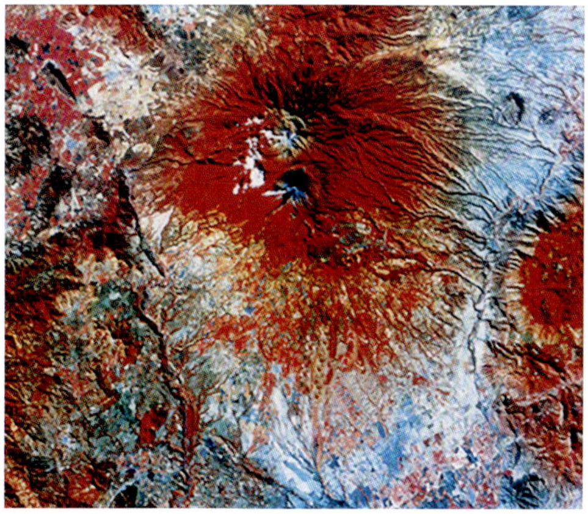

The two Volcanes de Colima, Nevado (at top) and Fuego (below), are distinguishable in this satellite view. (USGS)

There is risk from both the inactive and active volcanoes of Colima. The entire suite of eruption hazards is a constant threat at Fuego and has been since 1519. The Nevado, however, is sitting there, a massive edifice of progressively weakening rock, possibly on an unstable substrate and, over the long term, waiting to collapse from tectonic earthquakes, hurricane precipitation, tectonic spreading, edifice effects,[3] or simply gravity. The youngest eruption evidence is about 8000 BP in radiocarbon years.

Huge collapse events have occurred at the active volcanoes at each end of the volcanic belt, four at Popocatépetl, and even more from both volcanoes of the Colima complex. The collapses have been more frequent at Colima, possibly because of the greater rate of magma production there. Fuego is an ongoing case study, as is Popocatépetl, of repeated evacuations and offers of relocation, seemingly unappreciated and possibly resulting in increasing hostility to the authorities: "We fear scientists more than the volcano." With their colleagues, the staff of the Colima Volcano Observatory continues detailed studies on risk perception by the 5,000 people living within 15 km of Fuego. They report a complicated set of socio-cultural, historical, and political factors that mold villager attitudes.[4] A program of risk communication that began in 1997 has made progress.

Debris Avalanches and Their Mobility

Colima is an appropriate place for a detailed discussion of the features of debris avalanches and their mobility. Three of their most characteristic features are, one, a striking difference between the poorly sorted, angular detritus in a debris avalanche, and the better-sorted, rounded clasts in a deposit of coarse stream alluvium. Two, presence of the famous "jigsaw-puzzle" pattern produced by the intense collisions of megablocks in the violent flow. And finally, a mounded or hummocky surface that is considered diagnostic of volcanic debris avalanches, but which may characterize only the medial portion of the flow.

More than 300,000 people are at risk, most in the city of Colima. I get a little uncomfortable looking at a satellite view of the *volcán*, with the color of urban development spreading across the south flank. The city is constructed on multiple debris avalanches from sector collapses of both *Fuego* and *Nevado*. The largest of these has run to the ocean, and its distal hummocky configuration can be seen in submarine topography. If we think about a recurrence of one of these, it is solidly in the category of low-frequency, high-consequence events that "must be taken into account," according to Mike Sheridan. I agree, and should not Colima be a candidate for relocation just as its unofficial sister city of similar size, Beichuan,

Geologist Simon Hughes studies a sequence of block-and-ash flows from Nevado de Toluca. The flow deposits are overlain by interbedded tephra layers and dark paleosols (fossil soils).

China, had been before an earthquake destroyed the city in 2008? Too extreme? Of course—but an interesting topic for discussion. However, since the report of the huge debris avalanche by Sheridan and his student,[5] a different origin has been proposed for it, with significant risk implications.

Among these case studies, I have described debris avalanches that do not stop but run on and on, transforming in their entirety to more mobile lahars. The 1980 Mount St. Helens example did stop, only 27 km downstream, and it had a ratio of fall height to runout distance (H/L) of 0.10. With the understandable rush to identify and understand these potentially catastrophic monsters, this H/L unfortunately became a standard for the earliest hazard zonation. More than two hundred examples were quickly identified around the world, using the criteria of their hummocky topography.

Lee Siebert of the Smithsonian published an early definitive article on their general characteristics. Most notably, they included the world's largest landslide, the huge, ca. 45 km^3 debris avalanche running out along the I-5 freeway north from southern

Colleague Tom Pierson pauses by a "jigsaw-puzzle" pattern in a megablock of the 1792 debris avalanche from Mayuyama, near Mount Unzen on Kyushu, Japan. Running into the Ariaki Gulf, the flow triggered tsunamis killing 15,000 people—Japan's largest death toll from a volcano. Failure was associated with a magmatic eruption. Note the edge of megaclast defined by gray-pink color change at lower right.

California's Mount Shasta, in the Pleistocene.[6] By 1989, when USGS glacial geologist Dwight "Rocky" Crandell published his well-considered monograph on the astounding Shasta example (which he discovered), we were already recognizing their greater mobility, relative to Mount St. Helens, and Rocky was discussing a limiting H/L value of .075. But it had not yet dawned on most of us that their restricted extent might be based on the disappearance of their hummocks. The chunks of the mountain that formed the hummocks could disaggregate downstream or be shunted into backwater areas like beached icebergs. The flows themselves kept going, in cases unrecognized simply because the blocks had disaggregated. Colleague Jim Vallance and I had yet to report on the implications of the Greenwater lahar at Rainier. The flows at Rainier, seemingly except for the Greenwater, had also kept going. Some ran all the way into Puget Sound.

The Rio Ten debris avalanche down El Planchón Volcano, Central Chile, evident in the upper half of this photo, had a volume of about 10 cu km. It covered a layer of alluvium with rounded clasts, shown in the lower half, leaving a distinct line of contact visible. The debris avalanche ran from the crest of the Andes to the Pacific Ocean and is of Pleistocene age. (I noted glacial striations on proximal megablocks.) This image is tilted 15° to left; exposure measured 5-by-8 m.

Among the huge debris avalanches recognized after St. Helens were those from the Colima complex, as many as twelve, with perhaps nine from the active Fuego. The largest was from the older Nevado 18,500 years ago, traveling more than 120 km and inundating 2,200 square km. That 22- to 33-cu-km flow entered the ocean along a nearly 20-km-wide front, so a substantial portion of its deposits, and an unknown extension of its runout, are in the Pacific Ocean. The worrisome implication is that, even without knowledge of the submarine volume and extent, the H/L is 0.04. In other words, it flowed more than twice as far as expected (given the same fall height), based on the runout distances that were compiled after 1980.

In studying St. Helens and Rainier, we see that restricted runout distances of flows from sector collapses can be ascribed to overreliance on those photogenic hummocks, identifying chunks of the mountain buoyed along, to identify the flows. It seemed, however, by the early 1990s that the runout distance could be approaching theoretical infinity, given sufficient slope and the ability of the flows to keep maintaining or even growing in volume by bulking more material. Can the distal end of such giant flows be defined by only the body of water into which they must eventually flow? The idea that the runout distance must be related to the height of the proximal failure is appearing increasingly suspect; possibly the apparent correlation may reflect only that higher-altitude failures traverse steeper slopes, thus with a greater erosive power (or tractive force) to entrain material, and thus increase their volumes and their travel distances.

The H/L ratio, or coefficient of friction, is a useful concept for small landslides in alpine environments, but probably with little significance at the scale of sector collapses in volcanic terranes. For example, the topography of the runout terrain—whether it is a confining valley or an alluvial fan like the ring plains of New Zealand and the *faldas* of Nicaragua—is important. Generally this factor was not considered in early discussions of the H/L ratio.

Yet H/L has practical uses. CVO's brilliant experimentalist, Richard Iverson, studied the 2014 Oso landslide in the North Cascades, a failure of Pleistocene glacial drainage and lake sediment, showing with H/L ratios that it ran out about three times as far as a typical non-volcanic landslide in North America. The landslide killed forty-three people, making it the deadliest in U.S. history, and the search began for agencies and people to blame for why the landslide risk was not known. Because Richard established the uncommonly high runout distance, which thus could not have been predicted, the witch hunt deescalated. Survivors might have found some comfort in the view that apparently only an act of nature could be blamed. The conclusion also allowed Richard to search for other sources of the mobility, such as liquefaction at the base of the mass. The failure was preceded by high rainfall, and there was discussion of possible unpermitted logging on the pre-failure surface.

The failure occurred from a valley-side slope of the Stillaguamish River west of Glacier Peak volcano and south of Mount Baker volcano. There are a number of failures from analogous slopes underlain by glacial-outwash and lake deposits in the area, and I have done enough mapping of surficial deposits there for me to think that a detailed landslide map would have identified the risk of high mobility. Landslide mapping is now underway by the Washington Department of Natural Resources.

Lucia Capra, UNAM Professor and a coming star of TMVB volcanology (I was on her Ph.D. committee), along with her advisor, José Luis Macías, has proposed some interesting additions and possible modifications to the Colima story.[7] She interprets at

At Mount St. Helens, pieces of the of the mountain were buoyantly rafted down as megablocks, which formed hummocks. Don Swanson and companion explored the reshaped landscape in 1980. (USGS photo by Lyn Topinka, CVO)

least two debris avalanches from the Colima complex as stopping, damming tributary drainages, and releasing, with dam-breaching, breakout flood surges that bulked into debris flows. One is the flow from Nevado that was previously interpreted as the huge primary debris avalanche reaching the coast. She describes it as muddy or cohesive, the term applicable to all the clay-rich debris flows that form the runout phases of debris avalanches. That description has not been applied to a flow formed by the bulking of a dam-breakout surge, like those from the ancestral Spirit Lake near Mount St. Helens. If the Nevado flow were actually the result of failure of a debris avalanche dam, it would bulk enough surficial detritus to become a debris flow, but the deposits would be relatively low in clay—a granular or noncohesive debris flow with little clay-size material. These are commonly, if not entirely, formed by bulking of sediment into water surge(s), typically from eruption-induced meltwater as at Nevado del Ruiz, or as a lake breakout as at ancestral Mount St. Helens. Lucia describes the flow as both a breakout flow and as a remobilized debris avalanche.

Other examples of remobilized debris avalanches remain to be identified, and we should consider that direct flow of any debris avalanche from its collapse origin is more likely. One could consider that a breakout water surge would bulk its sediment from an older debris avalanche, but that surficial sediment would reflect selective sorting, so a granular, noncohesive lahar (and not a second debris avalanche) would result.

I joined Lucia and Los Guys in looking at these flows in the field before she embarked on her thesis work. There are several issues that I think need resolving before confirming that the flow that reached the coast was a lake-breakout flow. One is the relatively high clay content (3 to 4 percent), a level generally associated with lahars directly from flank or sector collapses. Another, the apparent lack of rounded clasts, which should have dominated if the flow increased a reported six times in volume. Lastly, hummocks in a lake-breakout lahar, especially 120 km downstream, would be highly unlikely. For the time being, however, I am assuming that Professor Capra is correct.

A lesson from the past at Colima is that collapses are usually extremely mobile, and possibly more so if from Nevado than from Fuego, given the presumably greater alteration of that older edifice. If Colima debris avalanches have dammed tributary damages that created secondary lahars, additional risk is possible. This risk, however, is notably less than that directly from the primary debris avalanches. Typically, it takes days to months or years before the resulting reservoir fills and breaks out, offering sufficient time for orderly evacuation and mitigation. Recall the several years of work by the U.S. Army Corps of Engineers to prevent the breakout of Spirit Lake after it was dammed the second time by a debris avalanche (2,500 years BP; and 1980).

More than 200,000 people live on the surfaces of debris avalanches from the Colima complex. This includes most of the city of Colima. This issue for long-term planning will evolve with time, with the experiences of new debris avalanches worldwide, and with further refinement of their recurrence interval at Colima. But the probability is definitely out of the "Black Swan" category. We would not be surprised if one occurred.

The communities at greatest short-term risk are, of course, the small villages near the active dome complex of Fuego, which have been repeatedly evacuated since around 1998. Some evacuations have gone well, especially with escalating dome collapse and pyroclastic flows, but in others not so well, with resulting suspicion of the scientists advising the Civil Protection Systems of Jalisco and Colima. Unfortunately, the state boundary crosses the summit of Fuego, and the two "Systems" operate coordinated but independent evacuation plans.

The 1888 failure at Mount Bandai in central Japan created hummocks, or mounds, that would form small islets in a lake created by the debris avalanche. These megablocks were deposited during the distal phase of a flow that was triggered by phreatic activity. It dammed drainages and formed at least four lakes.

Atenquique ('Flooded Place')

Atenquique is a town of fewer than a thousand souls on the east side of Nevado de Colima, located within Atenquique Ravine. The stream drains terrain on the flank of Nevado that is underlain by the largest debris avalanche from the complex. The pre-Columbian name means "flooded place" in the Nahuatl language, and its location in a broad, bedrock-walled alluvial wash should have been a clue. On October 16, 1955, residents were attending Mass. After a third day of heavy rainfall, at 10:45 A.M., a "gigantic muddy flood" destroyed the entire town except for the cathedral tower and a market building. Some worshipers climbed into the tower. However, twenty-three, including the priest, perished.

Geologists, including Ricardo Saucedo, reconstructed the event from its deposits.[8] They interpret the peak flow as in the range of hyperconcentrated flow possibly extending into debris flow. The flood was the result of rainfall runoff, and much of the sediment content was derived from bank erosion and small slumps resulting from bank undercutting near the flood peak.

Nevado de Colima is visible in the distance behind the Cathedral tower of Atenquique, before (left) and after the flood of 1955. (Ricardo Saucedo)

A combination of circumstances led to the tragedy, some related to the Nevado and some not. The Ravine, a wash of boulder-size bed material, conveys drainage from the youngest of three sector-collapse craters of Nevado.

Nine years earlier, in 1946, a large paper mill had been constructed at the townsite. Deforestation of the surrounding terrain then proceeded rapidly. The climate of the western half of the TMVB is very dry, and most of the forest is scrub. As you climb any of the volcanoes, including Tacaná on the border with Guatemala, you transition gradually into a forest of large and valuable softwood pine and oak. This is being incrementally logged, tree by tree, sawed by hand and man-hauled and skidded down the mountain by men as fit as mountain goats. Continuing forest destruction in other parts of the TMVB is a threat to the migratory Monarch butterfly that travels from as far as Canada.

Records show that despite Atenquique's repeated flooding since 1573, historical development was concentrated in the wash. Between 1906 and 1955, at least 325 people died. The population is declining (to 850 in the 2005 census). Deforestation of the flanks of Nevado continues and will increase the size of future floods. In preparation, Professor Lucia Capra is planning a lahar-warning system that would function even for floods because of the boulder-size clasts moved as bedload; ground tremor from that size of material is readily detected by Acoustic Flow Monitors.

NOTES:

1. Jim's summary paper: Luhr, J. F., Navarro-Ochoa, C., and Savov, I. P. 2010. Tephra chronology, petrology and geochemistry of Lake-Holocene pyroclastic deposits from Volcán de Colima, Mexico. *Journal of Volcanology and Geothermal Research* 197:1-32.
2. Guidebook for the 1997 IAVCEI conference: Komorowski, J.-C., Navarro, C., Cortés, A., Saucedo, R., Gavilanes, J. C., Siebe, C., Espíndola, J.-M., and Rodríguez, S. 1997. The Colima Volcanic Complex. *Field Guide to Pre-Conference Excursion 3, January 11-17, 1997.* International Association of Volcanology and Chemistry of the Earth's Interior.
3. A volcano is a constructed landform, poured and ejected onto the earth's surface, unlike other landforms carved by erosion. Picture a mold of Jell-O or a blancmange on a table quivering with the slightest movement. The quivering is the edifice effect.
4. More information on why the population on and around Fuego de Colima fears scientists more than the volcano:

   Gavilanes-Ruíz, J. C., Cuevas-Muniz, Varley, N., Gwynne, G. Stevenson, J., Saucedo-Girón, Peréz-Peréz, Aboukhalil, M., and Cortés-Cortés, A. 2007. The influence of increased activity on the perception of volcanic risk: The case of Volcán de Colima, Mexico (abs.), *in Espíndola*, J. M., Arce, J. L., and Macías, J. L., eds. *Proceedings of the Commemorative Conference El Chichón Volcano: Twenty-five years later.* San Cristóbal de Las Casas, Chiapas, México.

   Reyes-Davila, G.A., and De la Cruz-Reyna, S. 2002. Experience in the short-term eruption forecasting at Volcán de Colima, México, and public response to forecasts. *Journal of Volcanology and Geothermal Research* 117:121–27.
5. This astoundingly mobile debris avalanche is described by Stoopes, G. R., and Sheridan, M. F. 1992. Giant debris avalanches from the Colima Volcanic Complex, Mexico: Implications for long-runout landslides (>100 km) and hazard assessment. *Geology* 20:299-302.
6. Crandell, D. R. 1989. Gigantic debris avalanche of Pleistocene age from ancestral Mount Shasta volcano, California, and debris avalanche zonation. U.S. Geological Survey Bulletin 1861.
7. Lucia's papers:

   Capra, L., and Macías, J. L. 2002. The cohesive Naranjo debris-flow deposit (10 km^3); a dam breakout flow derived from the Pleistocene debris-avalanche deposit of Nevado de Colima Volcano (México). *Journal of Volcanology and Geothermal Resources* 117:213-235.

   Capra, L., Macías, J. L., Scott, K. M., and Garduño, V. H. 2002. Debris avalanches and debris flows transformed from collapses in the Trans-Mexican Volcanic Belt, México—behavior and implications for hazard assessment. *Journal of Volcanology and Geothermal Resources* 113:81-110.
8. Saucedo, R., Macías, J. L., Sarocchi, D., Bursik, M., and Rupp, B. 2007. The rain-triggered Atenquique debris flow (lahar) of October 16, 1955 at Nevado de Colima Volcano, México. *Journal of Volcanology and Geothermal Research* 173:69-85.

MEXICO

Chapter 11

El Chichón: A Surprise Volcano

In early 2007, my University of Mexico colleagues hosted a commemorative conference for the 1982 eruption of El Chichón, a small "bump" in Chiapas, Mexico. This "bump" (*chichón*), well away from lofty volcanic summits of the Trans-Mexican Volcanic Belt like Popocatépetl and Colima, was barely acknowledged as a volcano before 1980. Likewise little known, the surrounding state of Chiapas would later emerge in world consciousness as the home of the "Zapatistas," or Zapatista Army of National Liberation (ELZN). This was a movement for social justice by indigenous Mayans, organized by their charismatic, masked, Subcomandante Marcos. Not exactly a reincarnation of the peasant Emiliano Zapata, he would later be unmasked as a University of Mexico philosophy graduate of non-Mayan and privileged background.

Chiapas became a mecca for idealistic young supporters who, along with film director Oliver Stone, would visit the band in their wilderness lair. We would chat with their supporters from around the world in nearby airports. Stone, however, found that Marcos was no Ché Guevara, and the ELZN was thankfully no FARC (Revolutionary Armed Forces of Colombia), the ultraviolent revolutionaries of Colombia with whom I had later narrowly avoided becoming personally acquainted. At the 2007 conference, a road sign proclaimed that "Zapatistas Ride Again." They have become a tourist attraction.

El Chichón is one of those fortunately rare volcanoes, like Pinatubo. It erupts rarely, but when it does, be prepared. It is, according to John Eichelberger, Chief of the USGS Volcano Hazard Team, a very explosive end member of those volcanoes with long repose periods that respond explosively and periodically to the recharge of large, crust-resident magma systems.[1]

El Chichón sits by itself between the TMVB and the Central American Volcanic Arc (CAVA) in mountain rainforest, more than 100 km from the nearest volcano.

El Chichón as photographed in 2008. Note somma rim on the left, and 1982 crater at center. (José Luis Macías)

Pre-eruption air photos show a small, classically shaped central dome surrounded by a somma rim.[2] Unimpressive, and far from centers of population, the observations and unrest in 1980 and 1981 triggered warnings of a substantial hazard. The volcano, although discovered in 1928, had been promptly forgotten, and the new activity was a complete surprise. On our 2007 climb to the summit crater, containing the hot lake that we had bathed in a decade before, I introduced myself to Victor Rocha, who was carrying a copy of his and Rene Canul's now-legendary report and map. Victor was a utility company geologist who, with coworker Canul, had been looking for geothermal prospects before 1982. Their 1981 report had mapped the volcano in detail, identified the risk, and remains a classic example of the usefulness of field geology and geologic history to volcanology. Published in Spanish and what would have been regarded as the "gray literature" of a utility company, it had not penetrated to the consciousness of volcanologists with the influence to incite any action.

Thumbing through Victor's personal copy on the trail, I saw a beautifully crafted report.[3] Victor and Rene's alliance with Mexican and international volcanologists would have resulted in a very different and less tragic outcome, in that a larger and more experienced group of scientists would have been involved throughout the 1982 crisis, most importantly during the final day when the evacuation was rescinded. This is a reason why those of us who get paid to do this should go out of our way to develop collegial relationships with scientists and their students in less-developed countries.

Although the volcano was long forgotten after its first notice in 1928, in the late 1970s, after OPEC briefly held their oil hostage, hot springs in the area attracted attention as possible sources of geothermal energy. The Federal Electricity Commission began to map the area geologically with that idea. Victor and Rene heard reports of seismic unrest from the local villagers, then experienced them firsthand. At one point in 1981, ground tremor was so intense that they abandoned their camp on the *volcán* and fled.

The 1982 eruption changed the world's climate, but as interesting to me as Victor and Rene's story are the lessons from the tragic ending. After a long period of precursory seismicity, harmonic tremor began in earnest on Sunday, March 28. After an hour of complete calm, the eruption began with a 27-km Plinian column. The Army closed the area the following day according to preexisting plan. As many as 5,000 people had been evacuated in preceding weeks, but enforcement was apparently poor, and many leaked back, unmonitored, into the smaller settlements. From March 29 to April 2, activity decreased, although seismic activity remained constant, and on April 3, the military, apparently relying on a person or persons with scientific credentials, allowed villagers to return to the largest town, Francisco León. That night the final two cataclysmic eruptions occurred, killing 2,000 people just as they settled back into their homes, most of them in Francisco León.

Some of the 1.5 cu km of magma, in the form of pyroclastic flows, dammed the Magdalena River downstream from Francisco León during the night of April 3. A lake formed behind the 25- to 75-m dam, filling as the result of rainfall and upstream tributaries. It was 4 km long by the end of April. Anticipating the lake overtopping and breaching the dam, the Army evacuated 1,300 downstream residents. The dam failed on May 26 at 1:26 in the morning, producing debris flows transforming to a single large hyperconcentrated flow. Only a single fatality resulted, at the site of a hydroelectric plant under construction, where a 7-m rise in water level occurred. Towns along the route of the surge were severely damaged.

José Luis Macías, his student Lucia Capra, and I would in the 1990s study the 1982 stratigraphy in the sugar cane field that had replaced Francisco León. To me it seemed like a mini-Pompeii, but with the meters of the volcanic stratigraphy at

Pompeii transformed into centimeters. A basal 1-cm layer of a deadly pink-colored surge deposit overlay a floor of baked blue-and-white tile, reminding me of Pompeii mosaics. The pink basal ash, below several centimeters of pumice, recorded an ash flow just as deadly as those from Vesuvius.

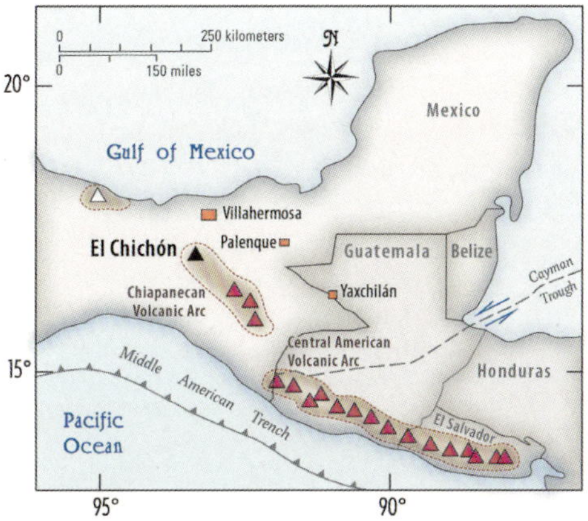

El Chichón lies at north end of the Chiapanecan Volcanic Arc, northwest of the Central American Volcanic Arc.

Wendell Duffield, USGS geologist (an accomplished novelist in retirement), joined his colleague Bob Tilling eight weeks after the eruption for the first helicopter recon of the destruction.[4] They were astonished at the total destruction by the hurricane of pyroclastic flows that had swept away Francisco León and its inhabitants. A massive stone church was the only recognizable ruin. Around the town, Wendell and Bob recalled seeing bathtub rings of the lake that had formed after the eruption and which had finally drained on May 26. Later, José Luis, Lucia, myself, and other colleagues reconstructed the lake dammed by the April 3 pyroclastic-flow deposits, and John Costa, USGS flood specialist, modeled the breakout surge.[5]

After returning to the United States, Wendell and Bob gave talks in response to the "nearly insatiable public thirst" for information on the eruption, only two years into the explosion of interest in volcanoes caused by Mount St. Helens in 1980. After one talk, a member of his audience told Wendell that he (Wendell) had just solved a two-decade mystery of Mesoamerican anthropology. A Harvard Ph.D. student, Gary Gosen, had written in 1974, referring to oral tradition of the destruction of an ancient culture of the Chamula Indians, Maya descendants, by a "boiling flood" in the mountains of Chiapas.[6] The estimated date was ca. 1300 CE, well after Maya collapse and a likely correlative of the previous eruption of El Chichón, dated as ca. 550 BP in radiocarbon years. Chamulan oral history included accounts of ground tremor "as though a god were repeatedly striking the ground to make it buzz like a musical gourd." Finally, there was a roar, and pumice was thrown into the air for several days. Flow in the river decreased to puddles. The people were busy harvesting now-catchable fish, when a roaring wall of water drowned large numbers of them. The story entered the lore and history of the people, unfortunately to be appreciated only in retrospect as indicating the presence of a dangerous explosive volcano upstream.

The church at Francisco León can be seen at the top of the upper photo, and as a ruin in 1982 in the lower photo. (Wendell Duffield and Robert Tilling)

That had undoubtedly been El Chichón, by the process of elimination. Wendell noted that some traditions may be fanciful tales, but many, perhaps most, are founded on actual events.

When the barrier damming the 1982 lake failed, only a single person was killed, with three seriously burned. That lake breakout, of course, had been expected, unlike the ca. 1300 CE example. The time to plan for the dam failure, as the lake progressively forms, is the saving grace of landslide- and debris-avalanche-dammed lakes, both earthquake- and volcano-related. Yet, historical examples have resulted in as many as 100,000 dead, as occurred in 1786 CE.

El Chichón had far more profound effects than the surge resulting from the pyroclastic-flow-dammed lake. Large explosive eruptions similar to and larger than 1982 inject sulphate-rich aerosols in the stratosphere, reducing solar radiation into the troposphere, causing reduced rainfall, and in this case reducing worldwide temperature nearly 1 degree C the following year. Benjamin Franklin may have been the first to relate climate to volcanic eruptions. In Paris in 1783, he noted the effects there of Icelandic eruptions that were killing one-fifth of that country's population, mainly by loss of livestock from emission of fluorine from Laki volcano.[7]

El Chichón is one of two volcanoes (with Popocatépetl) that may be accountable for the droughts that brought the Maya period to an end, the Classic Maya Collapse ca. 900 CE. Of the two, the location of El Chichón is closer to the Maya heartland, but a large eruption of either could have even influenced climate worldwide. Both volcanoes have rich sulphur dioxide emissions and both had major eruptions near that time, based on pyroclastic flow and ash cloud deposits dated by Macías, Siebe, Tilling, and others, and reviewed by anthropologist Richardson Gill.[8] Whether the deaths of civilizations can be attributed to a single factor or not, Gill's book is a fascinating account of eruption-induced droughts as the primary event that triggers a cascade of social effects. The social conflicts alone can, of course, appear as the primary causes, as attested by a huge anthropological literature.

On my first trip to El Chichón, a lesson that I would apparently have to relearn later at Casita was that, in the heat of the day in devastated, shadeless terrain, I can literally be cooked to death, or so it seemed at the time. Instead of a boulder to crawl beneath, returning from the crater, I had to find a gulley that was sufficiently deep enough to get my nearly nude self entirely in the shade and let evaporation do its work. In the mid-1990s, the terrain was still barren, and huge dune forms with wave lengths of 5 to 10 m recorded the passage of the final giant surge.

Bob Tilling would summarize the lessons of El Chichón at the retrospective conference.[9] These can be distilled to the fact that any young volcanic center (even if long dormant) must be studied in detail, initially with geologic mapping and concurrent volcanic stratigraphy. (Only 10 percent of the world's estimated 1,500 active volcanoes are mapped.) Then, a hazards map and assessment can be prepared before a crisis, and monitoring can be initiated to establish baseline behavior. Finally, and we might add above all, where the risk is high or where unrest appears, experienced scientists must be integrated in the research, planning, and especially in any evacuation management. Those involved at El Chichón in 1982 were not experienced; had they been, they would not have assumed that the decreased activity of March 29 to April 2 was the end of the eruption (especially with continuing seismicity), and they would not have rescinded the evacuation.

NOTES:

1. Eichelberger, J. 2007. El Chichón: An explosive end-member among long-repose period, recharged, crust-resident magma systems (abs.) *in Espíndola*, J. M., Arce, J. L., and Macías, J. L., eds. *Proceedings of the Commemorative Conference El Chichón Volcano: Twenty-five years later.* San Cristóbal de Las Casas, Chiapas, México, 27.
2. A somma is a segment of the rim of an earlier, larger volcano, within which the most recent edifice is constructed. After Monte Somma at Vesuvius.
3. Canul, R. F., and Rocha, V. L. 1981. *Informe geológico de la zona geotérmica de El Chichonal.* Chiapas: Comisión Federal de Electricidad, Morelia, Michoacán, Mexico. Only a few copies of this report are extant. The Library of Congress has lost its only copy.
4. Duffield, W. A., Tilling, R. I., and Canul, R. 1984. Geology of El Chichón volcano, Chiapas, México. *Journal of Volcanology and Geothermal Resources* 20:117–32.

   Duffield, W.A. 2001. At least Noah had some warning. EOS, *Transactions*, American Geophysical Union 82:305, 309.

   Duffield, W.A., 2007. Oral tradition, El Chichón, and beyond (abs.) *in Espíndola*, J. M., Arce, J. L., and Macías, J. L., eds. 2007. *Proceedings of the Commemorative Conference El Chichón Volcano: Twenty-five years later.* San Cristóbal de Las Casas, Chiapas, México, 26.
5. Macías, J. L., Capra, L., Scott, K. M., Espíndola, J. M., García-Palomo, A., and Costa, J. E. 2004. The May 26, 1982, breakout flow derived from failure of a volcanic dam at El Chichón Volcano, Chiapas, México. *Bulletin of the Geological Society of America* 116:233–46.
6. Gossen, G. H. 1974. *Chamulas in the World of the Sun, Time and Space in a Maya Oral Tradition.* Cambridge, MA: Harvard University Press.
7. Decker, R., and Decker, B. 1997. *Volcanoes*, 3rd ed. New York: W.H. Freeman and Co. Benjamin Franklin's observation is noted on p. 236.
8. Gill, R. B. 2000. *The Great Maya Droughts.* Albuquerque, NM: University of New Mexico Press.
9. Tilling, R. I. 2007. El Chichón's "surprise" eruption in 1982: lessons for reducing volcano risk. *Proceedings of the Commemorative Conference El Chichón volcano: Twenty-Five Years Later.* San Cristóbal de Las Casas, Special Pub. 6, Instituto de Geológía, Universidad Nacional Autonoma de México, 112.

NICARAGUA

Chapter 12

Casita and Mobacho: Volcano Collapses Unrelated to Eruptions

My long-time colleague José Luis Macías and I picked our way across the barren, boulder-strewn track of some sort of giant flow. José Luis, a professor of volcanology at the University of Mexico, was equally uncertain: We could not immediately tell if the flow was a water flood, lahar, or debris avalanche. Here at the base of long-dormant Volcán Casita in Nicaragua, desolation reigned. Downstream, what was unquestionably a lahar had destroyed almost every vestige of two towns on October 30, 1998. A single structure, an animal shed, was spared at the far edge of the flow track. Stains of ash line the track—the locations of hastily cremated bodies—surprising in both their number and their small quantities of ash. We met a *campesina* named Carmen Lopez carrying water from a spring on the volcano flank.

"The flow that took the people was water," Carmen said, sadly but resignedly. Her face is deformed, as if from a traumatic birth, but it has character, and she is clearly a survivor. "It was a black curtain of water with trees." She told us about her sister-in-law, Juana Rodriguez, who once stood only a few meters from where we are now, at the edge of the flow track. Juana had been "taken," she said, "along with her three children and her mother." But only Juana survived, holding onto trees at the edge of the flow as the others were swept away. The surge passed quickly, and Carmen dragged herself, childless and motherless, into the forest.

Less than 5 km downstream, however, the watery flow had become a 1.3-km-wide, 3.5-m-deep lahar described by survivors in press reports as "an infernal wave of mud, rocks, and trees," "an enormous mass of mud," and "pure mud." Witnesses saw a herd of panicked cattle running in front before the animals were engulfed. El Porvenir and Rolando Rodriguez, the two towns on the broad alluvial apron that surrounded

Flank collapse of Casita. (B. F. Molnia)

the volcano, were obliterated. Some 2,500 people were killed,[2] entombed in mud or remaining as only the anonymous little piles of ash where their bodies were cast into backwater at the edge of the flow.

The deadly flow had a unique beginning, one that would reveal lessons about flow and collapse-runout behavior that can save thousands in the future.[1] Unique features of Casita and the landscapes that surround volcanoes in Central America were also critical to the tragically large loss of life. How had two sizable communities been destroyed, almost to a man and a woman, absolutely without a trace? All that remained were a few PVC pipes protruding from the deeply scoured track of the flow.

On October 30, 1998, a relatively small landslide, or flank collapse, had been triggered by intense precipitation accompanying Class 5 Hurricane "Mitch," which then died over neighboring Honduras. What transformed this event, normally one of little consequence, to a genuine catastrophe were locations of the "new towns," El Porvenir and Rolando Rodriguez, which had been built in recent decades. The communities were constructed on the undulating surface of Casita's *faldas* (skirts), and the deciding factor for their locations may have been the spring that Carmen had been visiting when we met her; this is dry terrain and there is no money for drilling water wells.

Many farmers had returned home from nearby fields to take refuge from the storm of October 30, 1998. At 11:00 A.M., nearly all the residents (a few were visiting elsewhere) of both towns were "taken" by the lahar that transformed from the landslide. They were inside during the storm and could not have known what hit them when their homes were crushed and carried away in moments. Death was nearly instantaneous, like that from the pyroclastic flows and lahars elsewhere.

Later, on a very hot day, José Luis and I walked the 5 km from the volcano base to the townsites. We wanted to see how the flow had changed from a water surge to a roaring wall of mud. Gradually, levees appeared along the sides of the widening flow tract, a sure sign the sediment component was increasing. Within the track, the ground had been scoured of soil and overburden, the depth indicated by protruding roots. The flow grew by ingesting, or bulking, additional sediment. Within the first kilometers, it had changed completely to a lahar. For this change to occur from 100 percent water to a debris flow, typically with only 30 to 35 percent water, now told us that the volume had to have increased by at least three times. But damn, it was getting hot.

I felt the blinding onset of being cooked, even after soaking my hat and shirt. No shade from vegetation. All of that, like Juana's mother and children, had been "taken." It was like being locked in an oven, and someone had turned on the heat. I motioned to José Luis that I needed the shade of a large boulder resting on the surface. I needed to take off my clothes, to hopefully cool down by sweating. There was only room for one person per boulder, so he picked out another to do the same thing. I had done this before in barren terrain at El Chichón in Mexico, but then had crawled into a gulley, the only shade. By wrapping ourselves around the bases of the two largest boulders at Casita, we could each get entirely in shade.

Later, stumbling the rest of the way to our rendezvous point, it was easy to see how the flow had continued to scour the surface, continually growing in size as sediment was added. The lateral levees got progressively higher, recording the increasing size of the flow. This would be a great opportunity to document its "bulking factor," the magnitude of its volumetric increase from its origin on the volcano, to the towns, and then as it diminishes in the distal region of deposition.

Between the volcano and the towns, the wave had passed from a water surge, through the entire range of hyperconcentrated flow, and finally to a flow that was entirely debris flow, or a lahar, as it progressively ingested sediment. Now we know it as the normal behavior of granular, noncohesive lahars. Yet again, the importance of hyperconcentrated flow in volcanic terrains was documented, just as Dick Janda and I had seen it at the "spool locality" downstream from Mount St. Helens. As here at Casita, the sediment increase that formed the lahar was rapid. The reverse transformation, with loss of sediment, passage of flow from a lahar back through the range of hyperconcentrated flow, was much slower.

The press had reported low tolls for the loss of life at Casita, but these had been guesses based on out-of-date census records. That is common for volcano disasters as well as other disasters. Authorities may want to minimize fatalities, possibly to reduce their culpability; in others, they may want to exaggerate in order to encourage international aid. In response to my question about losses, the mayoress of the municipality that includes Rolando Rodriguez and El Porvenir, gives me the figure: 2,513, she says, adding "casi todo," or almost all, from the lahar.

I was amazed to see workers broiling in only baseball hats in this part of Nicaragua. Not a single hat with a brim. Local ears and necks seemed almost black with sunburn. I had a ratty and unraveling straw hat with a broad brim, originally one of those REI exotic-fiber creations. Later, talking with the friendly young mayor of Somotillo, a flood-damaged town a few kilometers north of Casita, I noticed him admiring it and apparently marveling at the concept of a brim on a hat. He seemed almost astounded that such a thing existed, and he immediately accepted it as a gift. I had a spare and hoped I had started a trend. Throughout the Trans-Mexican Volcanic Belt, I had searched several hat shops, hoping to find one of those white plastic *caballero* (cowboy)

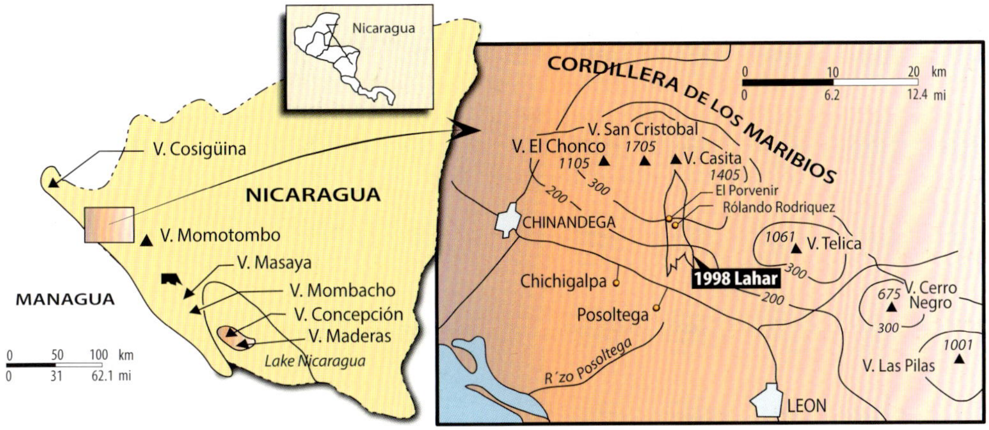

An outline of the Volcán Casita lahar shows its flow down the south flank. The towns of El Porvenir and Róland Rodriguez were obliterated from the face of the earth. (After Scott and others, 2005)

hats that the local guys in Mexico (but not Nicaragua) wear and that look very cool, both literally and figuratively. No fit yet. Such a hat would be both practical and add to my non-gringo persona.

The Cordillera de Los Baribios, containing Casita, is a 70-km segment of the Central American Volcanic Belt extending along the Pacific Coast of Nicaragua. The volcanoes occur in clusters, surrounded by the circular alluvial fans or aprons well described as *faldas* (skirts), or in New Zealand as "ring plains." On the other side of Managua, Volcán Momotombo is visible in the distance. It was active in 1905, and was the volcano shown erupting artistically, but not in reality, on a Nicaraguan postage stamp of 1900. In 1902, the route for a canal across Central America was under debate in the U.S. Senate. Then and today, a canal route across Nicaragua, through huge Lake Nicaragua, even with its freshwater sharks, was the logical choice. A clever lobbyist for the competing Panama route mailed each senator a pamphlet with the erupting-Momotombo stamp, thereby emphasizing the risk from volcanoes in Nicaragua and cleverly recalling the fresh disaster of Mount Pelée on May 8, 1902. There had been 30,000 deaths. Its most famous survivor had been a basement jail-cell prisoner, who later toured with the Barnum & Bailey Circus.

The Panama route was chosen on June 19, 1902, three days after the senators received the pamphlet and barely a month after Mount Pelée erupted. Ironically, Momotombo has not been seriously active since 1905; thousands died of yellow fever and malaria in building the canal through Panamanian jungle.

The destructive runout route of Casita's flank collapse left deep scars on the land and in the hearts of those who lost loved ones and property.

Casita is an inauspicious stratovolcano, its flank adjoining the higher, active San Cristóbal volcano. Casita's summit consists of the almost 1-km-wide La Ollada crater. Climbing through the collapse scar is a lesson in stratovolcano structure; lava and pyroclastic flows dip downslope parallel to the flank, their contacts forming many possible failure planes. After much searching, I was able to fine a single radiocarbon sample in a pyroclastic flow deposit in the collapse scar, giving an age of about 9,000 radiocarbon years. Rick Hazlett, geology professor at Pomona College and coauthor with Jack Lockwood of excellent *Volcanoes—a Planetary Perspective*, focused his master's thesis on Casita. I complained to him about preservation of wood for radiocarbon dating in tropical climates. No sympathy there; he had not found any, so I felt lucky with a single sample. Deposits exposed in gullies cut by the lahar revealed abundant but now-carbonless molds of large tropical plants.

The peak flow that came down the flank of the volcano was a water-rich flow and scarred trees like a flood. The rubbly debris that represented most of the failed bedrock mass formed only the basal part of the flow. A few survivors living at the volcano base, like Juana and Carmen, remembered the flow as a flood. This was in complete agreement with the hydrologic evidence, leading the first responding volcanologists to propose almost supernatural water sources ("cannons of water" shooting from the volcano). Later reconstruction of the sediment and water budget for the flow would show, however, that storm infiltration and runoff alone could explain its consistency and behavior.[1] The separation of the failed mass into a water-dominated flood peak and a basal "bedload" of coarse sediment took place on the flank of the volcano. Rainfall intensity in the five days preceding the collapse was unusual, but not unique, and not in itself of a magnitude portending a catastrophe. The fact is, had not so many died, the flow could easily have occurred unseen and unreported.

Less than three minutes after departing the base of the edifice, the watery flow had transformed entirely to a wave of debris flow, 1.3 km wide and an average of 3.5 m deep. At that point it removed El Porvenir and Rolando Rodriguez from the face of the earth. The few survivors from outside the flow track described a roaring noise like thunder or helicopters. Some thought an earthquake was occurring (a common but deadly response to the ground tremor of approaching lahars). The entire flow wave had transformed to what was a typical lahar from the runout of a flank collapse. It had a dispersed-phase in the pebble-size range and with very poor sorting, a measure of size variation.[3] The size and textural change in the flow wave resulted from the increase in volume as it spread across the alluvial apron, mobilizing the saturated soil profile.

The catastrophe is an especially well-documented example of how lahars can multiply in volume severalfold as they flow away from source. In the Casita example, bulking was facilitated by runout of the flow onto a saturated surface underlain by granular volcanogenic detritus that was easily eroded. In our technical report on the disaster,[1] I budgeted the sediment contribution of the lahar from source to deposit. Conservatively, the flow "bulked," or increased in volume, by at least a factor of 4.7 x from the failed mass to the area of deposition. This is just one example of the factors that make these flows so difficult to model or to extrapolate with any significance. The surfaces on which collapses run out vary greatly in their erodibility; at Casita, erodibility was probably near a maximum.

The 4.7 x volume change is probably as accurate a measure of bulking as is possible for any large-scale collapse runout and, relatively speaking, the Casita lahar is small. That bulking factor is a minimum-limiting figure for the flow, in that an unknown but significant amount of sediment would have been transported all the way to the ocean, beyond the main area of deposition and thus not included in the total distal volume.

Casita is also a discouraging example of how hard it is to make estimates or measurements of a failure volume at the scale, even of this relatively small volcano collapse. My

Casita coauthor Norman Kerle, studying the *volcán* for his Ph.D. thesis at Cambridge, used photogrammetry to determine our published figure of 1.6 million cu m. An early published estimate of the Casita collapse volume was only 200,000 cu m. That failure volume would have resulted in a bulking factor of over 20 times, using our figure for the deposit volume.

Just the difficulty of determining meaningful failure volumes on volcanoes, as well as what we see as wide variation in the bulking factor, should prohibit using volumes, extrapolated, averaged, or otherwise manipulated, for anything but approximate hazard zonation of lahar inundation areas elsewhere. But, the really interesting caveat that applies to the largest debris avalanches is the reason their distal portions have been unrecognized, both in extent and volume.

U.S. President Bill Clinton visited the site using the briefing sheet that the State Department had asked me to prepare. I had pointed out the pitiful and remarkably detailed mold left by the body of a seven-year-old girl. Her age had come from the mayoress who had first showed me the site and given me the fatality figures. The mold was truly an emotional site, and the press reported how sad the President appeared. A 1.5-m boulder with a brass plate commemorated President Clinton's visit, placed next to the girl's body impression and her partially cremated skull. In a later visit, I saw the plate was gone, and tropical vegetation was reclaiming the site. In a yet later visit, I couldn't find the boulder.

What are the lessons here, in addition to the caveats for those wanting to extrapolate and model lahar volumes? A small flank collapse, from a dormant volcano, triggered by unexceptional rainfall, nevertheless resulted in the most recent volcano-related catastrophe. Just incredibly bad luck? The basic reason was simply the modern siting of towns on an alluvial apron consisting of the deposits of numerous previous volcanic flows. By locating El Porvenir and Rolando Rodriguez several kilometers east, the townsites would have been in a flow "shadow" formed by the low rim of the ancient La Pelona caldera and out of the way of any lahars from Casita or San Cristóbal. That could have happened except for the water-supply problem.

The catastrophe is yet another variation of the hazard sites represented by broad alluvial surfaces in volcanic terrains, as in Sarno, Italy. Many volcanic complexes are surrounded by circular alluvial aprons like the faldas of Nicaragua, for which the techniques and approaches to mitigating flood hazards on alluvial fans are applicable, especially those relating to the distribution of risk. The art of risk management on alluvial fans has undergone a renaissance in the southwestern United States, especially in Southern California.[4] The transfer value to volcanic terrains is obvious.

A partial skull and the stark imprint of a young girl's body marks one death among the 2,500 victims of the 1998 flank collapse. U.S. President Bill Clinton visited the site in the aftermath.

§

Significant volcanic landslides yielding debris avalanches with large loss of life occur about every twenty-five years. Why are landslide runouts from volcanoes so different, so much more mobile, and therefore more dangerous, than those in alpine settings? Bulking is the first of four major reasons, for either the giant ones, which are called sector collapses, or the smaller flank collapses. They "bulk" additional material as they flow, becoming larger in the many cases where the amount of material added can exceed the amount deposited. I had developed, I thought, the term "bulking" for this process while working on debris flows in California years before Casita, and even long before Mount St. Helens in 1980. Researchers began to cite me for the term. After finding it in a Department of Agriculture publication from the 1950s, I formally renounced any credit for the term, but not for its importance in volcanic terrain.

A second reason is that volcanic landslides run out much farther than most reconnaissance field studies may discover. They have characteristic hummocky surfaces, revealing chunks of the mountain rafted by the flow. Where the hummocky surface ends, does the flow end? No, it most likely kept going—the chunks or megablocks of the mountain have simply broken up or been rafted into "backwater" areas. The flow has become in all respects a lahar, a volcanic mudflow capable of flowing many tens of kilometers beyond the presence of the last hummock.

Thirdly, and probably most intractably in forecasting risk, are collapse triggers other than magmatic activity, in the case of Casita and probably for a sister volcano in Nicaragua, Mombacho. With no warning possible, the potential for a catastrophe is huge. Nonvolcanic (tectonic) earthquakes are another such trigger.

This to me is the last but probably the worst possibility: the destabilizing effects of magmatic activity while it is still deep-seated. Emergency managers are beginning to discuss their risk strategies. As just one example, USGS scientist Mark Reid proposes the role of remote hydrothermal pressurization acting to destabilize an edifice.[5] Russian workers cite multiple cases where they believe sector collapses, mainly in Kamchatka, were triggered by magmatic intrusion before magma had risen to enter the edifice.[6] This introduces the nightmare of evacuating at the earliest sign of magma intrusion, at the time when they will be the most difficult to "call," and potentially the longest. At those times, during the normal waxing and waning of volcanic activity (as it may or may not progress to an eruption), the odds of a false alarm are the greatest. It is the time when emergency-response managers really earn their salaries.

The disaster of Casita was the result of precipitation and infiltration effects that are impossible to predict. Van Wyk de Vries of the Open University has proposed gravity-induced volcano spreading as an additional component of the instability both at Casita and Mombacho.[7] Progressive instability can be related not to magma injection, but simply to the huge forces acting on piles of volcanic rock poured out onto nonvolcanic substrates of varying rigidity and frictional resistance. The process is known as gravitational spreading, and it can operate in concert with other processes acting to increase the instability of volcanoes. In many stratovolcanoes, the originally hard rock, like lava, is progressively weakened, in cases all the way to a weak, gooey mush, by the hot acid water percolating through their internal plumbing.

Volcán Mombacho lies next to the colonial city of Granada, dating from 1524. It yielded a much larger debris avalanche than the one at Casita; hummocks, or mounds, stud the surface of the avalanche and form the group of small islands, Las Isletas, in Lake Nicaragua. The extent of the debris avalanche is known only from the observed isletas, so its actual extent is poorly constrained. Some individual isletas consist of basement ignimbrite, documenting the involvement of the subvolcano basement in the failure.[7] Thus, Van Wyk de Vries concludes that the spreading took place in a subvolcano zone representing about 20 percent of Mombacho's height. This contrasts with the idea of individual slip planes at Hawaiian volcanoes, for example, involved in the failures that produced gigantic debris avalanches running to the ocean depths. It also suggests that identification of active spreading can be a useful tool for assessing potential collapse hazard. It is reported from Kilauea and Etna and proposed by Chilean volcanologists for some debris avalanches at volcanoes there. GPS monitoring focused on volcano flanks appears to be the logical tool, but presently is used very selectively. Edifices with monolithologic and mobile substrates, such as limestone, would appear to be logical candidates.

Spreading is different from what seismologists identify for large volcanoes as "edifice effects," small-scale seismicity, the trembling of the huge mass of material loading the continental crust. The effects are something like the quivering of a blancmange, a molded gelatinous desert of British origin, when it is dumped out of its mold. Fans of the British comedy group Monty Python may remember a skit involving a tennis match between a blancmange and a Scotsman, who of course lost.

Van Wyk de Vries and Peter Francis, authors of the spreading attribution at Mombacho, note that collapse can occur without magmatic activity and thus "poses a significant risk even at unmonitored, inactive volcanoes."[7] Mombacho has failed twice, but the smaller flow originated entirely in the edifice and did not involve the basement.

NOTES:

1. The article in which we document the bulking factor: Scott, K. M., Vallance, J. W., Kerle, N., Macías, J. L., Strauch, W., and Devoli, G. 2005. Catastrophic precipitation-triggered lahar at Casita volcano, Nicaragua: occurrence, bulking, and transformation. *Earth Surface Processes and Landforms* 30:59-79.
2. To author from mayoress of Posoltega Municipality.
3. Sorting in phi units of 3.5 to 4.5 ϕ, a high value (meaning a large range in sediment size), typical of debris flows.
4. Committee on Alluvial Fan Flooding, National Research Council. 1996. *Alluvial fan flooding*. Washington, D.C.: National Academy Press. Probably outdated, but this is an excellent summary.
5. Reid, M.E. 2004. Massive collapse of volcano edifices triggered by hydrothermal pressurization. *Geology* 32:373–76. Excellent explanation of how collapse can be triggered at earliest stages of intrusion.
6. Example: Belousova, M., Belousova, A., and Voight, B. 1998. Relationships between failure of volcanic edifice and explosive activity: Case studies in Kurile-Kamchatka region, Russia (abs.) in *Abstract volume for Colima Volcano Sixth International Meeting*, Colima, January 26-30, 1998, unpaginated.
7. Van Wyk de Vries, B., and Francis, P. 1997. Catastrophic collapse at stratovolcanoes induced by gradual volcano spreading. *Nature* 387:387–90. This mechanism can be considered when collapse appears unrelated to eruptive activity.

At the dome in October 1993, heat radiating from every direction was intense.

Chapter 13

Mount Unzen—What Were They Thinking?

In southern Japan, a nearly flawless white granite monument—simple, but elegant, was dedicated at the base of Mount Unzen during the 2007 Cities on Volcanoes meeting. It remembered June 3, 1991, the terrible day when forty-three people were killed by one of numerous pyroclastic density flows.

Mount Unzen, with a maximum elevation of 4,875 ft (1,486 m), is a volcanic center consisting of several dome complexes near Nagasaki on the island of Kyushu in southern Japan. The complex had been active before, in 1792, when a debris avalanche from a satellite peak, Mayuyama, ran into the ocean to create a tsunami that was Japan's largest volcano disaster, causing 15,000 fatalities. Just offshore, many islets, collectively named Tsukumojima (99 islands) are hummocks formed by megablocks in the 1792 debris avalanche.

As seismologists had tracked the rising magma below Unzen in 1990, they expected another lava flow, not a lava dome. The collapse of the Mayuyama edifice had been preceded by a lava flow.

Speaking at a memorial dedication in 2007, the mayor of Shimabara, Teijiro Yoshioka, recalled when their community's "198 years of peaceful calm" ended. "This land was a quiet village," Yoshioka said. "As the people went about their daily lives they could see [Unzen] Fugendake to the west, and the Ariake Sea to the east. It was a very rich, fertile land that gave wonderful harvests in all seasons. . . . On November 17, 1990, we saw for the first time a narrow wisp of steam shooting straight to the sky from this exact spot. . . .

"On June 3, 1991, at 16:08, one enormous flow whose speed and size were beyond the limits of our imagination . . . took the precious lives of forty-three people who were working sincerely, firemen, policemen, press and volcano scientists, and forever changed the calm village into a charred barren landscape.

"From this place we honor the past and convey its history to the future. Wishing to live in close harmony with the mountain, we determine with all citizens of Shimabara to develop the city for posterity. Here we dedicate this monument."

Following the 1991 event, the bay, from which 25 percent of the sushi-wrapping black seaweed, *nori*, was grown, had been so polluted by runoff from the fresh volcanogenic sediment that production nearly ceased.

I had been near this site just two years later, in 1993, as flows were still forming, when pieces of the growing dome were breaking off and exploding into clouds of incandescent pyroclasts every few minutes. Finally, by 1995, the eruptions ceased. Standing at the memorial in 2007, we were looking directly up the flank, as if into the end of a gun barrel. The place was so obviously dangerous. What on earth had the Japanese and the scientists been doing here? But groups have a collective way of ignoring danger, sufficient to keep individuals from speaking up. Nobody wants to be a chicken, and it is always easiest to roll the dice.

Among those killed in 1991 at Unzen volcano was Harry Glicken, whom I knew well. The postdoc student had been pressured by his advisor at Utsunomiya University to guide two famous French volcano photographers, Maurice and Katia Krafft. The summit dome was shedding chunks of glowing lava that instantly exploded into pyroclastic clouds boiling into the emerald-green forest that lined the defile leading to the Mizunashi River. Pyroclastic flows were the weak suit in the Kraffts' oeuvre of dangerous volcanic hazards, and they were hoping to fill that gap at Unzen. Harry finally consented.

The flows had been occurring for ten days, and the media had selected their observation site: a small rise called Teiten. The barren, boulder-studded gulch leading directly from the dome to Teiten made it painfully obvious that the location was extremely vulnerable. That had not been clear to the media, but I was sure it would have been to Harry, and certainly to Maurice and Katia. Later, witnesses remembered that Maurice was joking about how the flows then occurring were much too small. He and Katia immediately headed closer.

At 3:57 P.M., some of the media members felt a gust of air. The seismic record would later show a pyroclastic flow, a PF, at that time, but those waiting below saw nothing because the summit was obscured. All seemed well. Small PFs had been regularly boiling part way down the flank. But then, exploding out of the mist around the summit, came a gigantic boiling cloud.

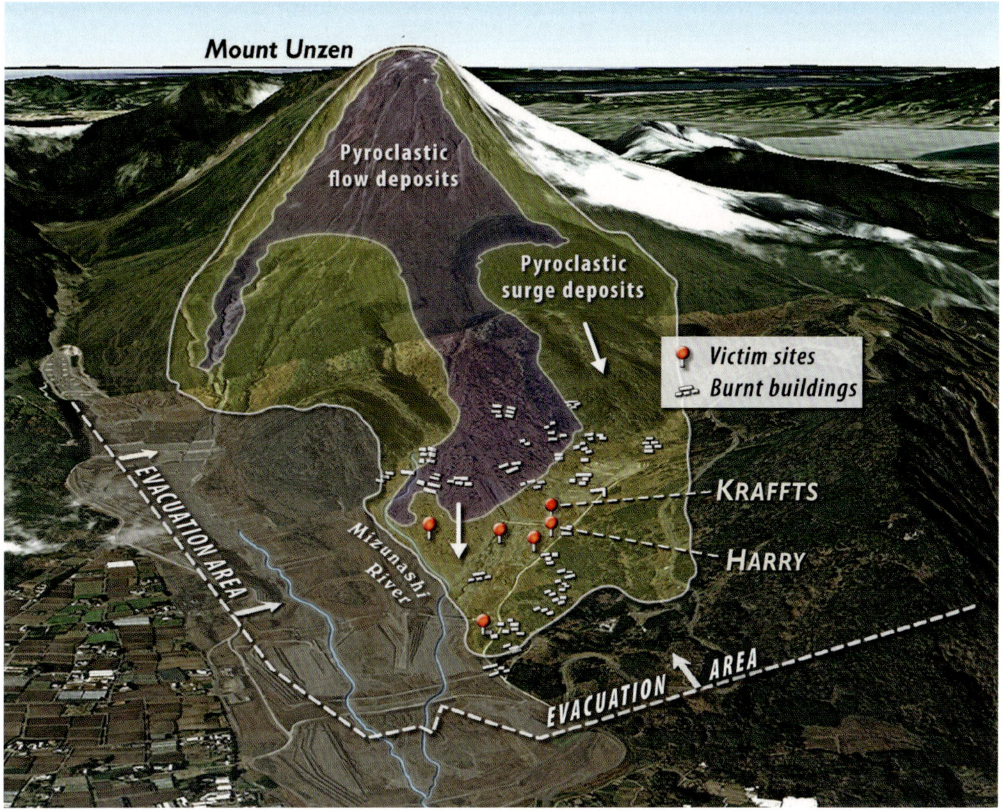

Mount Unzen, showing route and effects of the June 3, 1991, pyroclastic flow in a view looking west–northwest. (After Japanese sources)

It was an outlier—a much larger piece of the dome had broken off.

I have long imagined, incorrectly, that Harry and the Kraffts saw the piece of dome disintegrate into a huge cloud of initially incandescent particles and that they were initially in awe at their good fortune. This could be just the footage they wanted, and they would have immediately readied their cameras. Harry may have thought that at last the Kraffts would get the stuff they wanted, and he could get back to his new projects.

It probably took three to four minutes for the flow to reach the victims. During the first minute, Harry and Maurice and Katia Krafft might have been thinking, "Wow, this is great, what a shot!" Less than a minute later, so I imagined, Harry would be the first to recognize, in a moment between wonder and terror, that this billowing cloud impended an excruciating death. I imagined, hopefully but naively, that his body would have been found farthest from the others, well up the steep valley-side slope that began less than 20 m away. A person as fit as Harry could get a fair distance up that slope in less than a minute.

But he didn't. I would find later that you are literally paralyzed in that situation.

§

Standing before the sleek granite memorial in 2007, retired USGS scientist Jack Lockwood spoke a heartfelt tribute to the three volcanologists and laid three flowers at its base. We stood silently listening to Jack while the nightly news jockeyed for position. I was picturing the pre-eruption landscape below the embryonic dome as full of dense tropical vegetation. It would have been the misty mountain landscape inspiring serenity in Shinto tradition.

Jack Lockwood speaks to the Japanese press at the monument dedication, with Professor Nakamura to his left. Beyond them is the road on which Katia and Maurice Krafft perished about 200 m closer to the volcano.

The dead consisted of a group of eighteen media staff, their support crews (sixteen dead, two injured), twelve fire brigade staff (all dead), thirteen local residents (six dead, seven injured), four taxi drivers (all dead), two policemen (both dead), and the three volcanologists.

Our guides at the conference shared a map showing the flow's path and where the individual bodies were found. The Kraffts, ever pushing the envelope, had been together about 200 m farther up the valley, probably scouting a camera location for when the clouds dispersed. Harry was with the media, from where the flow had hurled several of their vehicles 80 m. The remains of a truck roasted by the blast are on display at the site of the Agricultural Training Center, another 350 m downstream.

The Kraffts were found up the road, and Harry and the Japanese were found clustered about the media site, probably at the last second seeking refuge behind their vehicles, with their bodies positioned defensively like the remains at Pompeii. It looked like a few may have started to run downhill. Asphyxiation, not heat, was quick and fatal for most. Nobody had run up the valley-side slope.

Actually, my fantasy of Harry's attempted escape had been dispelled earlier in the year when I met Setsuya Narada, who had been the chief geologist at Unzen in 1991 and who had identified the bodies of the three *gaijins* (foreigners) at the temple where they were taken the following day. According to Setsuya-san, their longer hair made the respective IDs clear, unlike many badly burned but sadly only temporary survivors, who could not speak to identify themselves through their horribly scorched airways before they finally died. I was glad to learn that Harry's death, unlike those of the short-term survivors farther away, was mercifully quick.

When I first met Setsuya Nakada in May 2007, we had been climbing and chatting on El Chichón, in Chiapas, Mexico, on a field trip commemorating the twenty-fifth anniversary of that eruption. The unimposing "surprise" volcano, known simply in Spanish as "the bump," had erupted violently in 1982. It had taken more than 2,000 lives and reduced world surface temperature the next year by nearly a degree C from injection of sulfate-rich aerosols into the stratosphere. Strolling away from the main group at the Unzen memorial gathering, Setsuya and I remembered El Chichón and recalled his role in identifying the bodies at Unzen in 1991. The next day, in an obscure shed in the valley containing Senbongi, Setsuya and I ran across an apparently forgotten 50-cm-high model of the new memorial, also carved from the luminescent white granite. I suggested that the model be recovered for the new Shimabara commemorative conference center.

Harry Glicken, the third volcanologist to die in 1991, had been my roommate at the Cascades Volcano Observatory in the early 1980s and was in Japan doing postdoctoral work on debris avalanches. His doctoral thesis had been on the huge debris avalanche that occurred at St. Helens with the main eruption of May 18, 1980.

Harry did not want to guide Maurice and Katia Krafft on their visit to Mount Unzen in 1991. He was instead excited about his work at Bandai-san, the famous volcano in central Japan, and particularly so about a possible lateral-blast deposit he believed he had found in a gulley on the east side of the massive 1888 crater. The crater was the source of a sector collapse like that of Mount St. Helens in 1980, running out as a debris avalanche emplacing megablocks that formed picturesque islands in a lake. Maybe that deposit, if it contained juvenile material, would be evidence that magmatic activity had triggered the failure, rather than only steam explosions as then (and now) believed. Like most examples, the 1980 debris avalanche at St. Helens had been magmatically triggered.

On Japanese TV videotape, Harry is on the flanks of Bandai with Yoichi Nakamura, his postdoctoral supervisor at Utsunomiya University. I see the Harry we knew in the hectic early days at CVO—awkward, excited, stealing looks at the camera with a shy smile. Yet he was remarkably interesting when it was his turn to explain the 1888 sector collapse at Bandai. Still, he was the quintessential lovable nerd, and for those who knew him, a troubled soul.

Harry had placed a large bookcase in front of his desk in our office. Periodically, a vocal outburst like a small explosion shook the room. I thought it was best ignored and never asked him about it, and he never spoke of it. But something was definitely wrong. He showed me an article about the strange, involuntary tics suffered by the eighteenth-century lexicographer, Dr. Samuel Johnson, whose strange movements were graphically reported by his equally famous biographer James Boswell. Harry told me he was sure that Dr. Johnson's symptoms were the same as his own. Years later, a medical acquaintance said he had heard that Dr. Johnson might have suffered from Tourette's Syndrome. On reflection, it did seem to apply to Harry. Only a small fraction of severe cases of Tourette's exhibit coprolalia, the involuntary, obscene speech for which the condition is known. Harry's periodic eruptions were similar, but never obscene. For Dr. Johnson, the diagnosis now seems confirmed to some, so Harry may have diagnosed himself correctly.[1]

Peter Baxter, M.D., retired from the faculty of Cambridge, has taken me to task for daring to make a medical diagnosis. Recent epidemiology indicates the condition may affect as many as one in a hundred people (greater than the incidence of Alzheimer's or autism), and it has been diagnosed in many accomplished scientists, musicians,

Seated in a chair labeled "Volcano Director," Harry Glicken played conductor as if orchestrating the bursts of steam from Mount St. Helens on May 17, 1980, one day before the catastrophe in Washington State. (Carolyn Driedger, USGS)

and athletes. It now may be approaching an "in-fashion" disease that people boast of on talk television. How Harry, with his insatiable curiosity, would have loved to put a name on his condition. One really felt for him, both because the USGS was not giving him a career job (never to be admitted, but in part because of his symptoms), and because a tenured faculty position for a *gaijin* at a Japanese university was then, as now, nearly unthinkable.[2]

"Harry, your salvation is obvious." I thought I had the solution, and I annoyed Harry in our correspondence. What he needed was what other young men working in Japan called a "walking dictionary"—a Japanese girlfriend. I met one lucky guy whose partner was the owner and abbottress of a Zen monastery, inherited from her father. I may have overdone the issue with Harry, but don't regret it. It is a shame that Harry did not find a compassionate companion. His behavior just did not charm the opposite sex; for example, at a spring festival, Harry joined Japanese friends in expounding on the beauty of the cherry blossoms, which triggered the comment from a non-Japanese girl, "Would you shut the f*** up?"

The Kraffts had found Harry when they contacted Yoichi Nakamura asking for a guide. In their film oeuvre of volcano hazards, pyroclastic flows were not well-represented, and those beginning on May 24, 1991, at Unzen were dramatic: glowing chunks of the dome (to be named Heisei-Shinzan) falling and disintegrating into gray clouds that boiled silently into the emerald green of the lower slopes and the channel of the Mizunashi River. The encroaching suburbs of Shimabara were brought to the foreground by telephoto lens. Harry was the logical candidate to guide them, and he consented only when asked a third time, as Nakamura-san finally made things clear, "The Kraffts really need you, Harry."[3]

I was traveling in the Midwest in 1991 when I read about Harry's death in a local newspaper. When I got back to the office there was a manila envelope from him, mailed from Japan. Inside was an 8-by-10 "glossy" of a beautiful young woman, with a note, "Kevin, here is my new girlfriend." Sadly, it was a publicity picture of a Japanese movie star.

§

Torii gates mark trails leading up many Japanese volcanoes, denoting the Shinto transition from the worldly to the sacred. I had come back to Unzen in October 1993 with an idea about a very different roadside marker: the melted remnants of vending machines that had once lined the roads around Unzen. Based on those remains, I had hoped to calibrate, at least relatively, the clear diminution of flow temperature with distance. That weekend in 1993, a Japanese companion and I entered the hazard zones at will, even approaching the approximate site of the 1991 fatalities.

Barry Voight, Emeritus Professor of Geology at Pennsylvania State, notes that the Japanese do not use the term "red zone." Journalists assert their right to communicate what is happening to the public and resist exclusion from hazardous areas—our "red zones." The Kraffts were advised by a Japanese scientist familiar with pyroclastic flows to move to a point farther away. They refused, citing a need to return to France, and being the Kraffts, immediately started to get even closer. Pyroclastic flows from the collapsing lava dome[4] had first entered the valley north of the east-flowing Mizunashi River, which conveyed the lethal flow. A new area of homes and businesses was being overrun just two years after the 1991 deaths.

A torii gate, associated with the Shinto tradition, marks the start of a trail to the overlook of Mount Unzen's flank.

As we explored, every few minutes the enlarging dome shed a solid mass of material, exploding into an incandescent cloud as it collapsed. These flows, fortunately for us, were small. The fatal outlier flow of 1991 can be seen in aerial video on YouTube, running out as a boiling cloud. My colleague and I unintentionally entered the poorly marked and unenforced hazard zone. We would shortly run like hell.

As the recipient of a Japanese Prime Minister's Research Award at Tsukuba, the "science city" of Japan northwest of Tokyo, I had been asked several times to return to Unzen. I had no particular desire to visit the site of my friend's death; it was a long flight to the southern island of Kyushu, and besides, Unzen was an example of hot, dry volcanic flows. I was a specialist in cold, wet volcanic flows. But I learned, and as anyone who has visited Japan knows, what the humorist-author of *Dave Barry Does Japan* found out the hard way. The third time you hear, "You want go Mount Unzen?"—you are absolutely positively going to Mount Unzen.

In October 1993, pyroclastic flows were still occurring. The first day my colleague and I climbed the volcano to stand, literally, only meters from the edge of the groaning, extruding dome. The radiant heat was burning, but a strong wind diverted the gas plume. The dome itself was not explosive, with pressure released by periodic collapses that disintegrated into pyroclastic flows on the steep opposite side; it seemed there was little risk, unlike the domes at Popocatépetl and Galeras that later killed the people standing near them when they exploded.

On our second day at Unzen in 1993, we gradually worked our way up the Mizunashi River draining the eastern, dome-collapse side of Unzen. Houses were partially buried by debris flows mobilized by tropical rainfall falling on loose volcaniclastic sediment. I was searching for ways to distinguish the hot basal avalanches of pyroclastic flows from deposits of their cold, water-mobilized secondary runouts.[5]

We entered, unrestrained, into the area inundated by primary pyroclastic flows. They were still occurring, but their runout direction had recently shifted north. We found the Okonoba elementary school, the scorched remains of which are today preserved as a monument. A lone ginko tree surviving in the schoolyard has become a national symbol of survival.[6] We got within a hundred meters of the then-unmarked site of the fatalities. I asked permission to collect a small, partially melted cup protruding from the ash. Looking directly up the flank of the volcano at the periodically collapsing dome, I had no doubt that Harry had also been very uneasy. I thought, as do many others, *My God, what were they thinking?* Some of the media reportedly thought they were safe because here they were on "Teiten," a small rise above the channel of a tributary to the Mizunashi River, but Harry and the Kraffts would have known that pyroclastic surges could cross mountain ranges, as well as ridges like that now known as Johnston Ridge on Mount St. Helens. Even their distal lobes, like those creating the distal "singed zone" in the forest around Mount St. Helens, could be fatal.

I felt fairly safe in the Mizunashi River valley, especially because there were strategically placed bunkers for emergency retreat. But when I tried one of their doors, I found it locked. "Oh . . . ," I uttered in surprise. *Where is the safety in a locked bunker?* I wondered. I would not know the answer for many years. In November 2007, I again tried a bunker door below Unzen, where I found it on a ridge separating the two watersheds that had conveyed the largest pyroclastic flows. It, too, was locked. Although dome growth and pyroclastic flows had ceased by 1995, it seemed that collapse of the inactive dome was still barely conceivable in 2007. I was told that the doors opened when triggered by seismic tremor. I probably missed something in translation. Knowing a little about the Japanese way, I am sure it made perfect sense, but I could not help suspecting humans would be involved (i.e., not involved) before the doors were unlocked. At that point I wrote the bunkers off at all Japanese volcanoes; if the implausible occurred, I would not waste time trying doors. I would simply run like hell.

I had always speculated that Harry had in the final minute run like hell up the valley-side slope, hoping to get above the flow. He did not try. On our 2007 revisit to the site, I frankly was relieved to verify that escape would have been impossible. That outlier 1991 flow was just too big.

In 1993, running was the only option for me and my colleague. On the third day of that trip, we traveled freely into the deserted Senbongi watershed, where flows had begun to enter three months earlier, in June. A broadcast news tape of a media van fleeing a boiling surge in the Senbongi area that month would become a staple of volcano videos. An upscale community of homes and a small shopping center, Senbongi had been evacuated before the first huge flows headed toward them on June 23. Images of the melted drink-vending machines showed what would have happened to people. We proceeded further into the area where the homes were destroyed. One home was burned, yet an arch remained over the entrance walkway. I framed an artistic shot of the volcano in the arch. I heard an oath in Japanese but ignored it. I fiddled with the exposure and finally took the shot. Turning, I saw my colleague sprinting down the valley in panic. *Well, he must know something I don't*, I thought, and when in Rome . . .

So I followed, leaping over the freshly deposited blocks of previous flows. After running downstream for nearly a kilometer, I caught my now-embarrassed companion, and he muttered something to the effect that it's the ones you don't hear that kill you. That, I reflected, is actually true of pyroclastic flows and surges, but not of lahars, and I would incorporate this bit of wisdom in the concept I would later promote as self-warning based on the ground tremor of lahars. I did not pursue exactly what triggered his flight—he'd seen, heard, or felt something that I did not. But the truth was, there is no way we should have been in that place at that time. That site was probably as dangerous as that of the June 3, 1991, tragedy.

In 2007, I would need a police escort to even get near where I could photograph the same deserted Senbongi ruins. The last pyroclastic flow from Unzen, among more than 10,000 recorded by their seismic signatures, was back in 1995.

At Daiyon Elementary School that November, a program of music, dance, and stories was titled "Living with a Volcano—Our History." The presentations brought tears to my eyes. One boy shared the story of his family farm near Senbongi: "We keep cows in my house. There were some cows when Mount Fugen [Unzen] erupted. On the morning of June 23, 1993, pyroclastic flow occurred. I heard that the hot air came down to Kamiori Bridge and caused burn injuries on the cows. Their [udders] melted and their eyes popped out. I felt very sorry for the cows. My mother looked very sad when she was telling me this story. I am sure my father had the hardest time even though he said nothing, because he really loves his cows."

The children also performed a song in praise of that remarkable, lone tree at the burned elementary school. The tree had somehow lived when all around was stark devastation. Their song was titled "You Survived—A Ginko Tree in the School Yard."[6]

> *A ginko tree at the corner of the school yard survived . . .*
> *The tree enjoyed the warm sunshine in spring and pushed out new sprouts.*
> *You survived—we want to look straight ahead and keep walking like you.*
> *The voices of the birds that disappeared in the buried mountain came with the spring wind . . .*
> *You survived—we want to look straight ahead and keep walking like you.*

§

As Jack Lockwood stood by the gleaming white monolith on a sunny afternoon, his spoken tribute to the Kraffts was eloquent. He recalled how, on June 3, 1991, he had been planning to meet Maurice and Katia at Pinatubo, just twelve days before its cataclysmic eruption. On June 4, Jack joined Chris Newhall in a meeting with USAF officials to advise about risk to Clark Air Force Base. The base had been constructed on what had only recently been recognized as the massive apron of geologically young pyroclastic flow deposits from the huge but infrequent eruptions of Pinatubo. Jack showed the Air Force brass some footage of pyroclastic flows that the Kraffts had taken to illustrate the hazard. Perhaps thinking the flows looked like dust clouds, the officers asked him if they were dangerous. He replied, "Well, the people who took these pictures were killed by flows just like them twenty-four hours ago." Only hours earlier, Jack had learned that that Maurice and Katia were missing after the large pyroclastic flow at Unzen, and he did not need for their deaths to be confirmed. As a result, at least in part, of the Unzen tragedy and what can be considered as a tribute to the Kraffts, the evacuation of Clark Air Force Base was ordered.

The author stands near the white granite sculpture that memorializes the victims of the Mount Unzen surge. Beyond him, the volcano's summit dome, still emitting steam, is a mere 3 kilometers away. (Dave Tucker)

Later, Jack confided to us that, as the Kraffts' reputations had risen and their opportunities increased, Maurice and Katia were forced to start making separate trips to active volcanoes. They had repeatedly expressed the hope that if death should come, they would be together and suffer the same fate. Neither wished to live without the other.

Returning from the 2007 ceremony, Jack asked me to say a few words about Harry, and I took the view that he had essentially received a "gift" of eleven years and sixteen days of life, measured from the morning of May 18, 1980, when he did *not* die on Mount St. Helens. If David Johnston had not replaced Harry at the new observation station one day earlier, Harry would have been on the ridge 8 km north of the volcano's bulging north side and instead, David died. But Harry was away, attending a May 18 meeting with his main graduate advisor, R. V. Fisher. Just months earlier, at his first meeting with Harry, the University of California-Santa Barbara volcanologist had made an immediate decision to award a research assistantship to the new Stanford graduate.

A final ironic twist comes to light. The reason why Professor Nakamura was pressuring Harry to accompany the Kraffts on Mount Unzen? His first choice was unable to go. As at St. Helens, while one man's life was spared, another's was lost. Nakamura's original choice was an English-speaking Japanese man who, with his wife, was hosting Harry in their home and teaching him Japanese.

The ultimate tribute to the forty-three people who died on June 3, 1991, is the fact that subsequent evacuations in Japan, and probably elsewhere, have been expedited by that tragedy. Japanese specifically cite a connection with Unzen for successful evacuations related to the eruption of Mount Usu in Hokaido in 2000. May that tribute continue elsewhere with more careful selection of volcano-observation sites.

Looking west onto an altered land, this is Unzen after cessation of its 1991–94 activity. Shimabara is cut by the Mizunashi River channel. The herringbone dike pattern continues to convey main flow when dikes are overtopped, and flood deposits are leveed in foreground. Visible at upper right is Mount Mayuyama, with its 1792 debris avalanche scar. Its deposit lobe, which triggered 15,000 tsunami deaths, lies at right in the foreground. (Setsuya Takada)

NOTES:

1. Tourette's Syndrome is now recognized, in a mild form, as associated with what society commonly thinks are obsessive-compulsive personalities, including that of Dr. Johnson specifically. Volcanology, in particular the subjects of sector collapses and debris avalanches, may well have lost significant contributions with Harry's death. A personal tragedy is that Harry did not survive to a time in which he would certainly have been diagnosed and treated and, above all, have an explanation of his behavior. He would actually have taken pride in the diagnosis, rather than the shame he felt when alive. I know that Harry was not considering Tourette's Syndrome while he was in Japan. He was treating himself with some early off-label antidepressants then being used for OCD. He had been getting them from Mexico, information that he may not have been sharing with his family or his advisor, R. V. Fisher.
2. Letter from R. V. "RV" Fisher to me, June 24, 1991. The letter was in thanks for a picture of Harry in the field, and a request for support of the idea of naming the 1980 debris avalanche at St. Helens after Harry (our letters did not help). U.S. Forest Service administrators were, in one of those bureaucratic spasms of officiousness, not wanting to "turn the monument into a graveyard." Nevertheless, I find such commemoration of interesting characters fascinating and unforgettable. In later obituaries, RV would note that Harry died happy, having in 1991 reportedly just been offered a research position at Tokyo Metropolitan University. Harry's anxiety about career security was acute, and I devoutly wish that was true. There is a trail named after Harry at St. Helens, and he would certainly have liked that. When hiking the blast zone, I remember him both fondly and sadly. It is the idealism and his joy in working with those in developing countries that I try to recall, instead of the angst of his post-1988 period when USGS employment had been denied.
3. Comments to me by Nakamura, during a 2005 visit to CVO.
4. A dome is a mound of lava that is so viscous it does not flow. Toothpaste is a common metaphor. Pieces of a growing dome, as at Unzen, may break off and immediately disintegrate into a boiling pyroclastic flow. They occur from volcanoes formed from lower-silica continental crust, like Mount St. Helens, in contrast to volcanoes from higher-silica oceanic crust, like Kilauea in Hawaii, where they extrude lava for which motor oil is a common metaphor.
5. This is a recurrent problem on volcanology field trips the world over—the group gets to a point where we start arguing, *Is this the deposit of a hot flow or a cold flow?* The best evidence (of heat) is charred wood that is not preexisting charcoal. The question would seem to be vital for hazard zonation but actually is not, in my opinion. "Hot lahars" can form both distally and secondarily from the basal debris avalanches of pyroclastic density flows and the coarse pyroclastic flows called block-and-ash flows. A boundary between hot flows and their cold transformations is interesting but not critical; once the primary pyroclastic flow or surge has been defined, for hazard zonation, the issue is simply the physical flow itself.
6. A song: *You Survived—A Ginko Tree in the School Yard*. From "Chapter VI—Hope and zest for living." Program for Delegates to COV5, Daiyon Elementary School, November 21, 2007.

THE PHILIPPINES

Chapter 14

Pinatubo: Second-Largest Eruption of the Twentieth Century

Pinatubo was a relatively unknown, forested volcano in the Philippines without records of historical eruptions, similar to El Chichón. Fifteen kilometers to the east lay Clark Air Force Base, the largest U.S. military base in the world, constructed on a large interfluve with a nearly horizontal stratigraphy that included thick beds of what looked like massive sand. In April 1991, thousands of small earthquakes were marking the start of a period of what we like to call "unrest," because we don't want to alarm people, and the jury is still out on what it could mean. Significant magmatic activity was confirmed by sulfur dioxide emissions beginning in early June. Preliminary hazard maps placed Clark at the east edge of a pyroclastic flow hazard zone, and the base was flanked by lahar hazard zones.[1]

At Clark, General William Studer boarded a helicopter with CVO volcanologist Rick Hoblitt and departed to literally see the lay of the land. Rick pointed out the extent of the pyroclastic flows of previous eruptions, and told him that Clark itself was probably constructed upon them. Rick made sure the four-star general knew what a PF was and what it was capable of doing. The implications were clear, and the general ordered plans for the evacuation of the base almost as soon as they touched down. After hearing Rick's risk assessment of Pinatubo, another Air Force officer asked a colleague, "Can we believe this guy?" The reply: "He's been right about everything else so far."

The final decision to evacuate was handed down on June 4 and most of the evacuation was accomplished only several days before the catastrophic event of June 15. The Air Force had finished evacuations of non-essential personnel on June 10, and on June 12, Pinatubo began the ramp up to its cataclysmic eruption. The final nine-hour

Nearly 60,000 people were successfully evacuated before Mount Pinatubo's cataclysmic eruption in 1991. (iStock.com / NaiveAngel)

eruption beginning after noon on June 15 would be the second-largest in the twentieth century (following Alaska's Mount Katmai). The tephra fall devastated the Clark aircraft hangers and fragile buildings in neighboring Angeles City. PFs swept down the adjacent Sacobia River valley to within a few hundred meters, but about 40 m below the interfluvial elevation of the Clark housing units. Only a handful of the original 30,000 military personnel remained. Evacuees were forced to leave their pets, assured by the military they would be back in a couple of days. All the pets then died of starvation and dehydration.

"Actually, the scary thing was watching the seismometers progressively go completely dead, first, away from Pinatubo and then in our direction at Clark," a noted CVO scientist told me later. The massive pyroclastic flows were boiling away from the volcano, scouring the landscape and devastating everything in their path. CVO tech genius Andy Lockhart, appearing in the final scenes of a National Geographic Society video on Pinatubo, remembered the runway lights at Clark. Once they began to go out, he said, he would know the flows were coming.

"I might have time to get to the opposite side of the room," he said. Who wouldn't be scared, in particular *just twelve days* after the deaths of the Kraffts, Harry Glicken, and many Japanese at Mount Unzen? As it was, by the time the hot flows nearly reached Clark, with the main housing high on an interfluve formed in part of the deposits of at least one previous pyroclastic flow, they had become channelized at the lower level of the adjacent Sacobia River channel. If the June 15 flows had been of comparable size and removed Clark from the face of the earth, I would again be writing, "Why on earth had anybody been staying in so vulnerable a location?" Like David Johnston on May 18, 1980, they had placed themselves at risk to monitor the run-up to what would very probably be a major eruption and disaster. They, like David, were very aware that they were placing their lives at risk.

More than 50,000 primitive Aetas were evacuated from the slopes around the edifice, most of whom would otherwise have died. Only an unknown few stayed, perhaps refusing to believe that their sacred mountain would harm them. I saw one of them while driving from Clark to the U.S. Navy base at Subic Bay with Tom Casadevall, later USGS director. The Aeta man was tiny, naked except for a loin cloth and an amulet, with a bow and about a dozen poison arrows clutched in his left hand, at the ready.

Later on a dark day flying back from field work on the volcano to Clark, as we skimmed the gray, ash-laden flank of the volcano, a deserted village high on stilts flashed by in the forest. There were no footprints in the desert of ash around it. During the Vietnam conflict, Aetas were hired to train U.S. troops in jungle survival, but that brief contact with the twentieth century had done little to nudge them out of the Stone Age.

Of the 300 or so people who died with the eruption, most perished in surrounding towns only because a tropical storm coincided with the eruption, and the extra weight of wet ash caused roofs to collapse.

In the months following the Pinatubo eruption, as we flew Hueys and the Navy version of the Blackhawk out of what remained of Clark, we passed over the ash-laden, collapsed but empty hangers that had housed the state-of-the-art aircraft making up the major U.S. fighter wing in the western Pacific. They had gotten out in time. Wet ash mantled the mainly deserted base housing, including the theater staging *The Last Days of Pompeii* before the eruption. They were certainly the last days of Clark.

Several weeks earlier, we had been checking a seismometer on a ridge between the jagged rim of the post-eruption Pinatubo caldera and Clark AFB, which had survived the June 15 eruption. The caldera was 2.5 km (1.4 mi) across and had formed

Evacuations from Clark Air Force Base were already underway on June 12, a few days before the volcano's massive eruption. (USGS photo by Richard P. Hoblitt)

by collapse during the 9-hour climax eruption. Our helicopter was a Navy version of the Blackhawk, the "screamin' machine" immortalized in the riveting film, *Blackhawk Down*. The aircraft has a large "belly hole," a manhole in the center of the fuselage, through which a squad could rapidly deploy. It was open that afternoon, and I was watching the ground come up as we flared to land. *My God, there were the shear lines of a lahar, and . . . they were shearing! A flowing lahar!* We were seconds away from touching down and sinking directly into a river of mud at least 10 m deep. It was flowing so slowly that the pilot had seen it as solid ground. Several of us yelled (screamed) in unison and instantly he pulled up.

§

In the years to follow, far more than 300 would die, mainly a result of lahars spawned by rainfall that began to mobilize portions of the cubic kilometers of ash. A large circular area of lahar inundation surrounded the volcano and would be progressively aggraded by many meters. Philippine sense of place is so profound that, if one house was buried, another would be constructed directly above it, and so on. At last count, the number of successively buried houses stacked vertically in one place was commonly three and possibly more.

The same was true for bridges, and the perfect illustration for this astounding rearrangement of the landscape could be found at what I call the "Three-Bridges Site," where the large first bridge across the Bamban River was progressively buried, visible in cross-section.[2] As that bridge was buried, a well-engineered steel truss bridge was constructed above it, with supports integrated with the trusses of the first bridge. This second bridge rapidly disappeared, to be replaced by a small wooden structure suitable for only pedestrians. The entire runout area was so aggraded to a uniform, nearly flat surface that flows were wide and shallow, and their deposits readily driven and walked on. There was no more need for a bridge at all.

The scale of the lahar deposition was so great that normal mitigation methods were not practical. For example, along the front of the Transverse Ranges in Southern California, a series of debris basins that I designed catch the flows, thereby debulking the sediment from the water, which is decanted into concrete channels leading to major rivers. When full, each basin must be excavated back to its original capacity. Early on, Dick Janda advocated what he called the "sacrificial lamb" approach. Large areas would be selected for deposition only, and channels would be constructed to route the debris-laden flows to them. The channels, however, were at least initially

The "Three-Bridges Site" illustrates the layers of newer bridges built as previous structures were no longer functional. The original truss bridge is no longer visible, and lies beneath the supports of the second bridge. The third, a wooden bridge, is at left.

formed of bulldozed lahar deposits and disappeared with erosion from the next storm runoff. All sediment management projects, textbook and *ad hoc*, were swamped by the deluge of sediment that continued in the years after 1991. The population gradually adjusted to a vertical, upward migration.

Farther away from the volcano, we landed to watch a major highway bridge stand like a rock in late 1991 as a massive lahar poured beneath. The ground was vibrating, and a group of perhaps forty chanting villagers appeared on the bridge, praying for its salvation. Unexpectedly, their prayers were answered, at least until the next rain. It disappeared from view during 1992.

A public works project on the broad lahar-runout fans consisted of many hundreds of villagers filling and placing sandbags, trying to stabilize the channels upstream from the bridges and funnel the flows under them. Soon there would be few bridges left to protect. Among the non-textbook methods suggested was the construction of flat-topped mounds that could serve in the Antarctic sense as *refugios*, places of refuge in case the main base burned during the Austral winter. The mounds would

Throughout Clark, structures and vegetation were severely damaged by tephra (ash) fall on June 15. This follow-up image was taken on June 24. (USGS photo by Willie Scott)

be *refugios* if an otherwise unescapable lahar arrived. Kelvin Rudolfo, a professor of oceanography at the University of Illinois at Chicago, advocated this approach.[3]

Kelvin wrote a charming book titled *Lahar* on the topic and was a successful advocate for defining the term at a 1993 Penrose Conference sponsored by the Geological Society of America. His definition stands but is not, to my knowledge, used by present-day students. It proposes that the entire flow be called a lahar, even when it is of the granular, noncohesive variety that transforms, first to the hyperconcentrated phase of the runout flow, and finally to sediment-laden streamflow. Deposits of the two distal phases, if seen only in the many kilometers of their distal phases beyond the actual debris flow, the extent of which may be only a few kilometers, will not have their origin recognized. The approach I have used, taught to my students, and proposed to many colleagues, is to describe the texture (such as sorting) and structures (grading, antidune cross-bedding, etc.) of the downstream deposits. This will reveal their flow process (such as hyperconcentrated flow) and thus their *probable* link to an upstream lahar. Or, start on the volcano and work downstream and, using stratigraphy, all will be clear.

§

Returning each day to Clark in a Huey, the gunship helicopters of Vietnam, Dick Janda and I passed over the flattened hangers that had housed the fleet of the most modern fighters in existence. The aircraft had gotten out, some to the naval base airfield at Subic Bay, southwest of Pinatubo, and many were flown back to the States. Aircraft are easily damaged by ash. In March 1944, the USAAF 340th Bombardment Group was based at Pompeii Airfield near Terzigno, Italy, a few kilometers from the east base of Vesuvius. Tephra and hot ash damaged control surfaces, engines, Plexiglas windshields, and gun turrets of the B-25 Mitchell medium bombers. An estimated 78 to 88 aircraft were destroyed.[4] That was the last eruption of Vesuvius to the present.

At Pinatubo two years later, I flew in from Manila to assist the U.S. Army Corps of Engineers in advising the Philippine government on lahar mitigation. I passed over a Philippine Air Force Base. A long row of unhangered fighters stood exactly where they'd been on June 15, 1991, covered by ash and now awaiting salvage. The Philippine Air Force had received a warning shortly before the eruption, but had been unable to act upon it.

§

The remarkable warning and forecasting effort at Pinatubo (I was not involved pre-eruption) was the work of the Volcano Disaster Assistance Program (VDAP), initiated by the efforts of CVO scientist Norman Banks after the Nevado del Ruiz tragedy.[5] USGS scientists had not been sent there because of other obligations following the Mount St. Helens eruptions. I think that our cachet, our tenacity, and our application of past volcano history to the present and future would have greatly mitigated that disaster. If I, or Tom Pierson, who went after the tragedy, had gone when first requested, there is not the slightest doubt that either of us would have recognized the sequences of "muddy" layers and the runout facies of lahars. We would not have just come, warned, and went, assuming that Colombian authorities would act. That would not happen again thanks to the VDAP mission statement and funding from the U.S. Agency for International Development (USAID).

The latest VDAP success story involves the 2010 eruptions of Merapi, the famous and frequently active volcano on the island of Java, Indonesia. There, VDAP staff and their leader, John Pallister, used satellite images to monitor dome growth and dome-collapse pyroclastic flows during the eruptions from September to November.

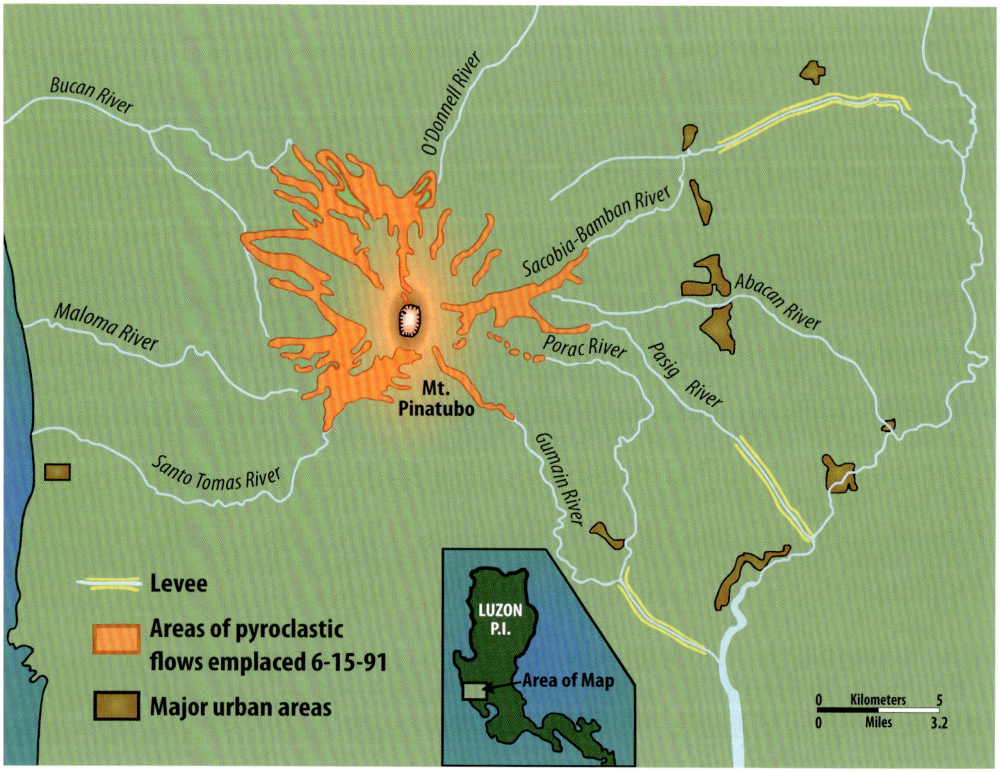

The reach of Pinatubo's destruction is visible in orange. (USGS)

Because of rainy season cloud cover, Synthetic Aperture Radar (SAR) was preferable to optical data and was used to issue even short-term (several hours) warnings. Well-established links to Indonesian authorities triggered the safe evacuation of 400,000 people.[6]

Enough credit can never be given to all those with USGS and PHIVOLCS for their dedication and sacrifice. The real heroes of this business are scientists like David Johnson who remain at their posts interpreting seismic, tilt-meter, and other data and relaying the implications to decision-makers as unrest escalates. Those who responded at Pinatubo when it first became restless, in their self-described *Year of Living Dangerously*, only privately wrote in their notes of the real dangers. In interviews, these were turned into dry humor that you had to have been there to appreciate.

The truth is, extraordinary risks were routine, in both installing instruments on the mountain's sharp ridges with helicopters, some of which were soaking their interiors with leaking hydraulic fluid, and at times without any flyable backup to extricate them if any of several varieties of hazard, including guerillas, arrived. They remained at Clark Air Force Base, a location fried in at least one previous eruption, for many hours before the main eruption. The seismic stations successively went dark, first to the west, and then to the east, indicating powerful PFs moving in the direction of Clark.

Evacuees totaled 60,000, and over 20,000 would have met certain death had they remained.[1] This was the most successful eruption prediction and mitigation in history and may well be for a long time.

NOTES:

1. The monumental volume by Chris Newhall and Ray Punongbayan, 1996, *Fire and Mud: The Eruptions and Lahars of Mount Pinatubo, Philippines*, PHIVOLCS and USGS, as well as the field notes by and conversations with my colleagues. It is greatly to be regretted that the field notes will not be published.
2. Article by Scott and others in Newhall and Punongbayan (1996), 971–88.
3. See Lagmay, A.M.F.A. 2010. Getting to know Kelvin. *Philippine Science Letters* 3:88-91. Kelvin Rodolfo was a marine geologist at the University of Illinois at Chicago but changed specialties as author of a book, *Lahar*, the story of his controversial experiences and theories of lahar mitigation at Pinatubo after the 1991 eruption.
4. Kaiser, D., www.warwingsart.com/12thAirForce/Vesuvius
5. Volcano Disaster Assistance Program (VDAP), formerly Volcano Crisis Assistance Team (VCAT), is a joint effort between the USGS and the U.S. Agency for International Development; Office of Foreign Disaster Assistance (USAID/OFDA).
6. Pallister, J. S., Schneider, D. J., Griswold, J. P., Keeler, R. H., Burton, W. C., Noyles, C., Newhall, C. G., Ratdomopurbo, A. 2013. Merapi 2010 eruption—Chronology and extrusion rates monitored with satellite radar and used in eruption forecasting. *Journal of Volcanology and Geothermal Research* 261:144–52.

Most of Pompeii's citizens were able to escape before Vesuvius erupted. The ruins of Pompeii and the sculpture-like figures of those who died are today part of a disaster museum. (iStock.com / DHuss)

Chapter 15

Mount Vesuvius and Campi Flegrei: The Parthenopean Megacity

In Campania, Italy, events at Vesuvius and Campi Flegrei are highly relevant to mitigating deaths at all volcanoes because of their long, well-documented history. Compared to Mount Rainier, the poster volcano for cold, wet volcanic hazards, Mount Vesuvius is the poster volcano for hot, dry eruption hazards, i.e., pyroclastic density currents and airfall. It dominates Campania, the country's second-largest populated region, with nearly 6 million inhabitants, including Naples with over 3 million.

Vesuvius, east of Naples, last erupted in 1944. Campi Flegrei (Phlegraean Fields), the huge and potentially dangerous supervolcano west of Naples, last erupted in 1538, but in 1983, inflated and threatened to erupt, triggering evacuations. It was the source of huge ash sheets, the Campanian Ignimbrite (age 40,000 years) and Campanian Yellow Tuff (12,000 years). The 150 km^3 of the ignimbrite spread over southern Europe is said to have caused the extinction of Neanderthals and their replacement by modern humans.[1,2] The Yellow Tuff covered much of southern Italy and forms the lovely yellow walls and buildings throughout the region. Campi Flegrei commonly ranks high, and higher than Vesuvius, in rankings of the ten most dangerous volcanoes.

Residents within the Campi Flegrei supervolcano caldera, however, are more worried about Vesuvius. A poll reported by Roberto Isaia at the 2018 Cities on Volcanoes meeting in Naples found that 70 percent of 1,008 respondents named Vesuvius as their greatest worry.[3]

Volcanologists make the obligatory mecca to Vesuvius and the cities it destroyed in 79 CE, Pompeii and Herculaneum. We dine in restaurants on the lower slopes of the edifice, especially on Tuesdays when the supply of fresh *mozzarella d' bufala* is released, made from the milk of water buffalos. To paraphrase a Japanese aphorism, a disaster will occur when all memory of the previous disaster has disappeared. We could rephrase that at Vesuvius and say that a disaster will occur when public concerns turn to more mundane and immediate issues than volcanic catastrophe.

Together, Vesuvius and Campi Flegrei are accountable for the deeply rooted fatalism of Campanians, and of Neopolitans in particular. But is it the cause or an effect of various reasons for fatalism? They might point to the seemingly invincible Camorra,[5] the powerful local mafia. Or the less-than-effective local government of an area ruled by foreigners for most of the last millennium. Not to mention the twenty-eight outbreaks of the Black Death between 1347 and 1647. Maybe a long history of volcanoes, the Camorra, and the Black Death fit together—irresistible forces, depressing in the futility of resistance.

On weekdays, villages in Campania have plenty of lounging single men with an attitude, astride Vespas, many unemployed and living with their mothers. They do not look happy. Others might call for *en masse* clinical psychology. I paraphrase from the guidebook to the 1998 Cities on Volcanoes meeting, discussing the unconsciously feared risk and fatalistic hope that Vesuvius will erupt far into the future: "The need of 'Greater Naples,' equally important to knowing the volcanoes and mitigating their hazards, is for social and psychological treatment of people living on and around them so that they can live in harmony, in a conscious, responsible, and rational way."

Or as the famed German writer Johann Wolfgang von Goethe so aptly said, "The Neopolitan [or Campanian] would certainly be a different creature if he did not feel himself wedged between Heaven and Hell."

In fact, the people are directly wedged between two potential Hells—Vesuvius and Campi Flegrei. Not to mention the Camorra.

§

Campi Flegrei, the broad (13 km) caldera complex west of Naples, is a volcano tourist wonderland—the Phlegrean Fields of the Greeks. At its center is Pozzuoli Bay from which Pliny the Elder, the Roman fleet commander, sailed across the Bay of Naples to die on the beach below the erupting Vesuvius in 79 CE. The most recent eruption in the main caldera of Campi Flegrei formed Monte Nuovo on the north side of Pozzuoli Bay during several days in 1538. Near the caldera center, Solfatara Crater is a steaming sulphurous pit 0.6 km wide. It was known to the Greeks, inspired Dante's Hell, and was where San Gennaro, patron saint of Naples, was beheaded in 305 CE after lions refused to harm him. A vial of the miraculously and regularly liquefied

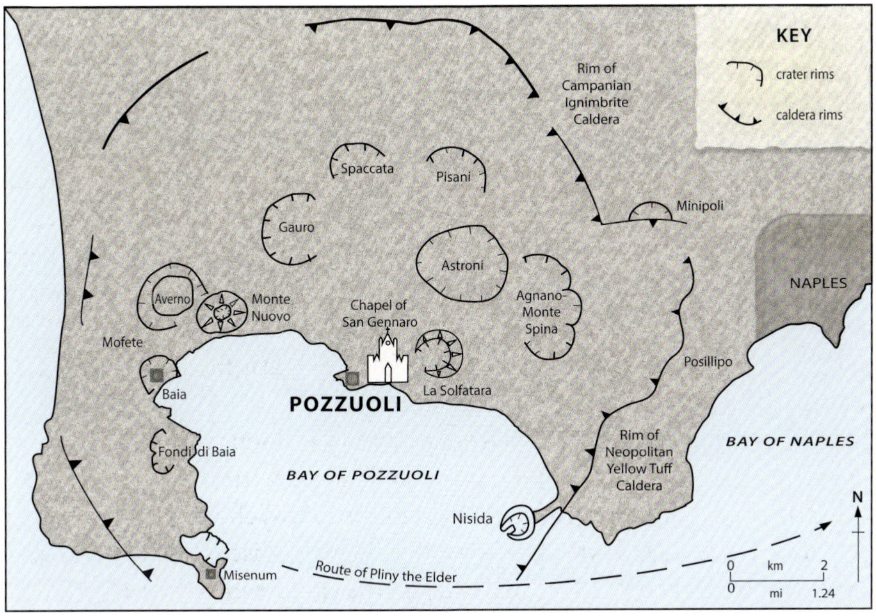

A map of Campi Flegrei indicates the epicenter of bradyseismic activity at Pozzuoli. (Adapted from multiple sources)

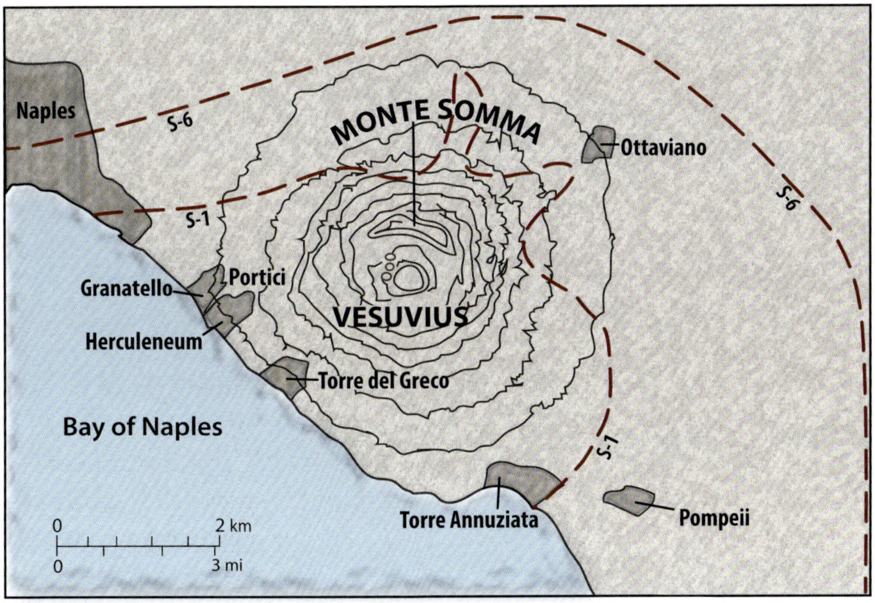

Mount Vesuvius. S-1 and S-6 are the first and last of the pyroclastic surges of 79 CE, mapped by Sigurdsson and others, 1985. (Adapted from multiple sources)

Campi Flegrei, where lions would not touch San Gennaro.

saint's blood is displayed three times a year in Naples to intimidate Vesuvius and reassure the faithful. We non-Campanians scoff at our peril when the blood reliquifies and the saint insures the area's safety.

The center of the Campi Flegrei caldera rises and falls with changes in magma volume at a depth of 5 to 6 km, causing the vertical oscillations called bradyseismism. The three columns of the "Temple of Serapis" (actually a Roman bazaar) are a standard photo in geology textbooks. Now above sea level, the borings of marine mollusks scar them to a height above sea level of 7 m, showing that they subsided to below sea level since construction. They were the frontispiece of what Stephen Jay Gould in his 1999 article, "Lyell's Pillars of Wisdom," described as *perhaps the most important scientific textbook ever written*.[6] That is Charles Lyell's *Principles of Geology* (1830 and many editions). Lyell, the most influential geologist of the nineteenth century (and believer in the importance of field geology), used the columns to illustrate catastrophism. That is the idea that the earth's surface is the product of a series of dramatic upheavals. Uniformitarianism, the competing idea and the explanation of the earth's surface through sustained, gradual change, was the idea that what was happening slowly now could explain the past—"the present is the key to the past." Our thesis here, of course, is that the "past is the key to the future."

Mollusk borings scar each of the three vertical Serapis columns to the same height, and thus act as a "tide gauge" to record initial, post-100 BCE bradyseismic[7] deflation and later inflation. Moorings for ships now stand above any useful height. Still underwater in the bay are the summer villas of Caesar and Nero, where Hadrian died in 138 CE. The most recent change, with magma injection (46 cm of uplift in last seven years)[7] is small, but any inflation cannot be good news. The caldera center has been higher in the past without a large eruption. An earthquake accompanying the uplift in 1983 triggered evacuation of 40,000 from the city of Pozzuoli (birthplace of Sophia Loren) when it looked like an eruption could occur. Many moved away permanently. The effects of that false alarm will resonate and may cause future deaths in ways inherent in the "false-alarm problem."

The Plinys (Elder and Younger)

No discussion of Vesuvius can ignore the roles of the Roman Commander Pliny and his nephew and later adopted son. About 2:30 the afternoon of August 24, 79 CE[8] the Roman Navy Commander Pliny (the Elder) boarded a small two-deck galley with his most powerful slaves at the oars, in the fleet anchorage at Misenum on Pozzuoli Bay west of Naples. He made ready to depart toward the rising mushroom cloud across the Bay of Naples. The author of the encyclopedic thirty-seven-volume *Naturalis Historia*, he had been alerted to the strange cloud by his wife, and he had to investigate. But as he was embarking, a messenger arrived by horse after a four-hour trip along the coastal road, asking for help from a friend on the coast south of Vesuvius then being threatened by falling ash. These events are recorded by a seventeen-year-old, Pliny's nephew (Pliny the Younger), in the first of two famous letters written many years later. If Pliny the Younger was not inventing a humanitarian excuse for his uncle's scientific curiosity, this story of the messenger is evidence that fallout was underway by about 9:00 to 10:00 A.M. south of the volcano on August 24. The news from the horseback messenger was ominous. The Commander then ordered the massive Imperial quadriremes (four-deck galleys, his "ships of the line") to depart their roadstead on what had now become a rescue mission. Whips cracked across the backs of the slaves chained to their rowing benches.

As they approached the coast, his helmsman wanted to turn back because of the floating ash. "Fortune favors the brave . . . " Pliny famously replied. The cutter had trouble approaching more closely because of the reef of fresh pumice, so he sailed farther south, disembarking to spend the night with his friend, Pomponianus, where little ash was falling. He dined and had a bath. He was awakened the next morning

At the center of Campi Flegrei, three large columns are scarred by mollusk borings below a level of ca. 35 percent of their height.

to flee, because earthquakes and the increasing pumice fall were threatening building collapse. His bedroom door would barely open because of the swiftly accumulating pumice. The party returned to the beach, pillows strapped to their heads, but they could not embark because of onshore wind and the cinder-charged sea. Near the time of the final surge that morning, killing the last of those remaining in Pompeii, the corpulent naturalist collapsed and died in the arms of slaves on the beach, apparently from suffocation but possibly from a heart attack.

Only on the second day would the distal surges reach 32 km westward across the Bay of Naples to Misenum, as Pliny the Younger would recall in the most widely quoted part of his second letter to Tacitus. His first letter had been confined to events concerning his uncle.

Two conclusions are possible, both obvious but not widely appreciated. In both of the "worst case" events—Avellino[9] and 79 CE—an initial, survivable period of pumice fall lasted many hours, sufficient for the "hundreds of footprints headed north" with the Avellino eruption, and in 79 CE for most of Pompeii and Herculaneum to escape the cities proper. Secondly, wind direction was critical in the two important Plinian eruptions, but opposite—to the north-northwest for Avellino, to the southwest for 79 CE.

That uncertainty casts a degree of doubt on most of the assumptions in a major future eruption, which logically focuses on the presently large coastal cities affected in 79, 472, and 1631 CE. Prevailing winds are to the south-southwest for ten months of the year (east-northeast in December and January), clearly placing the coastal cities in that direction again at risk, unprotected by Mount Somma. Volcanic stratigraphy reveals a range in both fall and surge directions of the seven largest eruptions of Vesuvius (actually of Somma–Vesuvius, thus including the huge pre-18,000-years BP stratovolcano). The Avellino eruption affected the area of Naples not previously included in high-priority hazard planning.

Planning—The Maximum Expectable Eruption

"Live in danger. Build your cities on the slopes of Vesuvius," said Friedrich Nietzsche, the German philosopher.

It's true that Vesuvius itself is the source of greatest present volcanic risk, because much of the population of Naples and of many smaller cities lives on its lower flank, and because of its record of more recent activity versus Campi Flegrei. The perspective of history yields the 236-sq-km *Zona Rossa* or Red Hazard Zone, likely to be hit by pyroclastic flows. At least 600,000 people in that zone would require evacuation in the event of impending eruption.

"We could have a few days' warning or we could have a few weeks," said Peter Baxter, the retired Cambridge M.D. who specializes in death at volcanoes. The official plan, however, hopes for three to five days to organize the evacuation, moving people from the coastal cities to "twinned" locations throughout Italy, probably to minimize leakage back to the zone as well as organized protests that will certainly evolve if time drags by without an eruption.[10]

Evacuations are practiced—in 2007, buses required ten hours to evacuate groups of one hundred from each of eighteen cities at risk. Keeping people completely out of the zone will be impossible. In spite of security before May 18, 1980, at St. Helens, some of the fifty-seven who died had used stealth to get inside the red zone.

Authorities admit that during the pre-evacuation period, proponents of the plan predicted "many deaths are to be expected, caused by road accidents, people being crushed, heart attacks, and shootings." In the 1997 movie *Dante's Peak*, a dramatic version of Mount St. Helens, the real lesson lies in the panic portrayed as people attempted to flee. The CVO staff largely approved the movie. After a joint viewing, we agreed to give it a passing grade when interviewed. The movie runs a tape in my head of what the Puyallup River valley downstream from Mount Rainier will look like when the lahar-warning sirens go off. The anti-establishment Italian volcanologist Professor Flavio Dobran makes a point—authorities could have used *Dante's Peak* as an educational video for Campania.

The *Zona Rossa* (Red Hazard Zone) at Vesuvius is based, not on the cataclysmic eruption of 79 CE that destroyed Pompeii and Herculaneum, but on the effects of smaller eruptions in 472 and 1631 CE and mainly on their areas of pyroclastic flows. These two eruptions are both categorized as sub-Plinian, smaller than the 79 CE type example of a Plinian eruption. Their combined effects yield the Maximum Expectable Eruption.

The red zone at risk of pyroclastic flows (Red Zone 1) contains 550,000 people; the red zone at risk of ash fall (previously in the yellow zone, now added to the red zone) adds another 300,000.[11] A second Yellow Hazard Zone of 1,125 sq km is at risk of lower probabilities of pyroclastic flows, but subject to heavy ash fall and lahars and floods. In the chapter on Sarno, Italy, we see the even more widespread effects of rainfall-triggered debris flows in the downwind, tephra-mantled regions. But that is not a hazard for evacuation with an impending eruption. A third, the Blue Zone, is later delineated north of Vesuvius, an area inundated previously by lahars.

The delineation of the *Zona Rossa* and the evacuation plans are more subjective and controversial than just the outlines of the areas of pyroclastic flows in 472 and 1631 CE. After the 1980s evacuation of Pozzuoli, the *Dipartimento della Protezione Civile* created a National Volcanology Group headed by Professor and later Undersecretary Franco Barberi. It created the eruptive scenario based on the 472 and 1631 eruptions by 1995, and in 1993 a committee prepared an emergency evacuation plan.

Authorities think a week is a good basis for planning and, after reviewing past histories, both that inference, as well as basing it on the 472 and 1631 eruptions, seems reasonable. In 1631, as early as in July residents were noticing earthquakes; in late November, shepherds reported the swelling cone, and several days before the eruption of December 16, they felt continuous shaking. From then on, there was time in 1631 to parade San Gennaro's relics, of both his blood and his skull, and intimidate the volcano into submission. As the eruption continued into December 17, Vesuvius did not seem to be listening, so a second procession was ordered: The Cardinal exposed the relics to the volcano and, accounts relate, "lo and behold, the immeasurable, high, and intemperate cloud fell from the summit, almost bowing its head to the holy relic . . . "

Incandescent clouds killed the people of Pompeii in 79 CE. (iStock.com / sestovic)

During a 1767 eruption, after a mob set fire to the gates of the Cardinal Archbishop because he refused to bring out the relic, the eruption worsened. Eventually, the head of San Gennaro was displayed, and the eruption ceased as the saint came in sight of the mountain.

The saint provides researchers with clues to smaller and later Vesuvius eruptions that would otherwise be unknown, by the times recorded in parish records when he was shown to the threatening volcano. In 79 CE, of course, he had not yet appeared—Christianity itself was just arriving. San Gennaro was beheaded at the Solfatara in Campi Flegrei in 305 CE, and one of his followers collected his blood in vials.

Franco Barberi, suave and respected both as scientist and politician, spoke at the 1998 Rome and Naples Cities on Volcanoes meeting. The relation between government and public attitudes to volcanic risk in Italy is often strained, and security was present in each corner of the meeting room. The room looked like it was the ballroom of the Bourbon Palace during the Kingdom of the Two Sicilies. I passed on the more boring papers, wondering if this room could be where Lady Emma, wife of the elderly English ambassador, Sir William Hamilton, first performed her "attitudes." These were poses from classical history that, with Emma's other talents, captured the heart of British Admiral Horatio Nelson, later hero of Trafalgar (1805). He had been recuperating from wounds suffered in his first and most brilliant naval victory over Napoleon, the Battle of the Nile in 1798. Sir William would become famous, not only as a cuckold, but as the first modern volcanologist. He spent thirty-six years in Naples happily studying and writing about a regularly active Vesuvius and probably pleased to see Emma diverted.

The 1995 Plan (updated in 2013) established alert levels and outlined the steps for each alert level, for which the responsibility rests with the Vesuvius Volcano Observatory. Various levels of evacuation are practiced, the first in 2006, when 2,000 people participated and fifteen foreign experts observed. Schoolchildren played the roles of foreign tourists touring the Pompeii ruins. Some of the practice evacuees couldn't reach the *autostrada* because it was raining, hardly a good omen, and a harbinger of reality. The citizenry of Pompeii would be evacuated entirely by boat to Liguria, the coastal province including Genoa, far to the north. Other destinations were similarly remote—Herculaneum to Tuscany; Torre del Greco, the largest city, to Sicily.

But otherwise? Peter Baxter told us in 2001 that the Naples *burocrazia* has only six hospital beds appropriate for volcanic trauma.

Professor Flavio Dobran, who was not among the consultants, countered with an alternative plan: Vesuvius 2000, in which he criticized the lack of appreciation for social and cultural issues, as well as the need for a phased, selective evacuation. A chief element is his idea of structures built on the side of the volcano to disperse future pyroclastic flows. He proposed modeling "all relevant parts of the volcano, starting from magma accumulation in [the] magma chamber, flow of magma through the volcanic conduit and interaction with the walls, and dispersion of gas and pyroclasts in the atmosphere and along the [flanks] . . . " integrated with a socio-economic risk educational philosophy, establishing a "serious debate culture" of local, national, and European Union leaders, and with "engineers, geophysicists, seismologists, physicists, computer scientists, historians, urban planners, sociologists, educators, telecommunications experts, economists, environmentalists, civil protection volunteers, and the exposed population," etc. Nearly everybody, that is, except the geologists and volcanologists who proposed the 1995 Plan. All this is ideally desirable, but it is easy to envision a perpetual "paralysis by analysis" with contentious dueling factions creating distrust within the public and endless excuses for non-action. To quite a few, the more Professor Dobran expostulates, the better the 1995 Vesuvius Plan appears, created by the commission of appointed experts, based on previous eruptions, and thus with geologic perspective. Logical, defensible plans, like the 1995 Vesuvius Plan and like the existing lahar-warning system and land-use plans

Across from the Naples church holding the crypt of San Gennaro, a sidewalk mural depicts the saint with vials of his blood as he calms Mount Vesuvius supernaturally. Also at the church, a museum houses his treasures, including a mitre encrusted with emeralds worth millions of dollars.

elsewhere, can become targets for self-promoting critics and, of course, endless funding of follow-up research. That is careful not to make any major shift in the basic existing plan, and thus not to become the new target. The net result is for no major changes in the basic plans, but the audience of critics gets so crowded that truly helpful refinements can get lost in the crowd.

The structures Dobran proposes to mitigate the disaster are 30 m-high barriers at 2.5 and 4.5 km from the crater rim. They are apparently a sort of baffle designed to disperse the ground-hugging pyroclastic flows upward into co-ignimbrite clouds, the finely dispersed ash rising (elutriating) from the coarse basal flow. I imagine the structures as quickly destroyed by crashing boulders in the high velocity, block-filled avalanche at the base of the initial flow. Were such structures possible, frankly, I am sure the Japanese would have invented them and tested them at Mount Unzen in the early 1990s. Their budgets for engineering solutions were then bottomless. Generally, proposals for engineering mitigation of large volcanic flows come from people with little conception of the nature of flow processes at a volcanic scale—those with no field experience. I recall attempts by Chris Newhall, retired USGS scientist and proposer of the VEI scale for calibrating eruption size, to make that point to a scientist proposing retention dams for volcano-scale lahars at Guagua Pichincha volcano in Ecuador, at the 2004 IAVCEI meeting in Chile.

Professor Dobran reports that he made his charges at the 1997 IAVCEI General Conference in Puerto Vallarta, where the proponents of the Plan "were unable to defend them." I apparently was responsible. Chairing a meeting at that conference, I recall him standing and beginning what seemed a long, attitudinally hostile diatribe. I was only marginally familiar with the issues at that time but took a non-verbal cue from colleague Bob Tilling and called for sticking to the schedule. To my knowledge, there was no promotion of the Plan, and thus no defense.

We can all agree that the population explosion on the lower flanks of the volcano is criminal. Vesuvius has collaborated in creating a trap by staying so quiet since 1944. This also subjects those connected to the Vesuvius Plan to even more criticism—they have not personally experienced an eruption, so they cannot know of what they speak. USGS geologist Rocky Crandell, along with well-recognized Italian volcanologists, and I would say that the events documented by volcanic stratigraphy speak plainly. Neither Rocky, nor his tephra-specialist colleague Don Mullineaux, had ever experienced an eruption, but they forecast the 1980 eruption of Mount St. Helens with an amazing and now legendary accuracy. No modeling, no crater studies, just geologic perspective gleaned from volcanic stratigraphy away from the volcano flanks.

Authorities chose not to use the larger 79 CE eruption for planning, requiring an evacuation of many more than 600,000 people. They regard that larger eruption as what planners see as a low-probability, high-consequence event—one for which, even with tiny odds, the consequences are so catastrophic that its occurrence cannot be ruled out. It must be considered at some level, but not necessarily as one for which evacuation must be planned in detail. It is similar to "worst-case." The important issue, to me, is that they have based the response on scenarios that have actually happened at Vesuvius (not extrapolated from other volcanoes), with consideration of a well-defined historic perspective. This should stand in the court of public opinion, regardless of the outcome. Italian volcanologists know what they are doing, but are they leaning, perhaps subconsciously, in the direction of smaller evacuations rather than larger? I probably would be. The more Draconian the evacuation, the more they will find themselves at the center of controversy. Activity has been minimal since 1944, so their jobs look safe from the perspective of career duration.

Footprints Headed North—a Second 'Worst Case'?

The eruption described as the "Avellino 3780-yr-BP catastrophe" was huge. Professor Maria Teresa Pareschi of Pisa told us in 2004 of the recent discovery of a well-preserved Bronze Age village 15 km northeast of Vesuvius; it was buried by ash, pyroclastic surges, and finally lahars from that volcano, not by the huge, much-older eruptions. Maria Teresa was not successful in getting me to the village site; it had been reburied and preserved to await intensive investigation. She had heard that the Bronze Age villagers confined their goats in pens and may have hauled them into trees at night because of wolves. Unlike human-shy North American wolves, European wolves are a threat to humans, as well as goats, having developed the taste from the dead of millennia of battlefields. That explained why I didn't worry when a big wolf with legs like stilts, along with his pack, had begged for food as I lunched at one of my study sites near the trans-Alaska pipeline haul road.

Mike Sheridan is as expert a volcanic stratigrapher and as patient and inspirational a teacher as exists. Now retired, he was head of the University of Buffalo Center for Geohazards, and a coauthor of the Avellino findings. Mike devoted much of his career to Vesuvius's 25,000-year history and recognizes the need for authorities to take the Avellino eruption "into account," because it is the first from Vesuvius to impact Naples itself. Roberto Santacroce, a major force in Italian volcanology, tells me that Mike was the inspiration for the "golden age" of reinterpretation of Italy's volcanic history that followed the renaissance in volcanic stratigraphy inspired by 1980 Mount St. Helens.

Thousands of human and animal footprints were preserved in the initial Avellino pumice fall, all heading north away from the volcano by survivors slogging through soupy volcanic ash. This was a mass exodus, beginning a socio-economic collapse from which the region *did not recover for more than two centuries.* Few bodies were found, and we can assume that most escaped. Apparently, the eruption evolved similarly to what had happened in 79 CE—an early pumice fall followed by multiple pyroclastic surges from collapse of the Plinian eruption cloud, giving people and animals time to get away before the last, most devastating surges. New "worst-case" or not, the long-term abandonment of the area after the Avellino eruption is a lesson in how profound the aftereffects of eruptions can be.

Some Italian volcanologists assert that the Avellino eruption is a worst-case "maximum possible" and urge Neopolitan authorities to plan for complete evacuation within 20 km of the volcano with signs of unrest.[12]

The Future of 'Greater Naples'

Questions that authorities should and doubtless have (maybe not completely) considered in not enforcing prohibition of further development on the flanks of this iconic volcano: Will it be possible to evacuate 600,000 (later 700,000) Neopolitans from their homes to scattered locales for what may be an extended period of elevated alert levels? And, should that prove a false alarm, will they evacuate a second time when unrest again escalates? Will the Camorra cooperate? I would like to ask the Godfathers what they think about Vesuvius. Meanwhile, the population at high risk has been edging up—each new villa, each restaurant, until recently every day, incrementally. In 2003, volcanologist Haraldur Sigurdsson asked, "Have we learned to live with the sleeping giant? Judging from the current urban sprawl and the rapid commercial and residential development that is creeping up the slopes of the volcano, I must sadly conclude that we have not yet learned the lesson."

Meanwhile, at Mount Rainier, Washington, each meeting of the Pierce County Planning Commission approves exceptions to the population-restricting, land-use standards in the valleys that I like to call lahar pathways. The population figure for Rainier's highest-risk town, Orting, is posted on signs at the city limits. It changes regularly, and it never goes down. The residents of both Naples and Orting are fated to decrease suddenly and dramatically, at some unknown but foreseeable day in the future. Fatalities or evacuees?

Will that which is immediately advantageous to individuals always going to transcend the long-term interests of a group, even their descendants? Maybe planners should appeal to people in terms of their grandchildren. As a well-known investment advisor found that getting people to do the right thing for their children's sake does not work, in his case minimizing inheritance taxes by selling them life insurance. He discovered that people, on average, really do not like their children much (the gift that keeps on taking)—but they love their grandkids! Changing his pitch to "Do it for your grandchildren," as opposed to "for your children," made his fortune.

What if the number of people who need evacuation is not 600,000 or 700,000, but 3 million, the population of the broad urban Neopolitan area affected by the Avellino eruption? The authors of a study looked at the 1991 eruption of Pinatubo

The modern cone of Vesuvius, with the somma rim of the huge, ancient volcano on upper left. Despite repeated catastrophic events, development has not slowed on the flanks of the volcano. (iStock.com / TatianaMironenko)

in the Philippines and its impact on Clark Air Base, the largest U.S. air base in the world, evacuated just days before. Will there be Italian volcanologists, like those of the USGS and the Philippine Institute of Volcanology, emerging justly as heroes? This analogy is a bit disingenuous. Most of the 30,000 personnel at Clark Air Base could be flown out, almost literally overnight, at the orders of the four-star general in charge, who fortunately believed the USGS scientists.[13] Separately, more than 50,000 people had been evacuated from the flanks of Pinatubo itself.

The simple, basic purpose for establishing a red zone is evolving—slowing growth if not reducing the population therein, monitoring the volcano, and evacuating from that zone at some to-be-decided point. An innovative 2008 paper by Peter Baxter and colleagues describes evidence- and risk-based approaches and methods from medical science, applying them as a new paradigm to volcanology.[14] It proposes mitigation, from more timely evacuation to strengthening buildings and preparing evacuation corridors.

Can all the new refinements in mitigation techniques be just too much detail for the massive, infinitely variable problems of saving lives at Vesuvius? At the 2018 Cities on Volcanoes (COV) conference, twenty years after the first COV conference in Naples, a room filled with several hundred delegates met only to discuss Volcano Alert Levels and their number (3 or 4?) and terminology. That packed meeting room convinces me that some aspects of volcanology are becoming intensely inbred.

The strengthening of buildings is wise but may encourage some to stay rather than evacuate, just as a minority did in Pompeii and Herculaneum. Doubtless, bunkers will be proposed, perhaps only to become pressure cookers. No worries there; when they are needed they are likely to be locked securely, as I found on Mount Unzen in Japan. In fairness to the Japanese, the locked bunkers existed for construction workers, not geologists, and they contained costly breathing equipment and fireproof garments. The Japanese were clearly students of death by pyroclastic flow after June 3, 1991.

So we can strategize with a greater perspective of the possibilities, especially with regard to "hardening the target." But with an Avellino or 79 CE "worst case," can we really reduce the risk outside of getting people out of the way permanently, and to facilitate their evacuation, both physically and psychologically, before that proves necessary? Maybe a workshop, in which residents are asked to role-play their feelings as volcanic unrest begins? Perhaps it might end with a role of the dice to determine their fate—escaped, cooked, choked by ash, or hit with a ballistic? Or, a permanent dinner theater playing *The Last Days of Pompeii*, (as was playing at Clark Air Force Base below Pinatubo in June 1991).[15] Is the potential for an eruption the size of that in 79 CE just too catastrophic to risk worrying about all those details proposed by Professor Dobran in his counter to the Vesuvius Plan? With the exception, of course, of tuning the approaches and techniques for evacuation as Dr. Peter Baxter suggests: Treat the volcano as an ill patient. One must like the simple and realistic idea of a logical red zone, keeping more people out of it, and when necessary, getting them out as orderly as possible.

Let's face it. The only fundamental mitigation is reversing the post-1944 growth that has doubled the numbers at risk and exponentially increased the evacuation difficulties.

The Granatello Epigraph

The importance of frequency in volcanic history was dramatically recognized at Mount Vesuvius. But not by an Italian. On January 16, 1632, a month after the major eruption of 1631, the ruling Spanish Viceroy Emmanuel Fonseca, Count of Monterey, erected three inscribed stone billboards (only one survives). That remaining plaque, inset in a wall in the Naples suburb of Portici, bears this message, paraphrased:

Descendants, descendants
It is about you . . . listen
Twenty times since the sun [first] rose if history does not tell stories
Vesuvius burst into flames always with huge extermination
of those who hesitated . . .
Sooner or later it catches fire . . .
It shakes itself and shakes the ground . . .
It punishes incautious and greedy people . . .
If you are wise listen to the voice of this stone
Do not care about your home and your belongings
Run away without delay . . .

Those twenty known eruptions may be an exaggeration, although few were the size of 1631, but the Viceroy had good reason. It is good advice, although it is in sharp contrast to the then-official attitude, probably including that of the Viceroy during the crisis, that the eruption was God's wrath toward sinners. The epigraph, as described in the guidebook to the 1998 COV meeting, "sounds a sorrowful warning to future generations and can be taken as the first civil defense manifesto of the Vesuvian area" or for any area around any volcano. The epigraph also reflects an early appreciation of volcanic earthquakes as warning signs. Pompeii had been so forewarned, and we can see evidence of seismic damage being repaired repeatedly in the years before 79 CE.

In April 2010, part of Naples proper was finally added to the zone from which evacuation will be ordered. Guido Bertolaso, the head of the Civil Protection Agency, made the decision. Although it was probably delayed fallout from the discovery of the Avellino eruption, it was likely related to the Icelandic eruptions then disrupting European air travel. There is nothing like one eruption for decision-makers to suddenly remember other volcanoes. The number to be evacuated has nearly doubled to more than 1 million.

Local schoolchildren depict the volcano as a monster.

The minister took a well-deserved shot at the Campanian regional laws ("a total failure"). Owners of property constructed illegally in the Red Zone will be allowed to keep it and rent it out, while getting public money to build new homes in safer areas. His solution to unlicensed building: "What's there is there. But anything new that goes up must be demolished."

What authorities are saying, especially the publicity about Parco Nazionale del Vesuvio, is reason to hope. Yet this is Campania, and palms crossed with silver or having your wife murdered by the Camorra can do wonders. Bertolaso, head of the Civil Protection Agency, is a national hero after his rescue efforts with the Abruzzo earthquake of 2007. However, he is accused of corruption, involving links between "megagalactic" sex parties and public contracts.

Greater Neopolitans, Save Yourselves?

At the 1998 COV meeting I saw a paper on the program by an official of a city on the volcano's flanks. It seemed to reinforce the idea that, in the spirit of the Granatello Epigraph, one should self-evacuate and not wait for word from the authorities. When the ground shakes, don't wait for the experts to meet and talk about it. I looked forward to meeting him. Unfortunately, he did not attend and the paper was not presented. Maybe questioning authority was unwise, but no—this is Italy, it's what you do.

As part of the 1998 COV meeting, we attended a program at a nearby elementary school on volcano awareness. It was wonderful; both the 1995 Vesuvius Plan and Professor Dobran have correctly deduced that the way to educate the populace is through their children. Students dramatized the evacuation by sliding down a volcano flank, a slide covered with red paper lava flows. Posters lined the walls, many showing the volcano as monster, leering down at innocent victims, waiting to devour them.

A New Role for San Gennaro?

There are enough polls taken, and enough questionnaires distributed, to know that a Vesuvius eruption is not among the first concerns of those who live on the volcano. Instead, it's garbage collection (always *numero uno*), the economy, crime, pollution, and waste disposal (all Camorra issues). All the usual non-volcanic suspects. Although about 45 percent of southern Italians attend Mass regularly, and most of Naples places faith in San Gennaro (but does not like to admit it to pollsters, apparently). The role of appealing for spiritual guidance and explanations in matters of natural hazards is ignored by most sociologists and scientists. It should not be, because it certainly provides a motive for doing nothing and waiting for divine guidance, and for interpreting disasters as divine punishment. Nevertheless, a substantial literature has evolved on the subject at both Vesuvius and Etna. I want to only mention the subject here, which is potentially the key to saving tens of thousands of lives in southern Italy.[16]

Naples' many patron saints do not seem to have provided much practical guidance. Campania needs a renaissance of optimistic action to replace the dark ages of fatalism. This idea occurs: an annual procession to the stone of Viceroy Fonseca with San Gennaro's relics? The saint and the Viceroy as a team. Effective, but unlikely.

The 1631 eruption that inspired the Viceroy's stone, and which is one of the two case histories for modern eruption planning, occurred at the height of the Counter Reformation, marking the end of the Renaissance. The Viceroy may have managed to keep the worst of the Inquisition away from Naples. For a time, he had barred the gates of Naples to those fleeing from the coastal cities to the south, fearing that the eruption was a carrier of disease. Beginning with the Age of Enlightenment of the next century, and the regular and mainly benign volcanic activity until 1944, a new appreciation of the volcano arose. Vesuvius, with the discovery of the remains of Pompeii and Herculaneum, and Grand Tour visits by Europe's intellectuals, became the lodestar of a golden age of awe, artistic expression, and the science of volcanoes. It was a period of small but spectacular eruptions that continued until 1944 when the volcano shut down.

A USGS-Style Fact Sheet for Greater Naples?—Wisdom and Faith

Much remains to be done about educating the public at risk. There have been reams of documents, manifestos, and well-meaning advice prepared for the living around Vesuvius. Why have those apparently not instilled any confidence? The answer is simple—*they were not endorsed by San Gennaro.*

Based on our Rainier experience, I suggest education-focused handouts, saturating every public place, and with annual, updated editions (for both Vesuvius and Campi Flegrei). The USGS publishes a series of two- or four-page "Fact Sheets," mainly on individual volcanoes. My colleagues and I have found them remarkably efficient and cost-effective for public education at Cascade Range volcanoes.[17] The *sine qua non* strategies of reducing numbers at risk and improving evacuation efficiency with practice and evacuation corridors will be clear, but they need to be repeated as often as possible. Similarly, New Zealand publishes a series of handouts called "Hazard Facts" for the Auckland volcanic field, a group of tuff rings and scoria cones from 60,000 to 600 years old.[18]

The title will be key, and ideally will include the name of San Gennaro (*A Tribute to . . .* , or *San Gennaro Warns . . .* , etc.).[19,20] Ideally, there would be an appeal from the Vatican Pontificate of Science, or the Pope himself (unthinkable before the present Pope Francis), to honor and integrate both spiritual faith and scientific wisdom—what in a biblical sense is God's and what is Caesar's. It can include a photo of the Granatello Epigraph, with Italian and English translations.

It can include a photograph of the skeletons in the Herculaneum boat houses, with a description by Peter Baxter of how and why they died (plenty of time to have escaped). Refer to the Viceroy's advice to leave your belongings behind. The Fact Sheet would address what polls and surveys show as the uncertainties about "twinned" evacuation destinations, with the planned means of getting people there. Frankly, twinned evacuations look like a permanent source of chaos to me. What happens when it's a false alarm and there is a demand to reverse them?

And finally, an optimistic forecast of a new Greater Naples once again rising from the ashes, this time with its residents having survived and prospered because of their faith and wisdom. Schools are clearly "with the program." Maybe an appeal from St. Augustine about suicide being an unforgivable sin, suggesting that to

At Herculaneum, bones of the dead were discovered in barrel vaults, or boat houses; they were subsequently replaced by replicas.

stay around Vesuvius is like committing suicide once the volcano becomes active. There may be citable points in Catholic theology relevant to martyrdom (i.e., death by pyroclastic flow). Sceptics to integration of scientific and spiritual issues can note that Naples in a recent year submitted 300 candidates for the initial stages of sainthood, more than all of France. And when saints speak, Naples listens.

Address the issue of property security. The present plan is for police to cordon the *Zona Rossa*, but will they stick around as precursory activity escalates, probably with their own families needing assistance? What about the locked bunkers at Unzen? What about the folding highways signs at Rainier without volunteers to unfold them? Bunkers may not be unlocked, signs may not be unfolded, and your property may not be guarded.

The idea that may be left unspoken: Move somewhere you don't need to worry about this, and don't build your home on the flanks of the volcano.

NOTES:

1. Oppenheimer, C. 2011. *Eruptions that Shook the World.* Cambridge, MA: Cambridge University Press. See section 9.1.2, Human impact. An excellent book.
2. Fedele, F. G., Giaccio, B., Isaia, R., and Orsi, G. 2002. Ecosystem impact of the Campanian Ignimbrite eruption in late Pleistocene Europe. *Quaternary Research* 7:420–24.
3. Isaia, R. 2018. The Campi Flegrei caldera (southern Italy): An active super-volcano with residents' low risk perception. Talk at COV10, Naples, Italy.
4. Sigurdsson, H., Cashdollar, S., and Sparks, S. R. J. The eruption of Vesuvius in AD 79: Reconstruction from historical and volcanological evidence. *American Journal of Archaeology* 86, no. 2 (1982): 39-51.

   See also: Sigurdsson, H., Carey, S., Cornell, W., Pescatore, T. 1985. The eruption of Vesuvius in AD 79. National Geographic Research.

   The best summaries of Vesuvius and Campi Flegrei, although not the most recent, are in the guidebook for the first COV meeting—Orsi, G., DiVito, M., and Isaia, R., eds. 1998. Volcanic hazards and risk in the Parthenopean megacity: *Guidebook, Field Excursion, July 5-7, 1998.* Cities on Volcanoes, International Meeting, Rome and Naples, Italy, June 28 to July 4, 1998.

   See also: Scarth, A., and Tanguy, J.-C. 2001. *Volcanoes of Europe.* Oxford: Oxford University Press.

   Scarth, A. 2009. *Vesuvius: A biography.* Princeton, NJ: Princeton University Press.

   Darley, G. 2012. *Vesuvius.* Cambridge, MA: Harvard University Press.
5. The Camorra, or Neopolitan mafia, is described in Chapter 16.
6. Gould, S. J. Article discussing Lyell's Pillars of Wisdom. *Natural History,* April 1999.
7. Bradyseismic activity is broad uplift over a large area. Recent amount of uplift is oral communication, Roberto Isaia, 2018.
8. The year of AD 79 is firm, but the actual date of the eruption is suspect. Garments and preserved fruit and produce are characteristic of a later month, and the Smithsonian Global Volcanism Program lists the eruption as ca. October 24-28.
9. The "Avellino 3780-yr-BP catastrophe" is described as larger than 79 CE by Mastrolorenzo, G., Thompson, G. A., Pappalardo, L., and Sheridan, M. F. 2006. The Avellino 3780-yr-BP catastrophe for a worst-case scenario for an eruption of Vesuvius. *Proceedings of the National Academy of Science* 103:4366–70.

   An *en masse* evacuation of thousands occurred at the beginning of the eruption, evidenced by their footprints "headed north" away from Vesuvius, and most of these likely survived. A late pyroclastic-surge sequence deposited 3 to 4 m of deposits in the present metropolitan district of Naples.
10. The evacuation plan, with the novel concept of twinning evacuated and existing populations on a possibly long-term basis, was probably motivated by continuing fallout from the widely publicized 1980 Mount St. Helens eruption as well as the 1983 Pozzuoli bradyseismic inflation and evacuation.
11. Peter Baxter, personal communication, 2018.
12. Guiseppe Mastrolorenzo, first author of the Avellino findings, promotes that eruption as the basis for planning.
13. The Commanding General at Clark general deserves a lot of credit. Post-eruption, he would visit our compound at Clark almost daily to inquire personally about how the military could help us. I went through many rolls of pre- and post-eruption aerial photographs of Pinatubo taken by a U2, the famous high-altitude spy plane.

14. Baxter, P. J., Aspinall, W. P., Neri, A., Zuccaro, G., Spence, R. J .S., Cioni, R., and Woo, G. 2008. Emergency planning and mitigation at Vesuvius: An evidence-based approach. *Journal of Volcanology and Geothermal Resources* 178:454–73.

15. *The Last Days of Pompeii* was an 1831 novel by Edward Bulwyr-Lytton (author of the line, "It was a dark and stormy night") made into a stage play.

16. Chester, D. K., Duncan, A. M., and Dibben, J. L. 2008. The importance of religion in shaping volcanic risk perception in Italy, with special reference to Vesuvius and Etna. *Journal of Volcanology and Geothermal Resources* 172:216-228. Introductory paper with a large bibliography.

17. Based on my coauthorships of Fact Sheets on Mount Rainier (with Carolyn Driedger) and Mount Baker (with Cynthia Gardner and Wes Hildreth).

18. Heiken, G. 2013. *Dangerous Neighbors*. Cambridge, MA: Cambridge University Press.

19. The literature on San Gennaro and the showing of his relics through the centuries is huge; just Google "Saint Gennaro." A host of explanations for logical, not magical explanations is proposed for liquefaction of the saint's blood.

20. Any form of Gennaro "coauthorship" must separate him as patron saint of Naples from his attributed power to reliquify his blood. The church position on Gennaro is that the thrice yearly processions in his honor as the patron saint of Naples are okay, but no imprimatur is given to the "magical" interpretations of the blood liquefaction that may occur. See the 1992 book by M. P. Carroll: *Madonnas that Maim: Popular Catholicism in Italy since the Fifteenth Century*. Baltimore, MA: Johns Hopkins University Press.

ITALY

Chapter 16

Sarno: Downwind of Vesuvius and Campi Flegrei

The Italian guard was stationed at the entrance to what looked like a large gravel-mining operation on the Campanian plain northeast of Vesuvius. There was a hint of menace in his voice, but he spoke calmly: "I know, young professors, that you will be good fathers for your sons. Sons should have fathers when they grow up. So, be good fathers to your sons, do not come back to this place."

Such is my paraphrased version of a conversation that my Italian colleagues had when they began work on downwind Vesuvian tephras. They simply did without that data point. It occurs to me that this is very like working around grizzly bears—you learn their habits and adjust accordingly.

Sarno is a city of 35,000, east of Vesuvius at the boundary of the Campanian plain and mountainous terrain. The area is ruled by the Camorra, the brutal central-Italian version of the Sicilian Mafia and five times its size. Among much else, the Camorra control anything to do with excavation, mining, and garbage and waste disposal, in short, any place where the airfall deposits of Vesuvius are going to be decently exposed without digging a new pit. Not that this is really an option—the surficial deposits are meters thick, and you would certainly attract the Camorra's attention. Based on warnings, my personable young colleagues, Roberto Sulpizio and Gianni Zanchetta, know well which gravel pits we can visit and which are off-limits. The latter may be sites for toxic-waste disposal or simply wholesaling centers for drug distribution. As of this writing, the author of the acclaimed book on the Camorra, *Gomorrah*, remains alive. And the Port of Naples continues to receive a large proportion of Europe's toxic waste for no legitimate reason.

The hazards of volcanoes can be far-reaching in space and time. In Italy, since 1640 and probably since Roman times, rain-triggered debris flows have periodically caused large losses of life along the steep fronts of the mountains above Sarno, rising sharply from the Campanian Plain 15 km east of Mount Vesuvius.[1] Wind has blown clouds of ash this way for millennia, and tephra have accumulated to depths of many meters. Even the carbonate bedrock on steep slopes is mantled with as much as 6 m of airfall, including the Agnano Pomici Principali (age 10,000 yrs) from the Campi Flegrei caldera west of Naples, and the Mercato (8,000 yrs) from Vesuvius.[2]

The most recent disaster occurred in May 1998, when about 150 lives were lost at several locations. Small but deadly slurries that began as shallow landslides during intense rain poured from mountain fronts into the developed parts of alluvial fans. Spectacular, they made our national television news. The sliding and subsequently flowing volumes grew rapidly as additional tephra was bulked into the flows downslope on their way to the fan head, or apex.[3]

Occurring at least once a century, these disasters of the Sarno region are sufficiently distributed in time and space, so that their devastating potential appears to have disappeared from the collective consciousness before the next. As in the Japanese proverb, "the time of the next disaster is when all memory of the last one has disappeared." A plaque down a Quindici street that became a flow channel, with 1998 peak-stage waves preserved by mud coatings high on building fronts, commemorates the twelve victims along that street. I read it twice, photographed it, and thought I saw a problem. It ascribed their deaths to "*causa della collate laviche del 5 Maggio 1998.*" *Laviche*—a lava flow? I checked this translation with UNAM Professora Lucia Capra. She iterated Roberto Sulpizio (University of Bara) who informed us that it was, of course, a *collate di fango*, a debris flow, and that people in the area commonly do not distinguish between them. Directly from Vesuvius, indirectly from Vesuvius—either is still deadly, so why quibble? It flows; it kills; don't worry about the name.

Once the debris flows reach the fan head, they can then spread to any part of the fan. The mitigation approach would mean building what is called a debris basin, in which the debris can settle from the water, at the fan head. The water then decants into a channel, lined with concrete to prevent the flow from gaining sediment, and finally it is conveyed it into a major drainage. This did not happen in Quindici because the debris basin and channel were much too small. The fatal result was that the street itself conveyed the debris flow.

Traveling along the mountain front, the mitigation measures that did exist at the time of the 1998 disaster—an uncoordinated collection of small dams, diversions, and channels—was clearly inadequate. Having designed the sediment capacities for a system of new debris basins in southern California,[4] I have a critical eye for the effectiveness of the structures.

Two years later, touring the broad valley fan containing the runouts of the rain-remobilized pyroclastic flows at Mount Unzen, I saw that the Japanese had invented and installed a herring-bone design of short, overlapping, vertical dikes which in aggregate, on each side, confine a large channel. If the conveyance of the main channel was exceeded, flow would just passively pour out laterally, between the individual dike segments. The central part of the flow would still proceed at maximum velocity directly into the ocean. Dike failure and overtopping would be nearly impossible, because a rise of the central discharge and stage would be continuously limited by the lateral loss of debris into backwater areas. It appeared an engineering design of genius, and I herewith promote a similar design for the engineering works after the Sarno disaster. It can be just as effective, conveying flow beyond the populated Sarno-area fans to distal runout areas. Where it is not economically feasible to build a huge debris basin at the fan head, it can be a way to get the flow across the fan and away from the critical potential diversion at the fan head.

At least in the Sarno region, the locations of Roman settlements seem to suggest a greater awareness of debris flow hazards, avoiding high-risk areas, than existed at the time of the 1998 tragedy. All the older debris basins around Sarno seem to underestimate the volumes of sediment that regularly sluice out of mountain fronts to devastate the towns and villages. I am glad to see new basins under construction, and they appear both larger and better designed. A report on the event described functional flood-control structures built during the Bourbon rule of the Kingdom of the Two Sicilies between 1830 and 1850. These had been filled-in and built-over by the late twentieth century.

Unlike earthquake-triggered debris flows, which can coalesce from the runouts of large numbers of landslides in similar terrain—such as Citlaltépetl, Mexico, in 1920, and Nevado del Huila, Colombia, in 1994—multiple rain-triggered flows cannot occur with the synchroneity necessary to coalesce into huge, catastrophic flows.

§

The village of Lauro, downwind of Vesuvius but untouched by the 1998 debris flows, has two patron saints. Sitting at a trattoria on the main street near noon having a soft drink with my Italian colleagues, we heard a band playing a Sicilian funeral dirge.

Somebody must have been watching one of the *Godfather* movies. But then the saints came marching down the street, their images on platforms shouldered by the faithful, followed by a charmingly amateur band playing the march. One of the two saints, San Rocco, had a similar role in the *Godfather*. The minor key was soul-stirring. Next in the procession, a priest and several nuns herded frisky and uniformed young scholars, happy to be out of school. Then several very large men in heavy black suits came strolling abreast. In spite of the heat, they had not taken off their coats. Were they respecting the saints? Possibly—but maybe also flaunting their confidence and authority. So completely does the Camorra and violence rule here, men may walk with coats folded over their left arms, the point of which is to show they have, or at least could have, an M-9 automatic pistol beneath. I was told by veteran Vesuvius researchers that a local chieftain had ordered four killings in the last year. Each was reportedly the wife of a man who needed to get with the program more enthusiastically. Could this be true? While hearing that funeral march, I am persuaded.

NOTES:

1. Migale, L. S., and Milone, A. Colate di fango in terrini piroclastici della Campania—prima dati della ricerca storica. *Rassegna Storica Salernitana* XV, no. 2 (1998):235–71.
2. Pareschi, M. T., Favalli, M., Giannini, F., Sulpezio, R., Zanchetta, G., and Santacroce, R. 2000. May 5, 1998 debris flows in circum-Vesuvian areas (southern Italy): insights for hazard assessment. *Geology* 28:639–42.

   See also: Pareschi, M. T., Santa Croce, R., Sulpizio, R., and Zanchetta, G. 2002. Volcaniclastic debris flows in the Clarno Valley (Campania, Italy): insights for the assessment of hazard potential. *Geomorphology* 43:219–31.
3. Revellino, R., Hungr, O., Guardagno, F. M., and Evans, S. G. 2004. Velocity and runout simulation of destructive debris flows and debris avalanches in pyroclastic deposits, Campanian region, Italy. *Environmental Geology* 45:295-311.
4. Scott, K. M., and Williams, R. P. 1978. Erosion and sediment yields in the Transverse Ranges, Ventura County, California. U.S. Geological Survey Professional Paper 1030.

The community of Orting, Washington, in 1994. The floor of the Puyallup and Carbon River valleys consists of about 1 to 5 m of Electron Mudflow deposits. (Dave Wieprecht)

Chapter 17

Mount Rainier: Recognizing America's Most Dangerous Volcano

Rainier and Vesuvius are examples of polar opposites on a risk spectrum. At one end is Vesuvius, prime among volcanoes that erupt, creating hot, dry flows. At the other is Rainier,[1] the perfect example of volcanoes that collapse, creating cold, wet runouts of large landslides. It threatens rapidly expanding populations in the lahar pathways that extend all the way to Puget Sound.

It was just by chance that Rocky Crandell would first uncover the evidence that Mount Rainier is America's most dangerous volcano. It is a great detective story that began in a mundane way. In 1953, the USGS assigned Rocky, a glacial geologist and artillery-officer veteran of the Battle of the Bulge, to map the Lake Tapps quadrangle.[2] This "quad," as we call them, was an area of 520 sq km (200 sq mi) at the southern end of Puget Sound. In 1867 Congress had mandated the brand-new USGS to prepare a geological map of the nation. In the mid-twentieth century, it was still doing its job, one latitude-and-longitude-defined quadrangle at a time. My own USGS career had begun as a field assistant on such a project, in the White-Inyo Mountains of eastern California, where the high-altitude, long-lived Bristlecone Pines were just gaining recognition for their importance in calibrating radiocarbon dates (converting radiocarbon years to calendar years).

Lake Tapps and the surrounding terrain north of Mount Rainier is an area of glacial deposits. A lobe of Pleistocene ice had excavated Puget Sound as far south as Olympia, Washington, branching from the 1.6-km-thick Canadian Ice Sheet (CIS) near the end of the last Ice Age. The Osceola till was considered a glacial deposit of isolated pebbles and cobbles set in a muddy matrix (the texture of a typical till) that had been mapped in the area by USGS geologist Bailey Willis. But the uncommonly flat surface of the poorly sorted deposit was troubling. Ice sheets rarely leave flat deposits. Rocky would trace the till east and south, following it up the White River Valley toward Mount Rainier, the icon of the Seattle–Tacoma skyline. He was shortly to discover why Mount Rainier was more than just gorgeous scenery.

Initially, Rocky saw that the till covered more than 200 sq km of flat terrain leading to Puget Sound. He could see the base of the deposit, 10 to 15 m thick, where it was incised by the White River and, overall, it seemed to contain more mud and be more consistent in composition and thickness than most of the tills from the CIS. There was an occasional hummock, about thirty all told, across the entire plain.[3] The top of the deposit was perfectly flat except where it had been eroded by streams. It looked like it had flowed across the landscape before solidifying.

As the upstream valley of the White River narrowed, however, the hummocks became more abundant, especially in embayments and backwater areas along the valley sides. The deposit extended from valley wall to valley wall. The hummocks were approximately symmetrical, typically with rounded tops, 3 to 5 m high, and 10 to 15 m across.

Osceola Mudflow

Farther upstream, the White River split, with both the main river and the West Fork headed up the east flank of Mount Rainier. Both were filled with the strange deposit. At last, Rocky found the highest deposit, at 9,600 ft altitude on the andiron-like cleaver known as Steamboat Prow. Now there was no doubt. The deposits were those of a gigantic mudflow that glacial geologist Bailey Willis named "the Osceola."[3] Willis was the glacial geologist who had mapped and named the Osceola deposit as a till. The mudflow represented the top 300 to 600 m of the mountain that had flowed away. Even though decapitated, Mount Rainier was still the highest volcano in the Cascade Range and, at 14,411 ft, the second-highest peak in the continental United States. Willis is honored by the Willis Wall, the formidably steep north side of the volcano.

The event was what we call a sector collapse, and this one involved approximately 3 cu km of rock. Because the failed rock was so clay-rich (altered by hydrothermal fluids), instead of forming a blocky landslide that would stop near the base of the mountain, it immediately mobilized and flowed all the way to Puget Sound. Its runout was prolonged by ingesting additional material along the way. Finally, it dumped more than a cubic kilometer of debris into the sound. Blocks of the mountain that did not immediately disaggregate to a muddy slurry were rafted on downstream to become lateral hummocks.

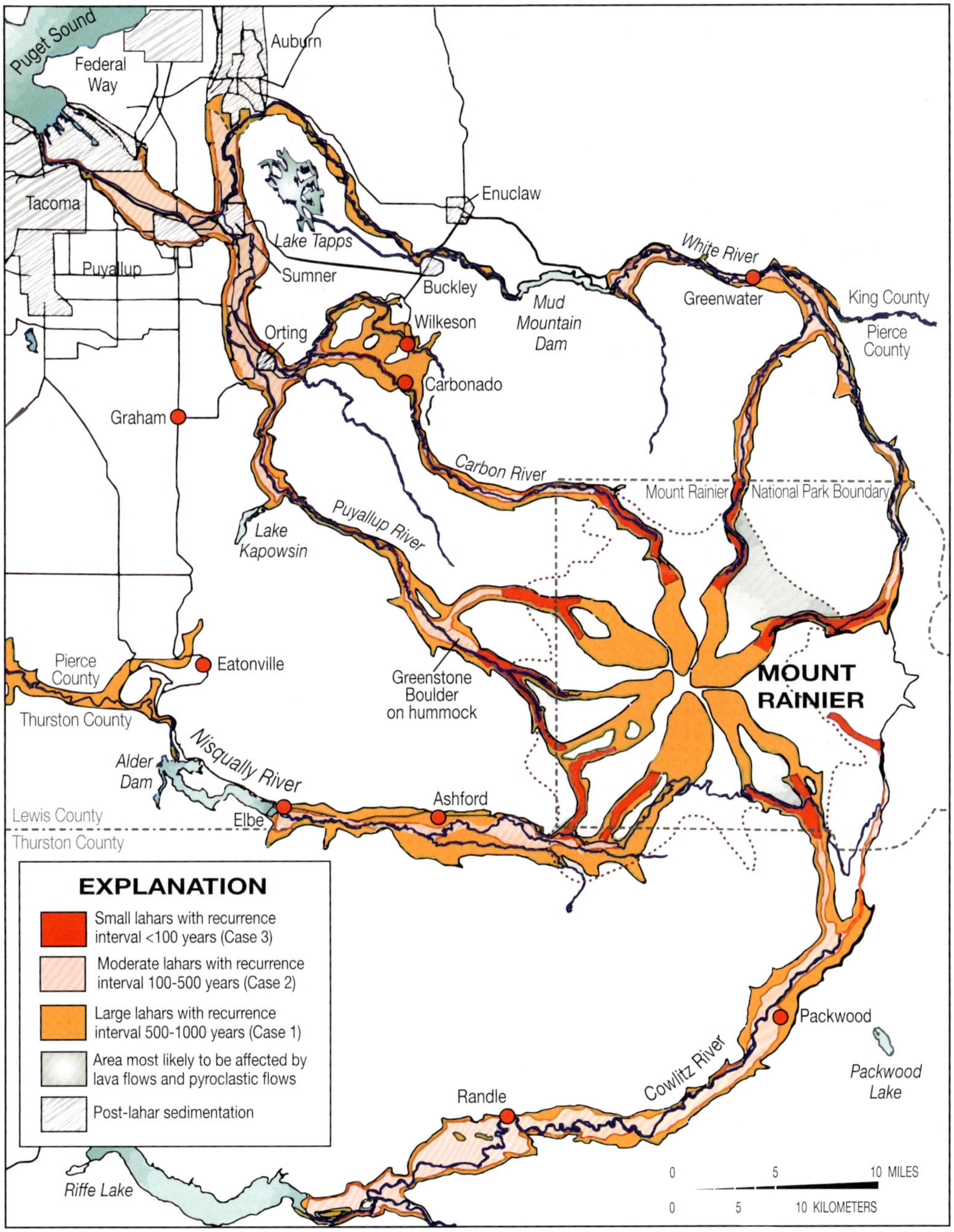

A map of Mount Rainier and vicinity shows lahar runouts from this classically shaped stratovolcano. The Electron Mudflow is a Case 1 example. (USGS map)

Sitting atop a Round Pass hummock in the Puyallup River watershed is a perfectly rounded, 2-m greenstone clast (arrow), just upstream of the hummock crest. The flow direction would have been from left to right.

The Osceola was the largest of the muddy, cohesive lahars that began as volcanic landslides at Rainier. Their recurrence interval is every 500 to 1,000 years over the last several thousand years. They would be major catastrophes (but not Black Swans) if recurring today because of their mobility, and ability to inundate valleys, wall-to-wall, to Puget Sound. They may or may not be triggered by eruptions. If they do correlate with eruptions, in the future there could hopefully be timely warnings through instrumental detection of moving magma. With this thought, our early work focused (incorrectly, as we now know) on correlating lahar dates with tephra ages.

Even with similar radiocarbon dates of lahars and tephras, however, actual differences in calendar years may be many decades apart. Russian researchers have postulated that collapses may reflect deep, early intrusion of magma. These collapses may lack obvious precursory activity, such as seismicity, ground deformation, or changing gas emissions.

The risk is that a collapse may be triggered while evacuation is still being debated. Little if any warning may occur in these cases because of the fear of a false alarm. This possibility dictates the novel approach to risk mitigation that I propose.

Rainier—the Next Generation

I recall the day in early 1986 when Dick Janda asked me to take on the job of a second-generation study of Mount Rainier. Well, of course. And, fortunately, two younger geologists were looking for jobs, which in each case would change their lives. Jim Vallance was looking for a Ph.D. project, so I asked him to take the northeast third of the volcano, thus including the intimidating Osceola as a thesis topic. He would write the definitive paper.[4] I also asked Pat Pringle, whom I thought also should take a shot at a Ph.D., to take the northwest third, including the young Electron Mudflow, only 500 years old. That flow would prove key to our making the project an example of how to do volcanic stratigraphy and combine it with the principles of flood-risk analysis. After all, were not lahars just rivers of mud? And was not 500 to 1,000 years a period easily conceivable as the return period of a flood—a frequency that spoke loudly to the need to prepare for its catastrophic recurrence?

National Lahar

We were fortunate in that all three sectors of the volcano, with the geologists I assigned to them, were good fits. I did not know it at the time, but by default I had given myself one of the few things Rocky had left for us to discover that was new, a flow I would name the National Lahar, from the name of a hamlet on the south side of the volcano. The National is yet another example of a lahar that would crystallize the fact that volcanic debris flows, or lahars, are of two different origins, textures, and behaviors. These two types are the muddy (cohesive) and granular (noncohesive) lahars, and their recognition is the *sine qua non* for any reconstruction of volcano history, and for legitimate hazard assessment, separating two radically different hazards—collapses (landslides) running out as lahars, and meltwater floods eroding (bulking) enough sediment to become lahars. Labeling both as simply "lahars" would not distinguish hazards that begin as two different processes and behave in two different ways. Ignoring those differences could either exaggerate the risk, or place lives at risk by focusing on only one of the two origins.

Jim Vallance tells me today that he found about twenty-five of these small granular, noncohesive lahars. With the exception of the National and one Jim reports as large or larger than the National, they did not extend far beyond the base of the volcano. And because they began with meltwater from an eruption, we would have seen them coming. The serious risk at Rainier is almost entirely from the huge clay-rich flows of collapse origin.

Greenwater Lahar

Rocky mapped the sections of the flat flow deposit from which hummocks protruded as parts of a pre-Osceola lahar, the Greenwater lahar. Strangely, however, when I looked at Rocky's cross sections of the White River Valley, the Osceola filled the valley to exactly the same level as the Greenwater. I could walk from one flow to the other, and not notice any change, except that when I got near the valley side, hummocks began to appear. The conclusion was inescapable—there was just a single flow, with only the lateral parts of it containing the chunks of the volcano that formed the hummocks. Either that, or by unlikely coincidence, the later Osceola managed to fill, to exactly the same level, the valley eroded in the earlier Osceola. For this to happen at every point was beyond reasonable doubt. The chunks, what I liked to call megaclasts (but most now prefer to call megablocks), were appearing exactly where they would have if they had all started out in a single flow. As the flow level rose, they had been shunted to the side to "beach" or "ground" themselves, like icebergs stranded on a beach. When the peak of the lahar had passed, they would settle to the pre-flow surface and would remain protruding from the flow surface.

Electron Mudflow

Five hundred years ago, high on the west flank of Rainier, a watery surge poured mainly into the headwaters of the South Fork of the Puyallup River. There was no obvious evidence on the flank of any landslide scar. Downstream, the wave flowed across the hummocks of an earlier lahar, the Round Pass, also named by Rocky. The Electron, however, left no hummocks, and deposited only a relatively thin layer of debris upstream that can best be ascribed to a flood. On one Round Pass hummock, poised on the upstream side, is a nearly 2-m, extremely well-rounded greenstone boulder, devoid of any associated matrix. It is just sitting on the top of the hummock. It had to have been washed there, probably rolled, by a relatively dilute flood, and its height above the Puyallup River, lying on top of the hummock, indicated a huge flow. The only possible source of the boulder rolled up the hummock was the Electron, which was far from a mudflow at that point. As in the case of El Chichón, a pre-Columbian Indian legend appears to hold clues. In her *Rainier Educator's Guide*, Carolyn Driedger included this summary of an American Indian legend titled "The Lake on Mount Rainier."[5]

"A young man carried shell offerings to the mountain's icy summit and camped by a lake within the crater rim. The presence of lake water at the summit impressed him, and he became convinced that the lake would one day drain. When the lake did drain, water swept away trees from where the city of Orting now exists, and left the area covered with stones."

The story is remarkable in several respects—the presence of a lake, the destruction of forest near Orting, and the deposition of "stones" far downstream. It explains the origin of the Electron by bulking of a flood or lake-discharge surge, and thus the deposition of the large greenstone boulder atop the Round Pass hummock.

Pat Pringle, now a retired college professor, continues to work on the age of the flow, even to the possible season of the year, and colleague Jim Vallance is preparing what will be the final answer, or at least a well-documented probability, of the Electron origin. But, of the group of collapse-initiated lahars at Rainier, there is a clear degree of doubt with this one. Neither a mudflow nor extraterrestrials left that greenstone boulder behind.

After completion of our Rainier studies that yielded the 1995 Professional Paper[6] and Hydrologic Atlas,[7] the USGS would have Lidar images made of the Round Pass surface for a very different purpose than the lahar history of the volcano. Lidar, the light analog of radar, denotes light detection and ranging, and yields surface images based on light reflection. A major fault zone, the West Rainier Seismic Zone, cuts north–south, just west of the volcano, and many small-to-intermediate earthquakes occur along the zone. Quake epicenters show a well-defined linear grouping.

Like the recent discovery of surface displacement of a marine terrace by the Seattle Fault, with activity dated to about 1,100 years ago, we hoped to see a displacement of the surface of the Round Pass lahar, well dated by Rocky and us at 2,600 radiocarbon years in age. I was disappointed when we saw no surface displacement disturbing the original and recently logged surface of the Round Pass.

The Growth-Management Boundary

We had our initial analysis completed in 1990 and had a report draft ready for review. Our changes in Rocky's results were not great, with the major exception of treating the lahar history as the analog of a flood record. Now, all the considerations that hydrologists apply to floods, such as recurrence interval (return period), inundation area, etc., could be applied to lahars. We were not warning of a Black Swan (the Osceola). Based on this traditional way of evaluating flood risk, especially applying the concept of a 500- to 1,000-year lahar such as the Electron, it was clear that lahars are a hazard well within the realm of those that require major policy considerations and mitigation. The valleys downstream from Rainier were being consumed in the

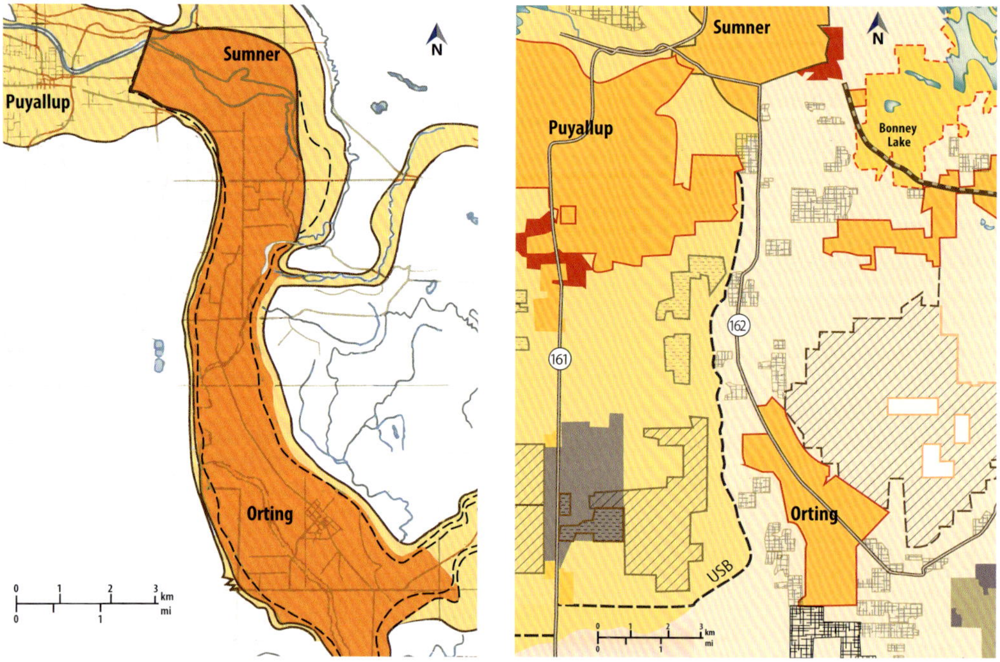

An analysis shows the projected route of lahar (left) compared with the Growth Management boundary (right), the heavy dashed line on the left side of the lahar pathway, showing where further growth is discouraged.

wave of growth expanding outward from Tacoma and Seattle. Lahars and their pathways were exactly the sort of natural hazard that the new Washington State Growth Management Act (GMA) of 1990 was designed to identify.

§

I asked Bill Lokey, head of the Pierce County Emergency Management Department, to be one of our reviewers. Bill immediately recognized the implications of the study, especially in terms of the GMA. He returned it to me but also referred it to his engineering staff. Bill had first been up Rainier decades earlier as one of the "climbing bums," many of them hippies with Volkswagen vans who were revolutionizing climbing with new techniques on the big walls of Yosemite. He told me how he'd once been lowered, roped up, down a "rathole" into the summit ice of Rainier that filled part of the crater remaining after the Osceola. Suddenly, he'd burst into a room the size of a basketball court.

After our report was approved by the Survey, the land-use map of Pierce County, which included nearly all the lahar pathways, could immediately include an Urban Growth Boundary (UGB). It would permit growth outside of the valley floors (the lahar pathways), but limit it in the choice, easy-to-develop, valley farmland that was calling to developers. It was a revolutionary reversal of the normal management of growth, and my Power Point presentations featured a comparison of the UGB map with the corresponding areas from our *Hydrologic Atlas 429.*

The UGB did not separate development from no-development, like a "no-fly" zone. The issue known to lawyers as "takings" deals with the debatable right of a government to control or prohibit land use, thereby reducing the value of the property affected. Some farmers in the lahar pathways may have been counting on riches when the development wave coming ever-outward from Seattle-Tacoma reached their property. So the potential for litigation required an allowance for some degree of development. Legal consultants therefore devised a level of growth density that would prevent anthill-like development, yet allow the property owners a just degree of reward.

The Warning System

The Electron had traveled nearly 50 km from the mountain before debouching onto the Puget Lowland and spreading completely across the valley plains of the Carbon and Puyallup rivers where they joined. There stood the town of Orting. In 2002, I was driving through, almost nostalgically, and stopped for a fast-food lunch. There beside the serving trays was a handout. It advised of a Lahar Warning Test scheduled for 10:00 A.M. on October 28, 2002.

"Test of the lahar warning and alert procedures for notifying citizens of the Puyallup River Valley of a potential mudflow," the handout advised, adding, "Outdoor Warning Sirens will be activated . . . you will hear sirens in Fife, Puyallup, Sumner, and Orting for three to five minutes." In addition, residents were told that local news and radio stations may be running the Emergency Alert Signal test and that NOAA weather radios would be activated.

Thanks to the GMA and the revolutionary delineation of the urban growth boundary, in the 1990s, Orting, the city closest to Mount Rainier, had become the poster child for cities at risk from lahars in the Cascade Range (and even around the world). The key to the public response, in my opinion, was presenting lahar probabilities like the recurrence probabilities of catastrophic floods, and in describing the valleys leading from Rainier as lahar pathways.

A Community Think Tank

In response to the public reaction to the threat of volcano hazards, especially lahars, the Mount Rainier Working Group (MRWG) was formed in 1995 by a consortium of agencies, chief among them the Pierce County Department of Emergency Management. Our interest-group was eclectic, including even the administrators of an Old Soldiers' home located on the valley floor, the Orting Fire Chief, and school principals and science teachers. Our first chairman was Bill Lokey, Department of Emergency Management, and Bill transitioned to Steve Bailey, an ex-Fire Chief in Seattle and a remarkable individual with the ability to put everybody in a good mood with slightly mocking but good-humored references to Chicken Little and a falling sky, i.e., a large lahar. The warning system evolved with this group and its meetings in the Longmire Community Building in Mount Rainier National Park.

The MRWG faced a crucial question: Could the lahars be foreseen by precursory signals of volcanic activity, triggering evacuations, or could they be "spontaneous lahars" that could not readily be foreseen? Rocky had not been able to connect most of the lahars with the eruptive activity, the beginnings of which might provide a precursory warning. Jim Vallance and later investigators were able to find closer but still equivocal correlations of some of the lahars with eruptions. Even with certain detection of the early intrusive activity, with increasingly sophisticated technology, great uncertainty still remains as to whether a large-scale evacuation can occur and be sustained throughout the unknown, and possibly extended period that collapse could occur. Eruption precursors are notorious for waxing and waning, and an evacuation of the areas at risk from Rainier lahars would disable an economy of regional scale. Some case histories elsewhere were indicating that large collapses could occur early in an eruptive cycle, as well as with little or no detectable intrusive activity, and even with only phreatic activity. Other nonvolcanic landslide triggers, including earthquakes and rainfall, could not be ruled out.

A Warning Network

The word "lahar" is only on advanced crossword puzzles in most of the world, but the average high-school teacher and even most school children in the Pacific Northwest know the term and its hazard implications.

A warning that triggered an evacuation of the far-reaching lahar pathways was certainly possible, but is it probable? Case histories elsewhere suggested that large collapses could occur early in an eruptive cycle, as well as with little or no detectable intrusive activity, and even with only phreatic activity. Other nonvolcanic landslide triggers, including earthquakes, could not be ruled out. Such lahars came to be known, in the Working Group and in public discussions about Rainier, as "spontaneous lahars." I do not like the term because it implies that a volcano just randomly sheds a lahar. I think the real issue is that, although there will probably be precursory signals, although possibly slight, can we act upon them in time?

The USGS and the MRWG responded to this apparent dilemma with a novel system of instrumentation to detect actual lahars near the base of the volcano, arrays of Acoustic Flow Monitors (AFMs)—small, geophone-based seismometers that could distinguish between the tremor frequency of a moving lahar and that of an earthquake.[8] Warning could be radioed downstream so that evacuation in response to an actual, real-time hazard could begin. The USGS's design of the warning-system software as an entirely automated system eliminated the possibility of a false-alarm or in human failure to relay warnings, which has happened elsewhere.

Because of the extreme difficulty of evacuating large populations for any length of time, evacuation would certainly occur only when a *lahar was actually on its way.* Orting would have about forty minutes for residents to evacuate to high ground. My first estimate was forty-five minutes to an hour, and the issue stimulated colleague Tom Pierson's compilation of velocities by flow size.[9] The system augmented standard approaches to eruption alerts; it did not replace them. All the normal instrumentation and procedures designed to yield information that could trigger preemptive evacuations would be in place.

My strategy with the AFM network was to defend the areas of high population, primarily the Puyallup and Carbon rivers systems. Both led into major cities, including Tacoma and Seattle. The White River had a flood reservoir, Mud Mountain Reservoir, which was almost always empty. That would retain much of any lahar the size of the Electron. Likewise, the Nisqually River had a large flood-control reservoir, Alder Reservoir, which could be drawn down when risk increased. Ed Wolfe and others, me included, selected the specific instrument sites, and Andy Lockhart and other colleagues made the installations. Each site on the two rivers consisted of three AFMs at a high level and two at a lower level. For the sirens to sound, the three high units would alarm in sequence. Two lower "deadmen" would need to go dark sequentially, thereby making sure the flow was of significant size and would endanger people downstream. False-alarm proof?

Pierce County authorities could not quite make the leap to eliminating the human element, the historical weak link in warning systems. A person at the 911 call center, where the radio-telemetered signals are received, would authenticate the signals before the sirens would sound and the reverse-911 and weather radio alerts would occur.

That center is manned 24/7 by more than one person. Once again I was asked, and once again the answer was yes, I would live in an area defended by this system, as long as—and here is the crucial caveat—I lived in a section of a lahar pathway from which evacuation was possible. Unfortunately, evacuation from Orting is not easy.

As part of the system, by 1996, sirens were being installed or planned from Orting downstream, and a total of twenty-three exist as of 2018. Periodic testing of the system has not been a total success—a surprising number of people living relatively close to them apparently do not hear them. A "reverse-911" system was in place, in which residents would be instantly auto-called with the evacuation mandate. NOAA weather radio would also broadcast the warning. And, two hundred warning signs indicated the evacuation routes. In the 1990s, those signs had been designed to fold in the middle by the Washington State Department of Transportation (DOT) so that the message, "Volcano Evacuation Route," was obscured. DOT did not want to alarm people (a common excuse for not warning them), and also the standard practice for temporary hazards (like ice). Only when an eruption threatened would the sign be unfolded and the message visible. Lahars were simply regarded as one on a list of volcano hazards, with hope that their probability or possibility could be foreseen. At a meeting to decide this issue, DOT promoted non-alarmist, folding signs. Noting their inflexibility on the subject, and recognizing the potential for "spontaneous" lahars, the MRWG then suggested that DOT be assigned an important mission. Their employees would quickly enter the area to be evacuated and unfold each sign when the AFM array signaled that a lahar, possibly of catastrophic size, *was on its way*. Needless to say, the DOT quickly decided that the signs should not fold.

Because of the extreme difficulty of evacuating large populations for any length of time, evacuation would certainly occur only when a lahar had departed the base of the volcano and triggered an AFM array. That is, "when a wolf is on the way." Orting would have forty minutes for residents to evacuate to high ground. The system augmented standard approaches to pre-eruption alerts; it did not replace them. All the normal instrumentation and procedures designed to monitor activity that could trigger a preemptive evacuation would be in place. Attention to monitoring should not decline because of the AFM event-warning system.

As the public reaction to our findings escalated, it was clear that a warning system based on Acoustic Flow Monitors (AFMs) would be a possibility. I had to start thinking about how many of Rainier's five major drainages should be instrumented. CVO colleague Rick LaHusen had been working for many years on applying these small instruments, which are essentially the geophones used by oil-company geophysicists,

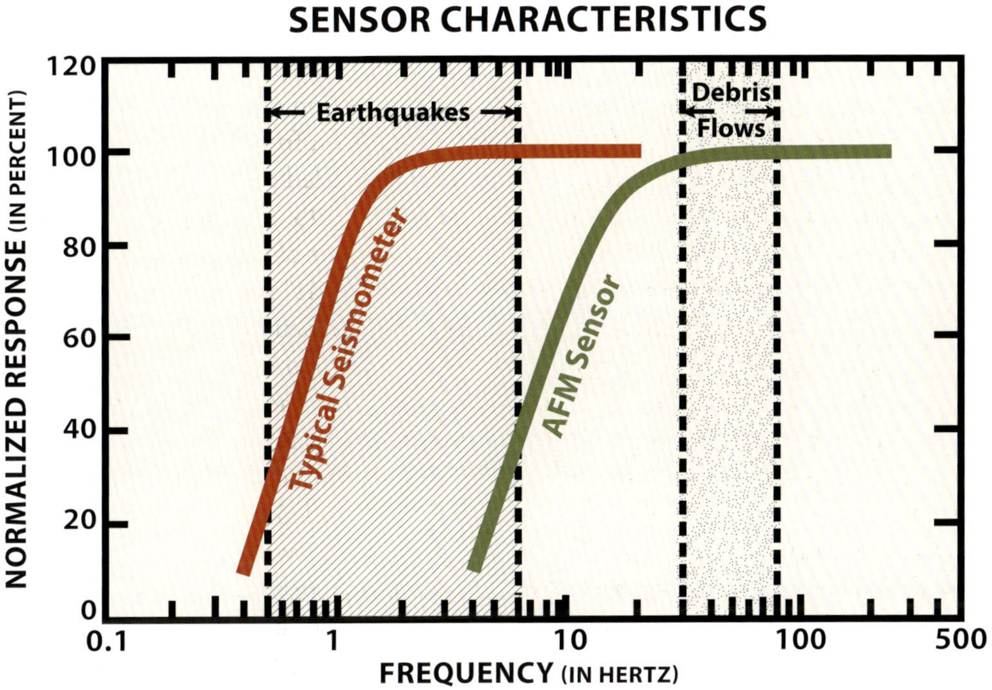

Comparison of frequencies of ground tremor detected by seismometers (on left) and Acoustic Flow Monitors. (USGS)

laid out sequentially in lines, to record seismic waves triggered by an artificial explosion, bouncing off resistant rock strata. A picture of the underground structure, in three dimensions, is revealed by many such "shots," and thus defines places where upward-migrating oil may be trapped.

After a lot of thought, it appeared to me that the idea of "defending" the major population centers had gravitas. So I proposed only the Carbon and Puyallup rivers. The Carbon River was not mentioned on the handout I found when I stopped for lunch that day in Orting, because it becomes part of the Puyallup, essentially at Orting.

I suggest that the two dams that form entire-or-partial lahar catchments have little risk of failure, explaining why I did not choose the White and Nisqually rivers systems. Only a debris avalanche, very unlikely to extend to the dams, could possibly cause them to fail. A well-known case history supports that conclusion—that of the 1963 overtopping of the seemingly delicate, high-arch Vaiont Dam north of Venice, Italy. At the top, the 260-m high structure was less than 4 m thick. The dam was impacted and overtopped by a ca. 250-m "tsunami" produced when a landslide of 250 million cu m entered the partially drawn-down reservoir from a mountain just upstream. The landslide was expected, and engineers were gathered on the dam to observe its effect. Cracks up to 1 m wide at the head of the slide were seen in the days preceding the failure. The slide occurred in less than a minute, contradicting engineers' prediction of a slow failure. More than 2,000 people, apparently lacking any warning, perished from the flood wave. The dam today stands unused and in original condition.

Dilemma of the Willis Wall

In defending the population in the mega-metropolises of Tacoma and Seattle by including the Carbon River for an AFM array, I violated my most basic premise. No large lahar had originated, or almost certainly never had, from the fearsome Willis Wall, named after USGS engineering geologist Bailey Willis and honoring his work on as-then-called Mount Tahoma. The huge, near-vertical scallop with his name has apparently failed progressively, stone by stone, onto the Carbon Glacier. The Carbon Glacier extends to the lowest elevation of any in the continental United States (about 4,300 ft) and conveys and crushes these contributions from the Wall to sizes that enable the Carbon River to remove them. Pat Pringle and I have searched every assessable reach of the valley downstream and have found no sign of a large lahar.

Why worry about the Willis Wall? It's clearly stable, as its geological history testifies. Well, here is geology as art and science—the art part. Or is it? You (or I) cannot look up at the formidable rock face and say, even if knowing little about volcanoes, "I would live here." Which means for me, of course, that I would not live anywhere along the Carbon River to its terminus. A flank collapse will bulk its way there. It is impossible to know the internal structure and alteration to the degree that you can be sure the Wall is stable. Every day, alteration, although slight, is progressively reducing the flank's stability.

I would not be entirely comfortable spending a vacation in the Ipsut River Campground near the glacier terminus, when magma, deep and perhaps only pulsing a little, might trigger a failure of the Wall. This could be long before an emergency manager feels the pressure to call an evacuation and prepare to defend his or her decision to lock down the regional economy.

So how do you define a potential inundation area to illustrate the hazard? The only logical view, in my opinion, is to study the lahar record of the volcano and select a logical and typical example to route down the channel. And that was what we did in *Hydrologic Atlas 429*, which Rocky grouped with our Rainier Professional Paper, as a "model of scientific writing."

Little Tahoma Debris Avalanche of 1963

Mount Rainier National Park rangers noticed that something funny had happened on the Emmons Glacier during the winter of 1962–63. They called Rocky when spring arrived, and he went to investigate. A debris avalanche had come off Little Tahoma Peak, the high point on the cleaver south of the Emmons Glacier. Rocky quickly decided it could be a mini-Osceola mudflow and as such deserved study. That summer and the next, he would collaborate with Ken Fahnestock, a recent hire at the University of Texas, and publish a USGS Bulletin that remains widely cited.

The avalanche poured over the end of the glacier and finally ramped up against a Little Ice Age terminal moraine, which probably prevented it from reaching the White River Campground. I have spent many nights there and always have my escape route planned, ready to run if the ground shakes. The Park Service has considered any advice to run as too alarmist (just like the Archbishop at Nevado del Ruiz); my own view is that knowledge of geologic hazards adds to the wilderness experience.

Public Response

In 1995, when both our reports (the Professional Paper and the *Hydrologic Atlas*) came out in enamel-paper versions, I was unprepared for the firestorm of interest that would result. Focused only on the lahar history, I had never thought about what I would do next. Well, to retire was one option, but before I got serious, my employers suggested a collaboration with a young glaciologist, Carolyn Driedger, who had spent most of the previous decade monitoring a series of glacial-outburst flows on Rainier. When nightly news needed a "talking head" I could force myself, which I did on each network, but Carolyn was much more skillful at handling the mass of press and public relations.

In response to my new publications, the USGS and others decided that they should inform local officials and residents about the findings and how future lahars might affect residents. So, in 1993, CVO scientist Steve Brantley, Pat Pringle (then with the Washington Division of Geology and Earth Resources), Bill Lokey, and Orting schoolteacher Marianne Smith joined forces at a public meeting to tell the Orting citizenry about the hazards. In less than two years, Marianne Smith and several teacher colleagues had joined with Carolyn to begin a series of Mount Rainier workshops for teachers and develop an educator's guide, a poster, and a bookmark. Each product received enthusiastic input and review by local teachers. Carolyn involved me in conducting the teacher workshops and community outreach events over the next decade. While I have retired from that effort, Carolyn continues to carry the story of Mount Rainier lahars to a new generation of teachers, public officials, park employees, and the news media.

This was tricky business, and I knew a single overly dramatic or alarmist statement would be on the nightly network news. I had all my answers carefully planned, especially for the inevitable "Would you live here?" But inspirational to me were the responses of the residents of the Whitehawk subdivision, with its media attractions of a huge boulder of Rainier, now a landscaping element near the subdivision entrance, and several stumps of the old-growth trees engulfed and mainly knocked flat and buried by the Electron. After finishing interviews, the producer suggested asking the people in the subdivision about living there. Only a few residents, suddenly confronted by a recognizable news personality and his or her camera crew at their door, drew a blank. Others made very reasoned answers, in the vein that they were aware of the risk but chose to live there in spite of it. Carolyn and I apparently had done an effective job in educating the public, and I must give great credit to her public-relations products.

An especially valuable product was the film commissioned by CVO scientist Steve Brantley, titled *Perilous Beauty—The Hidden Dangers of Mount Rainier*. The film opens and closes with segments of the video I had made of debris flows triggered by thunderstorms in remote Yunnan Province in broiling-hot southwest China. Not exactly lahars, but they certainly illustrated the power of debris flows. The film was shown on public broadcasting numerous times.

Other residents were less sanguine. Real estate salespeople did not publicize the issue, and a few home purchasers, having somehow missed our saturation of the Seattle–Tacoma media with the issue, found out only when they went to the Orting City Hall to request municipal services and saw this stamp on their paperwork:

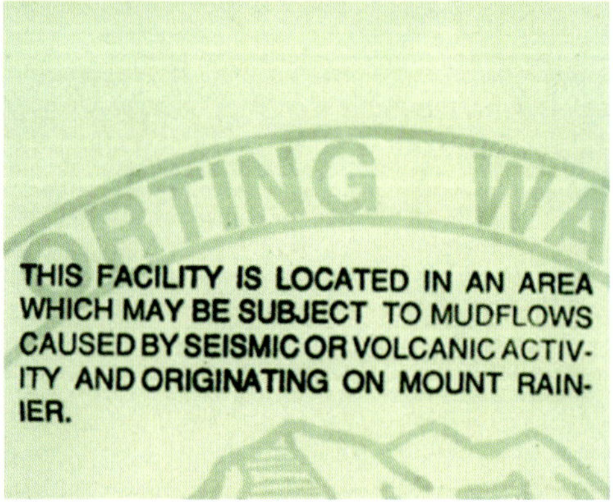

I did not suggest this wording, but I could not have said it better.

A few walked away and forfeited their down payments.

One vital member of the MRWG alliance was Orting Fire Chief Scott Fielding, a personable gentleman with wonderful charisma. My idea of a wise and friendly uncle. Scott, unfortunately, was suckered by a national news channel. They had filmed at one locality and, traveling to a second camera location, left Scott's "hot" microphone clipped to his collar. In conversation, he was asked, very comradely of course, by the videographer, something like, "Hey, Scott, what are the odds of most of Orting's citizens really being able to get to high ground when they get a lahar-warning signal or hear the sirens?" Scott, honest to a fault, replied in terms that may have included the words "snowball" and "hell." You can imagine the lead in that day's national news summary. Something like, "Government official admits mudflow from Mount Rainier volcano will be lethal, even with warning system!" Scott was reassigned.

The producer's job is to get you to say something dramatic, which will be something you definitely do not want to say. I do more than say, "It's off the record." I put my hand over the mic to make sure.

My favorite citizen response to the Rainier lahar risk, however, is the novel project called "Bridge 4 Kids," and its website at bridgeforkids.org. Just before its confluence with the Puyallup River, the Carbon River separates all of Orting's schools from a steep valley-side slope, scaled by an old road. The approximately forty-five minutes of warning would be enough time for students to evacuate across the river and get up the valley side, *if there were a bridge across the river.* Evidence of a long-ago road bridge, the central pier, still stands, but that's all. I recommended reusing the pier to save cost, but the volunteer designers had a better idea, one that was closer to the schools: a wide, single-span pedestrian suspension bridge. As of 2018, it was unclear if the new bridge would be built, or whether some road bridges would take its place. Still, the proposal has maintained attention on the hazards issues, and it is an example of how the gratis work of even a few residents like Marianne Smith can do much to educate a community and make it a safer place to live.

Subdivisions in lahar pathways increase in spite of the Urban Growth Boundary. The land inside the municipal limits of any town or city is exempt from the GMA restrictions, resolved at state level; the city fathers of Orting had created a large, optimistic area for the city limits, and the present city is taking full advantage.

I have wanted to be a fly on the wall of the unofficial City Council meetings—none of them have ever attended a MRWG meeting, and none of us has been invited to address the City Council. The unofficial position of Sumner, the next city downstream in the Puyallup drainage, is that they will worry when they see Orting floating by. This is not a good philosophy; let Orting worry, simply because they are at highest risk. However, Sumner would suffer the same fate as Orting within minutes; their fates are inseparable. Sumner officials should visit the Whitehawk subdivision in Orting to see the huge old-growth stumps of trees flattened by the Electron just several minutes of flow-travel time upstream from Sumner.

Again, the evacuation scenes from the Pierce Brosnan film *Dante's Peak* would be useful viewing for the Orting City Council and the Pierce County Planning Commission, who regularly approve exceptions to the UGB and thereby increase the numbers at risk. Sounding the sirens is the job of a person who must verify the AFM signal when it is received at the 911 center. They then push a button, knowing that people will probably die in the ensuing panic in much the way they do in the film. However, if the verification button is not pressed, thousands could die. The false-alarm problem is seemingly solved because the sirens will sound *only if a large flow is on the way*. But, there is that potentially fatal human link. When the AFM signal from the five instruments is received at the 911 center, *it is evaluated by a human*, who presses a button for the sirens to sound and the evacuation panic to ensue. Let's hope the button-pushers are not needing a smoke, constipated, or feeling sleepy.

The event-warning system clearly has legs, but we have to think that this is motivated by the need for developers, both in Orting and downstream, to reassure homebuyers that they are "protected." Just like the Bridge 4 Kids, of which four are now planned, each as the excuse for allowing development nearby, with the pretext that yet another bridge will allow it to be done safely. The land-use planning that looked so promising that resulted from our work in the early 1990s has clearly fallen by the wayside. Plans are underway to convert the current AFM system to a broadband system that can detect both earthquakes and lahars in every drainage. Local officials asked the State Legislature to double the number of sirens to more than forty at a cost of $2 million in 2017. It looks like every lahar pathway around the volcano is to be developed "safely." If you believe that, remember two words: *snowball* and *hell*.

NOTES:

1. In a spasm of stupidity, I did not include Pat as a coauthor of our 1995 *Hydrologic Atlas on Mount Rainier.* No apology can right this wrong.
2. Crandell, D. R. Undated. *This is My Life* (unpublished autobiography). Rocky reveals his transformation from glaciologist to volcanologist.
3. ---. 1971. Postglacial lahars from Mount Rainier volcano, Washington. U.S. Geological Survey Professional Paper 677. This is the seminal paper that brought lahars into focus as a major volcanic hazard in the Western Hemisphere.
4. Vallance, J. W., and Scott, K. M. 1997. The Osceola Mudflow from Mount Rainier: Sedimentology and hazard implications of a large clay-rich debris flow. *Geological Society of America Bulletin* 109:143–63. Jim's paper is the best and most comprehensive on this huge flow.
5. Dreidger, C., Doherty, A., and Dixon, C. 2005. *Living with a volcano in your backyard—An educator's guide with emphasis on Mount Rainier.* U.S. Geological Survey and National Park Service, General Interest Product 19. https://pubs.usgs.gov/gip/19/
6. Scott, K. M., Vallance, J. W., and Pringle, P. T. 1995. Sedimentology, behavior, and hazards of debris flows at Mount Rainier, Washington. U.S. Geological Survey Professional Paper 1547.
7. Scott, K. M., and Vallance, J. W. 1995. U.S. Geological Survey Hydrologic Atlas 429. Pat Pringle should be the third author of this Hydrologic Atlas.
8. LaHusen, R. G. 1998. Detecting debris flows using ground vibrations. U.S. Geological Survey Fact Sheet 236–96.
9. Pierson, T. C. 1998. An empirical method for estimating travel times for wet volcanic flows. *Bulletin of Volcanology* 60:98–109. Tom cleverly used the known travel times of past lahars to estimate travel times of future lahars by size.

CHINA and CANADA

Chapter 18

Disaster Museums and Relocating Cities

This chapter describes two unconventional ways of mitigating future disasters. In the first, a destroyed city is not rebuilt, but instead designated a "disaster museum," preserved in its destroyed state as a lesson in where not to build. In the second, a city existing in a dangerous location because of a natural hazard is moved to a location that is not at risk of that hazard.

Beichuan, China

Beichuan is an example of the first kind of mitigation. It was a city in southwest China of more than 200,000 before the earthquake of May 12, 2008, located 100 km south of the epicenter. The earthquake, known as "5-12," became China's "9-11."[1] The 8.0 M earthquake struck the eastern edge of the Qinghai–Tibet Plateau at 2:28 P.M., tragically during the school day. The city had been considered for relocation because of its hazardous location before the quake, and afterward Chinese officials designated it a disaster museum.

Between 15,000 and 20,000 bodies remained in the rubble of collapsed buildings. The large buildings that still stood were tilted, supporting each other like drunken sailors, giving a bizarre look to the city. Construction cranes suggested rescue operations, but no—all but one stood just where they were, frozen in building new construction at the moment of the quake. Spaced about the rubble were small red signs with the picture of a terrified boy fleeing a skull, asking that visitors respect the dead within. Small boys—or "little emperors"—give the warnings in China. I recalled a street sign showing a boy cowering beneath an angry, red-eyed beast. It was one of the water buffaloes that then, in 1990, roamed the streets of Kumming, apparently goring an occasional child. During World War II, this had been the large city in Yunnan Province

Beichuan is eerily quiet, and the buildings that have not fallen are severely damaged.

that marked the end of the Burma Road. Twenty years later, I watched a Golden Retriever perform modest tricks near the same site for a crowd of pet-starved Chinese, in a square surrounded by stores selling the likes of Rolex and Gucci.

Beichuan's geology was long recognized as so potentially disastrous that authorities had discussed moving the city and replacing it as the county seat. Two major faults intersected. The valley-side slopes that rose directly on each side of the city were steep and unstable.

A new city, without the high-rise building, was under construction, renamed Yongchuan (Eternal Prosperity). It is not at this location, but on a safer site, a flat alluvial plain 25 km away.[2] Sixty construction cranes at that site moved like a flock of storks. Residents will move into these new homes from modular units, after initially living in tents. Those who lost wives or husbands will have the services of matchmakers (combining two families reduces marginal housing needs by half). Those who lost children are receiving counseling, encouragement with new pregnancies, and modest reparations. Compensation depends on agreeing to "obey the law and maintain social order," i.e., do not mention the school that collapsed and killed your child again. Journalists who persist on raising the issue of the easily collapsed schools throughout the earthquake zone are not faring well.

Working throughout the region over the next six months, I saw many astonishing new schools—"Previously the worst, now the best," said a colleague. To be accurate, both the new habitation, mainly apartment buildings of several stories set in landscaped grounds, and the new schools appeared as marvels to my architecturally untutored eye.

I was reminded of China's recent return from their own Dark Ages when I met men of my age shuffling about the campus of Sichuan University and in the housing complex where I resided. *Were they among the persecuted or the persecutors during the insanity of the Cultural Revolution of 1966–1976?* The older generation in China seemed to have a wary, "survivor" kind of attitude, suspicious that those nightmare years could recur. I speculated, based on personality, that a dedicated colleague could have been a DI for the Red Guards.

Later in 2010, on the second anniversary of "5-12," I was still in Chengdu, capital of Sichuan Province and 80 km from the fault zone. Survivors were celebrated on CCTV; a band consisting of musicians disabled during the quake performed; an ongoing series, with English subtitles, portrayed the lives and problems of survivors. It was propaganda for internal, not external consumption, but the stories did not have happy endings and seemed to ring true.

Depressed women were a focus. Suicides by women in China, with no relation to natural disasters, were then five times the worldwide rate for women. We saw the indefatigable Premier Wen Jibao, himself a geologist and in his seventh year as Premier, China's number two—as ever, enthusiastically encouraging the country and comforting survivors. No disaster in China could occur without seeing the Premier leaping about on CCTV, survivors clutching him for stability in the rubble, within twenty-four hours. For new FEMA directors in the United States, this should be mandatory viewing.

Many of the Beichuan population were members of the Qiang ethnic minority ("people of the clouds"), one of more than fifty minorities that in China are being absorbed, one way or another, into a motherland. The Qiang are known for their Norman-like towers, a few still standing (surprisingly) from their construction ca. 1300–1400 CE.[3] On the highway between Beichuan and Yongchuan is such a tower, but on second look this one is brand new, and the center of a Disneyland-like village of apparently professional Qiang villagers. A *New York Times* article described the sixty-nine families who lived there as wearing Qiang costumes and dancing to Qiang music.[4]

In the rubble of Beichuan, a warning sign shows a boy fleeing a skull, symbolic of the thousands buried underfoot. Visitors are asked to respect the site as the cemetery that it is.

Deserted Beichuan remains, entrance guarded by police and razor wire against possible looters and unauthorized journalists; only a small number of survivor relatives, select tourists, and official groups of scientists were allowed in. I was advised to keep my head down at police checkpoints; foreigners suspected of doing stories on school construction are not welcome. The *New York Times* reporter was not allowed in, although he seemed to have been encouraged to visit the Qiang happy village, completed, he noted, within seven months of "5-12."

So, what to do with a gigantic mass grave consisting of bizarrely canted high-rises? Unlike Pompeii and Herculaneum, Beichuan is only partly buried, by landslides incorporating house-size rocks. Rebuilding is ruled out. The decision was made in late 2009: the city, as it stands, will become an "earthquake museum" and memorial mass grave. Will this work? I actually think so—the lessons to be learned about building big cities in dangerous places, and for allowing them to get endlessly bigger after the risk is known, will be eloquent. The signs of the boy fleeing the skull cannot be missed. But, I recall, the ruins of "volcano disaster museums" Pompeii and Herculaneum have not ended the growth of Naples and its suburbs up the flanks of Vesuvius. The lesson should be too obvious to be ignored at Beichuan.

There is an important difference between prehistoric and modern disaster museums. In Italy, Roman ruins are common, part of a long-ago epoch without clear links to events that could happen again. In Beichuan, analogies to the present cannot be missed. Children's toys litter the debris. Dust-covered cars waiting in vain for their owners deliver an obvious message. And the knowledge that thousands are entombed beneath cannot be disputed.

Is the museum plan hot air? I was at first skeptical of modern China PR, this being my sixth visit over twenty years. I have become fascinated by a 1,250-year-old series of inscriptions dating from the Tang Dynasty, carved in White Crane Rock, a sandstone ridge in a reach of the upper Chang Jiang ("Long River," the Yangtze). I was hoping to get them translated and see what they might tell about the drought history of southwestern China and the Tibetan Plateau. Unlike the more complete Nile inscriptions that record floods, these marked the times of low flow. The site was now drowned by the upstream reach of the Three Gorges Dam Reservoir, and during the planning process, a novel "underwater museum" was promised to preserve them. *Yeah, right*, I thought. Well, while watching CCTV English Channel news in 2010, there it was, the official opening of the subaqueous museum! Visitors could go down a tunnel to peer through portholes at carved images of giant carp. The fish, appearing to "leap from the river" at low-water, predicted the harvest.

I looked forward to international press coverage of a Beichuan Earthquake Museum as a graphic lesson of where not to build. I met a professor who proposed the gradual depopulation of China's mountain areas because of the costs of, and risks to, habitation there. Interesting man—he criticized the Three Gorges Dam in its early stages, lost his job, persevered, and was completing his career with still-controversial issues like this one. Such a plan would make economic sense in the 3,000- to 4,000-m escarpment along the east side of the Tibetan Plateau, lined and crisscrossed by active faults, transected by river gorges with youthful, unstable side slopes disappearing from view into high cloud cover. I get an altitude headache just writing this.

The museum idea can work in China, but probably not in the United States. Western cultures insist that every last body be recovered, even if not identified. The U.S. Army Corps of Engineers rapidly springs into action and begins reconstruction.

China was permanently changed, at some level yet to be seen, by that giant earthquake in 2008. Must this happen only individually, country by country, for seismic and volcanic disasters? Why must it wait for future disasters? Lessons are there, both in the geologic past and in the remarkable series of worldwide disasters over the last thirty-plus years, waiting to be read, combined with the history from volcanic stratigraphy, paleoseismology, and the deposits of both hot, dry, and cold, wet flows. Both have killed tens of thousands in the last century.

Can we actually move towns and cities from places we now recognize as dangerous? Probably not at the scale of Beichuan. In two Canadian examples, this actually happened with dramatically different results.

Garibaldi, British Columbia, Canada

Is it possible to completely move a community before a possible disaster? It has happened at Canada's best known volcano, Mount Garibaldi. Actually, Canada's best known volcano is Mount Baker, which many Vancouver residents think is in Canada. This includes reporters for Vancouver newspapers who appear shocked when I answer their inquiries with the news that it is south of the international boundary.

Only eleven days after the eruption of Mount St. Helens on May 18, 1980, land development in the area of the resort town of Garibaldi, British Columbia, was prohibited. Subsequently, all the property was expropriated. Residents were "bought out," a number of them unwillingly.

The town of Garibaldi was once located at the mouth of Rubble Creek, 4 km downstream from a lava cliff named The Barrier. The cliff was formed by a lava flow from Clinker Peak on the north side of Mount Garibaldi. Lava fractured as it was rapidly chilled by late-Pleistocene glacial ice.[5] Why did the provincial cabinet subsequently expropriate the developed properties in the town, and why did the process begin only days after the eruption of a volcano 300 km south, although the risk had been legally established for nearly seven years? Justice Thomas Berger of the Supreme Court of British Columbia had ruled against further development in denying the appeal of a previously denied expansion of Garibaldi in August 1973.

The site that was to become Garibaldi was an unusual rubbly deposit (in "Rubble Creek") known by explorers since 1858. They had encountered what they thought was a landslide in the creek, and local First Nations Canadians told them that it occurred three summers before. Later, by dating the scars on the trees, a date of fall or winter 1855–56 was determined. Beginning in the 1950s, associated both with development and the increasing recognition of geologic hazards, the potential recurrence of a landslide became a controversial issue that was first associated with the construction of a dam downstream. Could The Barrier fail again, and what exactly had been the nature of the 1855 "landslide"? Renowned engineer and the "Father of Soil Mechanics," Karl Terzagi,[6,7] in a 1960 consulting report for BC Hydro, expressed no concern about recurrence in supporting a dam and reservoir on the deposits downstream. Another consulting engineer, a University of British Columbia professor, posited that the "landslide" had been slow, composed of talus accumulated at the base of The Barrier.

Even Terzagi's biographer noted there was skepticism about building a dam on a "flow slide." Some asked why Terzagi had not considered the frightening possibility that the landslide, which had given birth to the Rubble Creek [deposit], might recur.[8] Terzagi's skeptics said that The Barrier, damming Lower Garibaldi Lake, from

In 1981, British Columbia officials declared The Barrier unsafe for those living below the formation. They relocated the threatened town of Garibaldi. (John Harvey, CC BY-SA 2.5)

which the giant, so-called flow slide had emerged, "continues to provide an extreme geological hazard, and one that construction of the Cheakamus Valley Dam may have worsened by placing a reservoir in its runout path."

Gradually, however, enough geologists examined the rubble of Rubble Creek to determine that it was emplaced by a volcanic debris flow, or lahar, and that neither dams nor people could be settled safely within the reach of a second flow. Justice Berger had denied the appeal of a prohibition of new development, and that 1973 ruling looks good today. The nature of the "slide" was thoroughly analyzed in 1978 by BC Hydro and University of British Columbia geologists. Although they continued to call it a landslide, they describe a textbook debris flow as much as 100 m deep. Flow velocity, they estimated from the amount of superelevation (runup or tilting of the flow surface) on the outside of bends by centrifugal force, was in the range of 18 to 24 m/s, between 40 and 54 mph.

There the matter rested until Mount St. Helens dominated the evening news in 1980.

This case history illustrates the ripple effects of volcanic hazards when they occur, or when evidence of catastrophic events has just been discovered in the geologic record. Dramatic footage of the huge debris avalanche in the North Fork Toutle River was repeatedly broadcast in the days following the Mount St. Helens eruption. It was convincing, and it provided both the impetus and the rationale for the otherwise difficult issue of moving the town.

Some of the displaced, as well as controversy-hungry journalists, thought this response was too Draconian, possibly in part because of the modest levels of the financial reparations. The wisdom in the "pettifogging screw-up" of the forced-but-compensated evacuation was debated by columnists on slow-news weeks thereafter. Will the future render a final verdict? For most people, even then probably not, but it won't matter providing the geological reasoning and inference were sound. Avoiding a potential hazard, even if it does not occur, can be like fire insurance and smoke detectors. Should you complain about their cost when you don't have a fire? Maybe we shouldn't complain about evacuations when the disasters do not occur, which is, of course, going to be most of the time. It clearly does not do government any credit to do it "on the cheap," as some thought occurred with the mandatory evacuation and confiscation of Garibaldi.

Later analysis would consider the possibility of the entire Barrier failing, and with the 4-sq-mi, 850-ft-deep Garibaldi Lake releasing a huge flood surge that would flood the populated Cheakamus and Squamish River valleys and reach the Pacific Ocean. With the fractured, ice-chilled lava plugging the valley, this could be a possibility, especially with a powerful seismic trigger. But, as scientists like to say, further study is needed, in this case of the blockage character and stability. Justice Berger decided to move the town, based on odds of 1 in 10,000, his calculation that the Rubble Creek lahar had occurred just once in postglacial time, the last 10,000 years. He qualified that seemingly tiny probability by noting that the town would be growing and probably last for hundreds of years. A remarkably enlightened jurist.

The "Garibaldi issue" is widespread in various incarnations. The more extreme version, forcibly moving people from harm's way, causes the greatest angst and anger, making future similar actions difficult. My favorite example is a protest demonstration scheduled for a Sunday afternoon (May 18, 1980) at a location along the Toutle River below Mount St. Helens. After having been locked out, residents would be allowed back in the "red zone" for a brief period. Fortunately, the paraders did not, or were not allowed, to arrive early—the site was obliterated by the "lateral blast" of the cataclysmic eruption that began at 8:32 that morning.

The mayor of Abuta, a Japanese town with a well-managed (and lucky) evacuation after a 1977 eruption of Usu volcano on Hokaido, stated, "Heads of municipalities should always be prepared to commit *hara-kiri* (ritual suicide by disembowelment). We obey the dictates of conscience and do what we think is right. If we are wrong and the people suffer as a result, then we should be prepared to atone for the error." The errors being, of course, waiting too long or revoking the evacuation too soon.

In Taiwan, at the final alert level for a rain-triggered debris flow with the approach of a typhoon, authorities can physically remove people from areas at risk. At Popocatéptl, the army has forced people to leave their villages when eruption threatened. Likewise at Colima. And downstream from Pinatubo, locally, without government incentive to either move or stay, the third levels of houses are being built atop the first two levels of ancestral property already buried by lahars since the 1991 eruption. These, and many similar cases, show how reluctant people are to leave their homes, and what a residue of ill will can remain when they are forced away.

Today, Rubble Creek crosses Highway 99, which in 2008 gave access to the Winter Olympic Games at Whistler, British Columbia. Parking along the highway near the creek is not permitted. Outside the potential flow path, new recreational subdivisions have been established several kilometers from the old town. People have been moved from harm's way. The dam and reservoir remain.

Canadian protestors of the 1980 "buy-out" ruling should note what happened a decade later in eastern Canada. Engineering studies in 1971 showed that the town of Lemieux in the Ottawa valley was sitting on a landslide-prone substrate. Those studies were initiated after a nearby landslide (every disaster has lessons). The ground beneath Lemieux was Leda Clay, a marine deposit formed by Ice Age meltwater depositing clay and silt into the Champlain Sea. Marine clays like the Leda are notably less stable than their non-marine, lacustrine equivalents. Lemieux was abandoned in 1991, and residents were relocated at government expense. At 3:30 P.M. on June 20, 1993, just two years later, a large but slow landslide consumed 17 hectares adjacent to the townsite. The slide advanced 680 m in one hour from a riverbank failure site—traveling 1.6 km downstream and 1.7 km upstream, blocking the river for several days and causing damages estimated at $12.5 million.

Geologists like me know that after you've identified an area at risk of a hazard, the television interviewers are going to ask, "And so, Doctor, would you live here?" The situation generally fits my rehearsed "It's a personal decision" answer, along the lines of: "Knowing the risk, I might still choose to live and raise my family in this lovely mountain valley (or whatever) rather than in a crime-ridden, polluted, urban setting." Considering the unstable, fractured nature of The Barrier, and the work

Dave Tucker and I have done on subaqueously chilled and fractured lavas in the Baker River valley, just south of the Canadian border,[9] I would really have to think about it in this case. A hike up Rubble Creek to look at The Barrier should be mandatory for any remaining skeptics.

NOTES:

1. Before officials could relocate Beichuan, "5-12" killed more than 10 percent of the population. Population statistics in China are so ephemeral, however, that absolute numbers are only approximations.
2. Rich eastern provinces are being taxed to rebuild portions of the devastated area. Guandong Province is paying and getting specific credit for this project. News on CCTV notes that twenty provinces are assessed a continuing 1 percent of their revenues to rebuild Sichuan.
3. Public Broadcasting System episode, "Secret Towers of Tibet," in the series *Secrets of the Dead.*
4. "China's Arranged Remarriages" *New York Times* article, May 3, 2010, by Brook Larmer. The government is encouraging remarriages of survivors (one new house is cheaper than two; families are more stable) into "restructured families" encouraged by their *danwei* (work units), to which everyone is still assigned.
5. Moore, D. P., and Mathews, W. H. The Rubble Creek landslide, southwestern British Columbia. *Canadian Journal of Earth Sciences* 15, no. 7 (1978):1039–52.
6. Mathews, W. H. 1958. Geology of the Mount Garibaldi map-area, southwestern British Columbia, Canada. *Geological Society of America Bulletin* 69:161–98.
7. Terzagi, K. 1960. Storage dam founded on landslide debris. *Boston Society of Civil Engineering Journal* 47:64-94.
8. Goodman, R. E. 1999. *Karl Terzagi, the engineer as artist.* Reston, VA: American Society of Civil Engineers Press, p. 323.
9. See suggested strategy regarding whether or not to drain a reservoir when a lava flow is approaching in Tucker, D. S., and Scott, K. M. 2009. Structures and facies associated with the flow of subaerial basaltic lava into a deep freshwater lake, North Cascades, Washington. *Journal of Volcanology and Geothermal Resources* 185:311–22.

Epilogue

Granatello Epigraph, Version 2

Two volcano disasters—Vesuvius and Nevado del Ruiz—dominate our thinking about hazards planning and emergency management. In these and other case studies from around the world, however, minor details can make the difference between a few and even thousands of deaths. Just as the Spanish Viceroy warned Neopolitans in 1732 with a stone billboard, *The Voice of This Stone* offers my own advice about how to think and behave in the event of a volcanic disaster.

Think of this chapter as a Granatello Epigraph, version 2.0. The remaining billboard in the Naples suburb of Portici continues to tell residents: When the volcano "roars, howls, thunders, . . . run away without delay."

First of all, treat the ground tremor of an approaching lahar as a "self-warning" to go to high ground. That is extremely important based on repeated cases of tremor felt at significant distances. Jack Lockwood believes it could have saved more than half of those who died at Nevado del Ruiz. Reports of tremor so powerful that people were knocked to their knees are convincing, particularly where the tremor was mistaken for an earthquake, or the aftershock of an earthquake. Repeatedly, as at Nevado del Ruiz, Nevado del Huilia, and Citlaltépetl, we think, *if they had only known*.

§

My other safety observations can be divided into two categories:

1. using the past history of a volcano to predict its future; and
2. dealing with the "false-alarm problem."

The Granatello Epigraph in Portici, Italy, compels us descendants to flee when the ground shakes.

Deciphering the Past

1. A letter written by Joaquin Acosta in 1850 plainly said, "It is astonishing that none of the inhabitants of these villages [destroyed in 1845], built on the solidified mud of old mass movements, has even suspected the origin of this vast terrain . . . although ancient traditions testify to the frequent mudflows in these regions . . . " If that observation was astonishing in 1850, it must have been even more astounding in 1985, when more than 20,000 died at Nevado del Ruiz because they again did not suspect the origin of the terrain.
2. Field geology allows us to reconstruct volcano behavior over millennia, which in turn lets us plan for the most probable future behavior. Examples are the land-use zoning of lahar pathways at Rainier, and the zoning for pyroclastic density currents at many volcanoes, including Vesuvius.
3. Even when a volcano's past urges wisdom in minimizing development in lahar pathways or on its flanks, areas at high risk will be filled with the unrelenting pressure for growth. Continuing public education is necessary to slow the rate of growth. I promote the use of USGS-style Fact Sheets as an effective means of accomplishing this. Vesuvius and Rainier are examples of unwise settlement.
4. The texture (size, shape, and arrangement of grains) in a lahar deposit reveals whether the lahar began as a surge of water (and thus as snowmelt from an eruption, or from a lake breakout); or as a collapse of a volcanic edifice not certainly with an eruption. The difference is in clay content, if low (commonly <1 percent) or high (>3 percent, commonly 5 to 6 percent)—producing granular, low-clay, or noncohesive lahars, or muddy, high-clay, or cohesive lahars, respectively. Examples and further discussion can be found in the chapter on Mount Rainier and in the Mount St. Helens chapter about a lahar larger than the Amazon River.
5. Hyperconcentrated flow deposits (with their unique characteristics) reveal the nearly certain presence of an upstream noncohesive (granular or low-clay) lahar, and thus of a past eruption. Nevertheless, transformation, with our ability to recognize it, is the most useful finding in our post-1980 study of debris flow behavior. More on hyperconcentrated flow can be found in the Mount St. Helens chapter.
6. Clast rounding yields crucial evidence about the origin of a lahar and whether it can be correlated with an eruption. If most of a lahar's clasts are rounded, they were entrained in a surge of water that most likely was produced by eruption-induced snowmelt. The rounding occurred during previous stream

transport. If a lahar's clasts are angular, it originated by a collapse of a volcano edifice. That collapse may not be related to an eruption. We saw this on the giant Mount St. Helens lahar and in the story of Bandai in the Colima chapter.

7. Official "disaster museums" can preserve a past disaster as a reminder of what led to that disaster, and how we can avoid it from happening again. The stories from Vesuvius and Beichuan are testimonies.
8. Recognition of a potential hazard, past or present, may trigger complete removal of a town. This was considered at Beichuan, but the city was too large. The town of Garibaldi, British Columbia, below the volcano of the same name, was in effect moved (all development was made illegal). Owners received compensation but were dissatisfied with the amount.

The False-Alarm Problem

1. The worst case is that an eruption or collapse occurs with no warning. Sector collapses may occur with no warning, emphasizing the need for an event-warning system (It is happening *now*!) at volcanoes like Rainier. Also see more in the Colima (Bandai) and Rainier chapters.
2. Calls for evacuation tend to be too late, because officials fear looking foolish if there is no eruption or collapse. Officials may want to err on the side of being too early, combined with public education on how precursory volcanic activity can wax and wane, justifying their "call" on the side of caution. Education is essential to prevent potential evacuees from fearing scientists more than the volcano. Again, USGS-style Fact Sheets will be effective. More detail on this idea may be found in the chapters on Colima, Popocatéptl, and Garibaldi.
3. Nevado del Ruiz was visited by a number of scientists who came, warned, and went, apparently assuming authorities would take action. No evacuation occurred, even as deadly lahars were snaking down the volcano, and more than 20,000 died in Armero. Scientists who identify risk from precursory activity and the past history of a volcano must "cry wolf" and stick around to advise authorities.
4. After an eruption, calling off an evacuation and allowing people to return home can be equally difficult. At El Chichón in 1982, the return of 2,000 people to Francisco León just before the climactic eruption was caused by inexperienced advisors.

5. After one false alarm, again "crying wolf" is likely to meet skepticism and non-compliance. Education about the periodic nature of volcanic hazards seems to be the only answer. The chapters on Popocatéptl, Colima, and Campi Flegrei offer more detail.
6. In ordering large evacuations, emergency managers may consider, when the volcanic hazard does not occur, likening the evacuation to buying fire insurance. We do not complain about the cost when a fire does not occur, so we should likewise support the evacuations. See more within the chapters on Popocatéptl, Colima, and Garibaldi.
7. Beware when authorities do nothing, with the excuse that a warning is *too alarmist or may lower real estate values*. Those excuses were spoken at Nevado del Ruiz and continue at Mount Rainier.

At the foot of Nevado del Huila, Colombia, a sign in Toez translates to "Valley of the Forgotten." This building suffered cracks in the 1994 earthquake and shows mud splashes from the gigantic lahar called *La Avalancha*.

Glossary

Ash (volcanic)—Pyroclasts <2 mm in diameter.

Bedform (or bed form)—Three dimensional configuration of shapes repeatedly occurring in nature, such as ripples (<5 cm amplitude) and dunes (>5 cm amplitude), plane beds, and antidunes, representing lower flow, transitional, and upper flow regimes, respectively. Bedforms are preserved in deposits as cross-stratification, layers seen in cross section preserving successive positions of the forms through time.

Black Swan—The highly improbable.

Blast—See ***Lateral blast***.

Block-and-ash flow—Rubbly pyroclastic flow characterized by a large fraction of juvenile blocks in an ash matrix.

Bulking—Entrainment of sediment during flow; debulking is the progressive loss of sediment.

Catastrophism—Explanation of the geologic past as the result of short-lived, violent convulsions with their effects felt worldwide.

Clast—Fragment of rock produced by mechanical weathering of a larger mass.

Clay—Size term for particles finer than 0.004 mm; may also refer to a layer-lattice silicate (clay mineral).

Cohesive lahar (deposit)—Common international term more strictly applied only to a lahar deposit containing a significant amount of clay- or of silt- and clay-size material. Common synonyms of cohesive: muddy, high-clay, clay-rich. Approximately equivalent to viscous debris flows and their deposits in Chinese literature. Clay content commonly reflects origin as a lahar runout of a *collapse* (*sector* or *flank*) in which the clay originated by hydrothermal alteration in a volcanic edifice. Some huge cohesive lahars begin as transformations of collapse-derived debris avalanches. See ***Noncohesive lahar***.

Collapse—Volcanic landslide; may be of flank (flank collapse) or of summit, leaving a horseshoe-shaped crater (sector collapse).

Cross-bedding (or cross-stratification)—Strata occurring at an angle to the contact; may be low-angle (<15°) or high-angle. Evidence of bed forms and flow regime.

Debris avalanche (volcanic)—Rapidly flowing, incoherent, unsorted mixture of rock debris (commonly hydrothermally altered in volcanic debris avalanches), soil, and varying amounts of water that move downslope under the influence of gravity. *Rock avalanche* is an alpine analog with commonly unaltered blocks.

Debris-dammed lakes—Lakes formed when drainages are blocked by landslides, debris avalanches, or lahars. Blockage is commonly temporary, with eventual breaching and release of a flood surge unless mitigated, as in the case of Spirit Lake.

Dish structure—sedimentary structure found in thick sand units (e.g., deposits of HF lahars) consisting of vertical sequences of overlapping, concave-upward bowl-like structures, commonly 10–15 cm across, defined by thin, dark concentrations of fine sediment concentrated by dewatering after deposition. The structures record the waves of upward flow of water as a sediment deposit settles and compacts; especially common where deposition is *en masse* or extremely rapid. Commonly associated with vertical *water-escape pipes* to form *dish-and-pillar structure*.

Dome (lava)—Mound of extruded, relatively viscous lava amassing over a vent.

Facies—Deposit with similar characteristics and origin.

Flood plain (floodplain)—Low-lying area peripheral to stream channels, periodically inundated by floods.

Flow transformation—Change in flow state, as from debris flow to hyperconcentrated flow.

Forecast—General description of future events. See ***Prediction***.

Fumarole—Vent or fissure releasing volcanic gas and steam.

H/L ratio—Ratio of fall height to runout distance of a volcanic landslide or debris avalanche.

Hazards—Natural physical processes with the potential to cause injury or death to people and loss or damage to property.

Hummocks—Mounds (also *cerrillos*) and conical hills on the surface of a debris avalanche or muddy DF lahar transformed from a debris avalanche, reflecting the protrusions of blocks transported by the flow.

Juvenile (particle)—Particle formed directly from erupting magma; equivalent to primary volcaniclastic particle.

Lahar—Volcanic debris flow.

Lateral blast—High-velocity pyroclastic surge directed laterally by collapsing landslide blocks; type example at Mount St. Helens, May 18, 1980.

Matrix—Finer-grained material enclosing, suspending, or filling the interstices between larger grains of a sedimentary deposit or rock.

Noncohesive lahars (deposits)—Common international term more strictly applied to the deposit of a lahar with a relatively small proportion of silt and clay. Common synonyms: granular, low-clay, clay-poor. Approximately equivalent to non-viscous debris flow in Chinese usage, where this term is also common. Many noncohesive lahars begin as water surges that entrain alluvial material from which fine sediment has previously been winnowed or removed by previous selective sorting during transport. See ***Cohesive lahar.***

Prediction—Specific description of future events as to time and place. See ***Forecast***.

Phreatic—A phreatic eruption is a *hydrovolcanic* eruption resulting from interaction of water with hot rock. See ***Phreatomagmatic***.

Phreatomagmatic—Referring to interaction of ground water and magma; a phreatomagmatic eruption is a eruption resulting from interaction of water with magma, and is defined by a tephra with a significant component of *juvenile* material.

Plinian eruption (column)—Eruption characterized by high, convective eruption column resulting in atmospheric particle injection and dispersal over large areas.

Pumice—Light-colored, glassy rock, commonly less dense than water because of the large proportion of bubbles (vesicles).

Pyroclastic density flow—Flow (density current) of fragmental, mainly juvenile material. Same as pyroclastic flow (PF).

Pyroclastic surge—Turbulent, high-velocity pyroclastic density current, less dense and less confined by topography than a pyroclastic flow.

Pyroclastic particles, or pyroclasts—Fragmentary, juvenile material ejected during a magmatic eruption.

Risk—Probability of loss or harm to property or human life, with the occurrence of a physical process or event.

Scoria (cinder)—Pyroclast containing >ca. 50 percent void space (vesicles) and at least several mm in diameter.

Stratovolcano (stratocone)—Large volcanic edifice composed of many layers of deposits by multiple eruptions.

Tephra—Pyroclasts of any size, shape, or origin ejected by volcanic eruptions. Term commonly applied only to pyroclastic-fall (or airfall) deposits.

Uniformitarianism—Explanation of the earth's landscapes by the same processes we see today. The present is the key to the past.

Index

Notes are indicated by n after the page number.

About the Author

Kevin Scott is associated with the David A. Johnston Cascade Volcano Observatory (CVO) in Vancouver, Washington, as a Scientist Emeritus. He earned a B.A. and an M.A. in geology from the University of California, Los Angeles. For his Ph.D. from Wisconsin, he mapped by horseback the volcaniclastic sequence around the spectacular granite towers, the Torres de Paine, in southern Chile.

Kevin has received the Distinguished Service gold medal, the highest award of the U.S. Department of the Interior; the Meritorious Service silver medal, the Kirk Bryan Award of the Geological Society of America, a Japanese Prime Minister's Research Award, the Antarctic Service Medal, and a NATO Postdoctoral Fellowship at the University of Edinburgh. He was employed as a Senior International Professor by the Chinese Academy of Sciences from 2009 to 2011.

Kevin has written what is probably the record number (more than ten) of first- or solely authored USGS Professional Papers, the most prestigious publication series of the USGS. A final Professional Paper, on Mount Baker, is in review.

He lives in Portland, Oregon, with two large dogs, his wife, and family.